Foreword

Alex Arteaga

Boris Hassenstein

Gunnar Green

Klangumwelt
Ernst-Reuter-Platz

A project of the
Auditory Architecture
Research Unit

Alex Arteaga
Boris Hassenstein
Gunnar Green
(eds.)

This book concludes the research/design project "Klangumwelt Ernst-Reuter-Platz."[1] The project was initiated by Alex Arteaga and Thomas Kusitzky in 2010 with two interlaced goals: the realization of a design for the transformation of Ernst-Reuter-Platz, a city square situated in Berlin's Charlottenburg-Wilmersdorf district, and the development of practices and strategies of architectural research and design based on the aural experience of an environment. Pursuing this second goal, we intended to enhance the concept and practice of *auditory architecture*. This term denotes a new approach in research into the relationships between the aural and the built environment, defined and developed at the Auditory Architecture Research Unit of the Berlin University of the Arts.[2] This approach is based on theories of embodied and situated cognition,[3] and on the performance of aural-aesthetic practices as research practices.[4] It aims to identify and develop efficient procedures of environmental transformation, actualizing the cognitive potentialities of different varieties of auditory action.

The first goal—the realization of a design for the transformation of Ernst-Reuter-Platz—was set in the context of deliberations about the new definition of Berlin's City West and, more specifically, Campus West.[5] Within this framework, Ernst-Reuter-Platz appears to be a problematic urban space, pulled between wishes to preserve it as architectural and urbanistic heritage—it is classified as landmark—and the necessity of its integration into the current urban paradigm, radically different from the paradigm in which the square was designed.

After the long period of time required to conclude this project—six years—we can affirm that we have attained both goals. On the one hand, the Auditory Architecture Research Unit's design for Ernst-Reuter-Platz offers an integrative alternative to the conflict between protection and renewal, presenting a viable and efficient proposal for sustainable transformation of this urban space in the form of a network of constructive and non-constructive measures. On the other hand, the concepts and practices developed for, and due to, this process of research/design have consolidated the theoretical configuration and operativity of auditory architecture, clarifying both its position in the framework of established architectural design practices, and the ways in which it can contribute to their reinterpretation and development. This book, whose production was understood and performed as another opportunity to reflect on the whole project rather than merely to document it, presents not only the final results but also significant contributions to those results. The project "Klangumwelt Ernst-Reuter-Platz" has been articulated in four phases. The first consisted in a basic and systematic inquiry into this square through practices developed in previous projects. The results of this initial research phase were presented publicly at the first "Standortskonferenz Ernst-Reuter-Platz" at the Technische Universität Berlin. In the second phase, the ideas thus developed were synthesized in a provisory design, presented in the form of an experimental installation at the Ars Electronica

1 For more on the terms "research/design" and "Klangumwelt," see footnotes 4 and 2, respectively, in the chapter "Towards an Architecture of Embodiment: thinking the environment aurally" (p.13). 2 www.udk-berlin.de/forschung/forschungseinrichtungen/auditory-architecture-research-unit/ 3 The most basic idea of these theories is that cognition requires the activity of a body—an embodied living unit—coupled with its surroundings. For an overview of these theories, see: Shapiro, L. (ed): *The Routledge Handbook of Embodied Cognition*. Oxon 2014; Robbins, P. and Murat Aydede, M. (eds.): *The Cambridge Handbook of Situated Cognition*. Cambridge 2009. For an overview of "enactivism," the specific approach that constitutes our main reference in this context, see: Stewart, J., Gapenne, O. and Di Paolo, E. (eds.): *Enaction: Toward a New Paradigm for Cognitive Science*. Cambridge, MA 2010. 4 Research at the Auditory Architecture Research Unit is characterized by a hybrid methodology resulting from a combination of practices of the humanities—in particular phenomenology and philosophy—social sciences, and artistic research practices. 5 For more information on City-West and Campus-West, see footnotes 2 and 3, respectively, in the chapter "The Auditory Architecture Research Unit's design for Ernst-Reuter-Platz" (page 169).

Center in Linz. In the third phase—"Lab ERP"—this design was reconsidered from different perspectives, on diverse platforms: four seminars conceived and realized as a cooperation between the master programm Sound Studies and Sonic Arts (Berlin University of the Arts) and the Department of Landscape Architecture and Environmental Planning (Technische Universität Berlin); six forums about related topics with the participation of experts of different disciplines; and a design group. In the last phase of this project, the final design of the Auditory Architecture Research Unit was conclusively defined, select student projects were further developed and completed, and the final public presentation of the results was designed. This presentation took place at the glass gallery of the former IBM-Building on Ernst-Reuter-Platz, providing direct contact between design and its object. This last phase was integrated into Alex Arteaga's wider-range research project, "Architecture of Embodiment."[6]

As a clear example of transdisciplinarity—or, as we prefer to understand it, *non-disciplinarity*, that is, deep and integrative cooperation beyond any disciplinary boundaries—this project was realized by numerous participants. Together with Alex Arteaga and Thomas Kusitzky, the following people contributed in varying constellations: Boris Hassenstein, Gunnar Green, Willy Sengewald, Frédéric Eyl, Hans-Peter Tennhardt, Laura Vahl, Jürgen Weidinger, Uta Graff, Annette Matthias, Gabriele Dolff-Bonekämper, Oliver Bormann, Saskia Hebert, Stephan Günzel, Frank Eckhardt, Lucas Hövelmann, Maria Horn, Anna Bogner, Marco Mattelig, Harald Fugmann, Andreas Quednau, Peter Cusack, Stefan Horn, Christian von Wissel, Peter Fischer, Philipp Oswalt, Klaus Lingenauber, and Wulf-Holger Arndt.

The present book is structured in five chapters. In the first—"Steps towards an architecture of embodiment: thinking the environment aurally"—you find a comprehensive description of auditory architecture's current state of development as a research/design approach. This description is articulated through the specification of our concepts object of design and design process, a comprehensive outline of our main research/design practices—*auditory diagramming*—and a concluding reflection on the function of this approach in relation to the general field of architectural design practices. The second chapter—"Model 1"—describes the experimental installation through which we presented our first provisory design for Ernst-Reuter-Platz at the Ars Electronica in Linz. The third chapter—"dialogues"— includes the transcriptions of three conversations dealing respectively with possible connections between the practice of architecture and phenomenology as practice, the idea of providing access as a form of landmark protection, and a socio-historical view of Ernst-Reuter-Platz. The fourth chapter—"projects"—consists of four student projects developed in the framework of the seminars integrated into "Lab ERP." Not only did these projects contribute to the conception of our design, they themselves constitute viable approaches to, and/or proposals for, the transformation of this public space. The title of the last section—"The Auditory Architecture Research Unit's design for Ernst-Reuter-Platz"—already reveals its content: the object of design co-constituted by our research practices and our proposals for the square's transformation. Although these five chapters are interconnected, each of them is conceived autonomously and can be read separately.

The project "Klangumwelt Ernst-Reuter-Platz" would not have been possible without the support of several people and institutions. We would like to thank: Martin Supper, former head of the master programm Sound Studies and Sonic Arts (Berlin University of the Arts), for institutional and intellectual support and especially for integrating auditory architecture into this program; Volker Straebel, current director of this master program, for his advice during the production of this book; Thomas Schildhauer and Mirko Behrens, respectively executive director and head of administration of the Berlin Career College and Susanne Hauser, head of the Institut for History and Theory of Design (both at the Berlin University of the Arts), for providing the necessary framework not only for the realization of this project but also for the development of the Auditory Architecture Research Unit and the research project "Architecture of Embodiment"; the Einstein Foundation for supporting the project "Architecture of Embodiment" with an Einstein Junior Fellowship, which made possible the publication of the present book; the Federal Institute for Research on Building, Urban Affairs and Spatial Development for financing the first two phases of this project through the research initiative "Zukunft Bau"; Rainer Emenlauer, director of ProStadt, for making possible our participation in the first "Standortskonferenz Ernst-Reuter-Platz"; Frank Tanaka, head of the Deutsche Bank at Otto-Suhr-Allee in Berlin, for supporting the realization of "Lab ERP"; Dirk Spender, head of Regionalmanagement City West, for supporting and co-organizing the final presentation of this project; and, last but not least, Lucas Hövelmann for the coordination of this book project, and, especially, Brandon LaBelle for including this book in the series "Surface Tension" and for his inspiring advice during the conception, design, and production process.

Steps towards an architecture of embodiment: thinking the environment aurally[1]

Alex Arteaga

13

"Klangumwelt Ernst-Reuter-Platz"[2] is the first project realized at the Auditory Architecture Research Unit, in which an architectural design has been fully accomplished. In this project we have completed a whole cycle, from the first contact with the object of design to the definition of measures for its transformation. Accomplishing it over a long period of time—at least long enough to critically observe each move—has helped me to clarify the goals, the conceptual framework, and the practices, strategies, and methods of a possible auditory architecture, as well as its position and function in the general context of architecture and of artistic research. Although I have published some texts on this topic,[3] the one I present here, reinforced by the context of this book, provides the most comprehensive and coherent account of what auditory architecture is and aims to be.

In order to explain this topic I am going to address three basic questions. The first refers to the subject matter of auditory architecture: What is an *aural environment*? The second addresses the operations to be performed on this object: What does *researching/designing*[4] an aural environment mean? And the third addresses the specific performance of these operations: How can an aural environment be researched/designed? After addressing these questions, I will describe in detail the main practice of research/design as it has been conceived and performed in the framework of the project "Klangumwelt Ernst-Reuter-Platz"—namely *auditory diagramming*—as a way of exemplifying the response to the third question, and presenting the operative context in which my position regarding the first two has been developed. In conclusion, I will briefly look at the potential contributions of an auditory architecture to general architectural design practice.

FROM SOUNDSCAPE TO AURAL ENVIRONMENT

The concept of *aural environment* was developed at the Auditory Architecture Research Unit as a radical alternative to the concept of soundscape.[5] The latter concept has been used during the last forty years to deal with the relationships between sound and environment. The need to base auditory architecture on an alternative concept stems from a shift of paradigm in the underpinning cognitive approach. Whereas "soundscape" belongs, implicitly, to a realistic paradigm, the concept of aural environment is developed according to the *enactive approach to cognition*.[6]

A soundscape is understood as an entity that exists in itself, independent of the acts of hearing and listening. A soundscape is "out there," topologically localized, fully configured, clearly contoured, and ready to be heard, analyzed, and recorded. It is defined and formed exclusively by its objective components, and the act of listening to it is understood in terms of its apprehension, as an act of mental representation.

1 I would like to thank Mika Elo and Lidia Gasperoni for their contributions to this text. 2 "Klangumwelt" is a basic term in auditory architecture. The possibility of differentiating in German between "Umgebung"—which I translate in English as "surroundings"—and "Umwelt"—which I translate as "environment"—although these words are commonly used as synonyms, is conceptually relevant in this context. This differentiation and the explicit references to the term "world"—"Welt"—disappear in the English translation: "aural environment." For this reason we decided to maintain the original German in the title of this book. I will use the English formulation in this text to ease the flow of reading. 3 A selection of articles about auditory architecture, all in German: Arteaga, A.: Bildgeneriende Bildlosigkeit. Klangumwelt Ernst-Reuter-Platz: ein auditiv-architektonisches Forschungs- und Entwurfsprojekt, in: Hillnhütter, S. (ed.): *Planbilder, Medien der Architekturgestaltung,, Series: Bildwelten des Wissens*, vol. 11, Berlin 2015, pp. 107-109; Arteaga, A.: Auditive Architektur, in: *kunsttexte.de*, 4, 2011 (http://edoc.hu-berlin.de/kunsttexte/2010-4/arteaga-alex-1/PDF/arteaga.pdf); Arteaga, A. and Kusitzky, T.: Ernst-Reuter-Platz als Klangumwelt, in: *Ausdruck und Gebrauch. Wissenschaftliche Hefte für Architektur Wohnen Umwelt*, 9, 2010, pp. 84-96; Arteaga, A. and Kusitzky, T.: Auditive Architektur: Erforschung und Gestaltung architektonischer Klangumwelten, in: *Archithèse*, 37, 2010, pp. 34-35; Arteaga, A. and Kusitzky, T.: Hörend gestalten, in: *TEC 21*, 2008, p. 134; Arteaga, A. and Kusitzky, T.: Klangumwelten. Auditive Architektur als Artistic Research, in: H. Schulze (ed.), *Sound Studies. Traditionen — Methoden — Desideraten*, 2008, pp. 247-265. 4 In this text I use "research/design" to express the kind of relationship between these traditionally differentiated terms as it is established in the framework of auditory architecture. In this context there is no categorical differentiation between research and design that would allow these terms to be related to each other in formulations like "research-based design" or "design-based research." As I will explain later, the generation of knowledge about the object of design—research—and the transformation of this object—design—can be considered one single activity, articulated through different practices performed in iterative continuity. 5 For the original concept of soundscape see: Schafer Murray, R.: *The Tuning of the World*, New York 1977 6 The enactive approach to cognition was defined in: Varela, F. J., Thompson, E. and Rosch, E.: *The Embodied Mind: Cognitive Science and Human Experience*, Cambridge MA 1991. For an exhaustive description see: Thompson, E.: Mind in Life. *Biology, Phenomenology and the Sciences of Mind*, Cambridge MA 2007. For its further development from different perspectives see: Steward, J., Gapenne, O. and Di Paolo, E. A.: *Enaction*, Cambridge MA 2010. And: Hutto, D. D. and Myin, E.: *Radicalizing Enactivism: Basic Minds without Content*, Cambridge MA 2013.

In this context, to listen and to record appear as operations that are similar to each other. They differ only through the medium of representation. Only on a realist-representationalist basis can a recording be understood as a means to represent and store a listened soundscape.

The aural environment, in contrast, does not exist independently of the actions the listener performers in touch with it and its material substrate. The aural environment is not present independently of all kinds of dynamic relationships—not only the aural ones—that the listener and her environment together establish from the very moment of their encounter. Although the aural environment first appears as something given, the reflective interaction reveals that it is *phenomenal*. In other words, it is a presence that does not exist in itself but is *constituted*, or more precisely, *co*-constituted. It arises out of the encounter of heteronomously organized matter—the physico-chemical, material components of the designer's surroundings—and autonomously organized matter—the designer and those inhabiting and referring to her surroundings.[7] Getting in touch with each other, both parties initiate an intimate coupling that will mutually condition their shared process of embodiment. The confluence of multiple processes, articulated by previous convergences and participating concurrently in other junctions of processes, configures the horizon in which the phenomenal presence appears. Like a new texture or a different, perhaps unexpected color variation that a piece of fabric acquires through the interweaving of multiple threads, the object of design emerges out of the interaction of an objective correlate and a subjective correlate. More precisely, it emerges out of the interaction between a dynamic and complex field of objective correlates and a dynamic and complex network of intersubjective correlates centered on a main one: the designer. The object of design—the aural environment—is a temporarily stabilized but ever-changing configuration of emergent qualities manifesting for the designer in their interactions. In turn, the designer emerges for herself simultaneously with her object of design in a relation of mutual dependence or reciprocal determination. Both, designer and object of design, manifest as their respective actual specificities—as a specific self and as its specific world or environment—fundamentally conditioning each other: they *co-emerge*.[8]

The term "co-emergence" expresses on the one hand the mutual dependence between object and designer—there can be neither object of design without designer nor designer without object of design. On the other hand, and more fundamentally, considering the system the two configure, it denotes the relation of mutual conditioning between emerging qualities and the intertwined dynamic constraints that enable their appearance. The arising of some qualities—the object of design appearing as "structurally complex," for example, and the designer experiencing herself as "a designer able to organize complexity"—constrains the activities of the system's agents: the designer experiencing her object of design as "complex" will not try to establish simple causal relationships between its components, and will chose adequate practices and tools to treat the manifesting complexity, which in turn will enable the emergence of new qualities. Designer and object of design are therefore immersed in a ceaseless

7 To lighten the text flow I use the singular "designer," although design processes are always, more or less explicitly, performed by a collective. 8 The concept of "co-emergence" has been defined by Evan Thompson in the framework of the enactive approach to cognition as a specification of the term "emergence," developed in the framework of theories of dynamic and complex systems. For its definition see: Thompson, E.: op. cit., chapter 3, "Autonomy and Emergence."

and closed circular relationship of mutual transformation generated by their very specific interactions, which in turn are conditioned by their respective forms of organization and their current embodiment, as well as the very specific way both—designer and her object—manifest as such. The aural environment—the object of design—therefore does not exist prior to the process of design, but emerges by virtue of it.

In the project presented in this book, Ernst-Reuter-Platz came to be what it was for us—a radical space of circulation, a functionally used and perceived environment, a potential place for aesthetic observation[9]—in the course and by virtue of the process of research/design. In the same way, we came to be what we were with it: auditory architects able to develop and perform practices to understand this square, that is, to configure-it-for-us, and to identify adequate measures for its transformation through design. Therefore, neither the object of design nor the designer are understood here as a priori clearly contoured objects,[10] fully configured in isolation from each other. Furthermore, they are not linked to one another by a unidirectional operation—the designer forming the object—but rather through the intertwined, co-dependent processes of their emerging embodiments. Accordingly, their respective stable appearances in any given moment are understood as temporary stabilizations of these processes, that is, as provisionally steady states. These presences will be destabilized again and again due to their common development, giving way in turn to new configurations, new stable appearances, new forms and meanings. To summarize: designer and object of design configure a dynamic, complex system—a system of co-emergence.

Their internal forms of organization are enabling conditions that allow the logic of the system and, in turn, according to this logic, their respective presences to emerge. These emerging presences constrain the dynamic organization of the enabling conditions, which in turn condition the further development of the system. Therefore, the object of design needs to be understood as a radical processual and relational presence. It brings about form and meaning for the designer by virtue of their process of co-emergence.

ARCHITECTURAL DESIGN AS ENVIRONMENTAL TRANSFORMATION

Elaborating on this interpretation of the aural environment as co-emerging presence, a further specification must be undertaken. I will develop this specification, questioning its objectual nature in two steps: firstly by delving into its definition as environment, and secondly by questioning its perceptual nature. Along with these reflections I will present the basic traits of my concept of architectural design.

The object of architectural design is never a single entity. It is never a distinct, clearly contoured phenomenon, isolated and independent from other phenomena and from the relations they—and with them, we—establish to one another. Affirming that, I am explicitly negating the definition of architecture as a set of operations of design and construction of individual three-dimensional and large-scale artifacts. The object of architectural design is always an *environment*.

Accordingly, and based on the concept of environment I am going to characterize in what follows, architectural design

9 See the chapter "The Auditory Architecture Research Unit's design for Ernst-Reuter-Platz" for an exhaustive description **10** The term "object" here is not to be understood as the opposite of subject, but as an entity that can be recognized as such by a subject. Accordingly, the subject becomes an object when it recognizes itself as such.

cannot be defined as the creation of new architectural objects—new isolated forms and volumes in a range of sizes larger than a group of human bodies, able to include and exclude them—by a designer. Architectural design here is not understood as the productive activity of a single agent—an activity initiated in and by the "inside" of a designer, which she "leads to the outside" (*pro-ducere*), generating an objectified entity—but rather as an *intervention* in ongoing processes of emergence, from and with which these actions and the current states of their agents arise. Consequently, the resulting design is not thought to be an out-come or a pro-duct, but rather the *trans-formation* of the object of design, which has been co-constituted through the same processes that led to its transformation. The architectural design is immanent to the system in which it emerges. Therefore, to design architecturally means firstly and most basically to *vary the conduct* of the designer in and towards the environment that she has co-constituted as her object of design: that is, to modify the ways she interacts with it.

Furthermore, looking deeper into the emerging structure of the environment, this change of conduct should not be understood as the beginning of the process of its transformation. It is simply a point of inflection, a change in the way the designer transforms her environment. It is a variation but not a beginning. The transformation of the environment does not start when the architect, expressed in traditional terms, "begins to design"—and consequently neither does it begin with its possible material alteration through construction. It begins—if a beginning can be identified at all in this radically processual framework—when the architect gets in touch with the surroundings that are going to become her environment, that is, her object of design. It begins, thus, with the emergence of the environment as such: the result of a process of transformation inherent and definitional not only to the process of architectural design, but more fundamentally to the process of *life*.

The development of an autonomous system—of a living unit like a monocellular bacteria or a human being—inexorably implies the transformation of its *surroundings*—the physicochemical context with which the living unit interacts—into an *environment*—a senseful, allover field in, with, and through which the autonomous unit becomes a self. In other words, the process of living implies the transformation of the surroundings-*of*-the-living-unit into an environment-*for*-the-living-unit. The living unit introduces a fundamental difference—a vector, a directionality, a valence, a value in the most basic meaning of this term—to its surroundings by giving its own "answers" to the "questions" "asked" by them. It transforms a field of neutral possibilities into a senseful—eventually also meaningful—meshwork of significant actualities. For example, a complex process of periodical changes in air pressure can be transformed by a living unit affected by it into sound—maybe "the sound of a car," maybe "an unpleasant, aggressive or even dangerous but familiar sound," maybe "beautiful music." And this transformation does not occur because the living unit "composes," that is, actively manipulates the disturbances of its surroundings by combining them in a target-oriented manner, but primarily because it "hears"—and maybe also "listens." Our surroundings are transformed into our environment first of all because we live, because we perform the skills embodied through a long phylogenetic history and a short ontogenetic one, that is, embodied in and through the very process of life itself. Our surroundings, thus, are (in) a constant and inexorable process of transformation, initiated and led by the logic of the living itself—the *bio*-logic.[11]

This very same logic of transformation also articulates cultural life, that is, the life of those particular living beings that, without ceasing to be autonomously organized matter and due to the logic generated by this form of organization, develop their existence in symbolic environments—networks of signs endowed with forms and meanings. These symbolic environments, which are themselves transformative processes, are subject to the same kind of transmutative dynamics.

Taking this account of the relationship between living beings and their environments as a framework within which to think architectural design, this can be understood basically as the introduction of a *modulation* in a continuum of environmental transformation.[12] The beginning of a process of design, therefore, can be understood as a transition from a passive and implicit variety of environmental transformation—which does not cease, but withdraws into the background—to an active and explicit one. [13] It can be understood primarily as a change of attitude towards the environment.[14] And this gesture—a change of position towards the object of design, a variation in the way the designer approaches an ever-changing environment—characterizes not only its beginning, but the whole process of design. Accordingly, *participation*,[15] *transformation*, and *intervention* are more suitable terms to describe this process than production, creation, or formalization. The first group of concepts expresses the operative relation of *immanent transformation*—or *transformative immanence*—that designer and object of design intimately share as constitutive parts of a common system, in contrast to the idea, implicit in the second set of terms, of a subject fundamentally separated from its object, relating to that object exclusively through its own actions. Architectural design is understood here as a mutual transformative dialogue between the designer and the environment, which, by virtue of their interaction, becomes her object of design and, furthermore, the consequence of the process of design: the environment transformed through design. Between the object of design and the results of the design process there is no substantial difference; both emerge due to the interaction between the designer and the environment as states of transformation of the latter.

VARIETIES OF REFLECTION

Building on this basis, the next relevant concepts in the approach to architectural design developed through the practice of auditory architecture are *reflection* and *adaptation*—two deeply interlaced concepts, as I am going to show. These concepts are denoted here in their very basic and minimal meaning.

11 The biological roots of the enactive approach are to be found in the theory of autopoiesis, defined by Humberto Maturana. For a first definition see: Maturana, H. R.: Biology of Cognition, in: Maturana, H. R. and Varela, F. J.: *Autopoiesis and Cognition: The Realization of the Living*, Boston 1970, pp. 2-58. For its generalization as a theory of biological autonomy see: Varela, F. J.: *Principles of Biological Autonomy*, New York 1979. For a summarized description of this approach see: Varela, F. J.: Organism: A Meshwork of Selfless Selves, in: Tauber, A. I.: *Organism and the Origin of Self*, Dordrecht 1991, pp. 79-107. 12 "Environmental transformation" can be understood here in two apparently different but confluent senses: as the transformation of the environment, and as the emergence of the environment through transformation. 13 The term "passive" as used here does not mean the absence of activity. As I will explain later, I use this term to qualify those activities that are not volitional and target-oriented. 14 Notice the similitude between this definition of the beginning of the process of architectural design and the first phase of the phenomenological method: the epoché. The change of attitude towards the world, suspending its validity as such in order to recognize how it appears, that is, to go from a naive or natural attitude to a phenomenological or reflexive one, is the first step in every phenomenological inquiry. For an introduction to the main concepts of the phenomenological method see: Gallagher, S. and Zahavi, D.: *The Phenomenological Mind: An Introduction to Philosophy of Mind and Cognitive Science*, New York 2008, chapter 2, "Methodologies." For a very inspiring description of this method as practice see: Depraz, N.: *Comprendre la phénoménologie: une practique concrete*, Paris 2006. 15 "Participation" here does not mean the involvement of users, neighbors, or other non-professional architects in the process of design as the formulation "participatory architecture" designates. I use the term here in a more fundamental sense, to express the constitutive, inherent, and inexorable implication of the designer in the system she configures with her environment.

"Reflection" does not refer here to a language-based process of interpretation or elucidation of a subject matter through logical and rhetorical operations. Instead, this term is used in its most fundamental meaning of *becoming aware*.[16] The operative core of this concept of reflection consists of the reorientation and sharpening of our perceptual skills in order to achieve awareness of the ongoing processes that manifest as our environment, without interrupting or disturbing their course. In this sense, reflection is not performed as an addition of intentional actions to the ongoing process of perception, but rather as a change in our perceptual attitude and our perceptual performance in a way that allows the environment to manifest as such. In other words, reflection as becoming aware is also a relational process of transformation—a variation of the course of the perceptual process that makes possible the presence of the environment as emergent process.

This variety of reflection is not based on the generation of new intentional objects through the processing of arising perceptions, but on *adaptation* to the very process of their arising. Its goal is not to produce artifacts clearly differentiated from the object of reflection, like explanations or interpretations, but to *let* the environment "manifest itself" exhaustively in its relational and dynamic complexion. Reflection, therefore, is understood here as the adjustment or con-formation of two processes deeply connected to each other, two processes mutually determining each other—the emergence of the environment as presence and the processes of constitution of intentional objects—that allows an adequate manifestation of the first through the second.

Although a good metaphor to describe this concept of reflection is the mirror—due to the passivity of its surface, allowing what comes into its scope to be seen, ideally, without adding to or modifying the reflected object, but simply enabling its own image to manifest—it would be necessary to complement this metaphor with another one: the touching hand, a soft, flexible, and trained hand able to follow the movements of the object being touched without losing contact, constantly adapting to its movements and arising forms. A hand moved by the touched object—endowed thus with the passivity of the mirror—finely sensitive to its continuous changes. *Passive adaptivity*, thus, is the main operative trait of this variety of reflection.

Understanding the process of auditory-architectural research/design as an intervention in the system of emergence configured by the designer and her environment, the performance of this kind of passive, adaptive reflection introduces new conditions into the system, altering it as a whole and expanding the possibilities of its transformation and the transformation of its components. The performance of practices of this variety of reflection—like the auditory diagramming I will present later—constitutes the fundamental layer of the whole process of auditory-architectural research/design. The realization of auditory-architectural projects is therefore led by reflection from their very beginning, and throughout their entire course.

DO WE PERCEIVE THE ENVIRONMENT?

Before I describe a concrete reflective practice, a further explanation of its object—the environment—must be undertaken. The need to specify a particular kind of reflection on

16 For an exhaustive exposition of this term in phenomenological/enactivist context see: Depraz, N., Varela, F. J. and Vermersch, P.: *On Becoming Aware: A Pragmatics of Experience*, Amsterdam 2003

(or better, *of*) the environment results from the definition of the environment as the all-over *horizon* of all our actions and perceptions that co-emerges with and through the coupling of our actions with the actions of our surroundings.[17] This definition requires us to address a question, commonly overlooked, in order to further specify the concept of reflection I am positing. This question can be phrased as follows: How objectual is the object of design? Or in more concrete terms: Is the environment an object? According to what I have been describing, the answer is clear: no, the environment is not an object, but rather the *dynamics of coherence* between phenomena that on the one hand emerges from the complex interaction between different intentional objects, and on the other hand allows all these objects to appear the very way they do. The conclusion I draw from this answer is one of the most fundamental hypotheses—and probably the most controversial—that I posit in this text: we do not perceive our environment.[18]

This conclusion is based on a very fundamental principle: we just perceive objects. Perceiving means to perceive something—to perceive some-thing. It means to be aware of a singular presence, a presence we differentiate, or better, a presence that appears to us as such, that is, as differentiated from its circumstances.[19] Therefore, although we perceive objects *in* an environment—objects the perception of which enables the emergence of the environment as presence—we do not perceive the environment as such. We perceive in and, mainly, with the environment, and the presence of an environment depends on these perceptions, but the environment as such is not one of these perceptual objects.

17 In this definition of "environment" I am referring to Merleau-Ponty's definition of world, interpreting it from an enactivist perspective: "The world is not an object such that I have in my possession the law of its making; it is the natural setting of, and field for, all my thoughts and all my explicit perceptions" (Merleau-Ponty, M.: *Phenomenology of Perception*, London 1962, p. xii). The difference between environment and world is not substantial but spatiotemporal: the environment is the immediate world, the world we experience in the current moment and the actual surroundings—the present world-around. **18** Positing this hypothesis, I contradict, for once, Merleau-Ponty: "We must not, therefore, wonder whether we really perceive a world, we must instead say: the world is what we perceive" (Merleau-Ponty, M.: op. cit., p xviii). **19** I am referring here, again in agreement, to the most basic definition of perception as provided by Merleau-Ponty: "the patterning of data, the imposition of meaning on a chaos of sense-data" (Merleau-Ponty, M.: op. cit., pp. 22-23). **20** In this regard: "[…] Husserl distinguishes between intentionality of act, which is that of our judgments and of those occasions when we voluntarily take up a position – the only intentionality discussed in the *Critique of Pure Reason* – and operative intentionality *(fungierende Intentionalität)* or that which produces the natural and antipredicative unity of the world and of our life, being apparent in our desires, our evaluations and in the landscape we see, more clearly than in objective knowledge, and furnishing the text which our knowledge tries to translate into precise language" (Merleau-Ponty, M.: op. cit., p. XX, italics in original).

Nevertheless, the environment is present for us and consequently the question now is: How is the environment present, if not perceptually? The first step towards an answer is to state that the environment does not come to be present due to the performance of intentional acts based on processing perceptually constituted objects: the environment does not manifest firstly through imagination, fantasy, categorization, composition, deduction, induction, or judgment. The environment is not constituted through any objectifying form of intentionality, but through the performance of *operative intentionality*: a variety of aboutness, a way to refer to what we tend to be aware of that presents it as a whole instead of configuring it as an object or a collection of singular objects.[20]

The term "whole" here does not designate another kind of object—a big, complex one, an object of objects—but the dynamics that bring and hold all present objects together and, more fundamentally, allow the constitution of every single one by virtue of a double and simultaneous relation of coherence: between the different objects and between each of them and the subject to whom they manifest—the subject that co-constitutes them, the subject that co-emerges with them. Understood as a whole, the environment is not composed of perceptions. It is not a configuration of singular perceptual objects. It does not appear after perception. It is present as the *manner* in which all perceptions achieve their respective objective pres-ences together. It is present as the implicit, dynamics of coherence of all co-emerging perceptions. The environment, therefore, is the dynamic and relational condition of possibility required for perceptions to appear.

This transcendental formulation is not meant in the temporal sense, that is, it does not mean that the environment appears before perception. The envi-ronment is not an a priori—neither in the empirical nor in the ideal sense. As their condition of possibility, the environment appears simultaneously to the perceptions as their *dynamic and relational horizon*. The singular perceptions are, in turn, the condition of possibility of that horizon. Perceptual objects and the environment in, with, and through which they appear—as well as the subject to whom both manifest—co-emerge. Similarly to the figure and its ground, perceptions and their environment become present at the same time and through mutual conditioning.

Perceptual objects cannot become present if we do not participate in the dynamics of their coherent appearance. In turn, these dynamics cannot be established if we do not perceive objects. But the presences of the perceptual objects and these dynamics are of a different kind. While the objects are pri-marily perceptual, the environment is present in, through, and as our partic-ipation: that is, in, through, and as our acting-in/with-it. Our environment—this is my thesis—is not perceptually but *operatively* present. It is present in and through our actions, in the performance of the mutually enabling con-nection between our actions and our perceptions. It is present in, through, and as the constant actualization of our sensory-motor skills, as our most fun-damental *cognitive domain*. It is not present in an objectified way—as some-thing thrown (*-ject*) against or in front (*ob-*) of us—but implicitly, immanently in our con-duct: in the actual way we lead (*-duct*) ourselves with (*con-*) the objects we perceive, the objects we co-constitute through our interactions, the objects that, as the environment, co-emerge with us. In summary: I posit that our environment—our "Umwelt": our world-around—is the non-objec-tified, operative presence of the process of coherence, of coming-to-be and "sticking-together" (*co-haerere*) of all our perceptions and actions. It is their dynamic, enabling horizon. It is the fragile, always temporary, ever-renewed stabilization of the dynamics of co-emergence of all objects that inhabit it as its conditions of possibility, being in turn enabled by it. The environment is, primarily, implicitly present in our active, sensuous, and emotional being-in-the-world. This presence is also the condition of possibility for us to be in our world—to become ourselves-in-the-world—and for this world and its/our objects to appear as such—as our world-and-its/our-objects—to us.

TRANSITIONAL AWARENESS

Based on this further concretization of the environment as being opera-tively present, it is possible to further specify the concept of reflection I have described. To reflect the environment requires being intensively in touch with its operative, implicit presence in a way that facilitates the transition between this variety of presence and an objectual, explicit one. To reflect the environment means to *mediate* between both varieties of presence, to be reflectively active—in a passive and adaptive manner—on the permeable edge between the dynamics of configuration and the already configured objects.

To adopt this intermediating position is necessary for two reasons. Firstly, to not falsify the object of reflection, that is, to reflect the environment as an operative whole and not as an objectified substitutive. Secondly, to perform this reflection in a way that makes possible the arising of objectified presences, which will enable the performance of those intentional operations also performed in the process of design, like categorization, judgment, logical inference, or composition. To reflect the environment, therefore, requires the establishment of a specific *variety of awareness* that allows mutual transitions between the processes of objectification and the objectified entities to become present, that is, the presence of the transitions between the process of emergence and the emerging qualities, between the unstable and non-formalized processes and the stabilized and formalized objects, between the implicit non-sign—the not-yet-sign—and the explicit sign. I call this variety of awareness *transitional awareness* and define it as the kind of awareness that mediates reciprocally between the operational and the perceptual.

When we are transitionally aware, the objectified presences partially lose their stability. Their contours, their clear and firm forms and meanings become blurry, and consequently the objectified presences become open to redefinition. Transitional awareness does not present the operative presences in an objectified way—it is transitional and not translational—but rather presents the already objectified ones *according* to their operative, that is, processual and relational—emerging—substrate. It presents the perceptual objects emerging in an environment on the edge of their constitution as such, that is, on the edge of their perception. It presents them as being mutually dependent, fitting in with each other in their shared process of coming to be—of becoming coherent. It presents them—it continues presenting them—but on the edge between their objectification in the foreground of our perceptual awareness and their relational dynamics of coherence in the background of our operative awareness. It presents them in their *communication*, in their mutually conditioning constitution, and, beyond, in their participation in the constitution of the whole that, in turn, constrains their respective appearance. Strongly anchored in our sensory and emotional experience of the world, transitional awareness allows us to realize the dynamics of stabilization and destabilization of the phenomena that participate in the environment we are trying to reflect und thus the logic of the environment—the environmental logic, the environment as logic—that enables their manifestation.

Due to the strong, reciprocal continuity between processes of constitution and constituted objects, the sign-based expressions of the latter that appear through the reflection performed in transitional awareness—single words, groups of words, lines, forms, visual configurations: text, drawings, diagrams—are characterized by an undeniable and immediate *sense of identity* with their operational ground.[21] Simultaneously experiencing the object of reflection—the environment—and its reflection—constellations of sign-based objects[22]—we recognize the first through the second. To perform this variety of passive, adaptive, transitional

21 I use the term "expression" as interpreted by Merleau-Ponty. For a summarized explanation of this interpretation: Landes, D. A.: Expression, in: *The Merleau-Ponty Dictionary*, London 2013, pp. 73-74. For an exhaustive description: Landes, D. A.: *Merleau-Ponty and the Paradoxes of Expression*, London 2013. In regard to language: Merleau-Ponty, M.: Indirect Language and the Voice of Silence, in: Merleau-Ponty, M.: *Signs*, Evanston 1964, pp. 39-83.

reflection allows the configuration of objective *analogies* to the environment as an emerging whole. Therefore, the performance of this variety of reflection is a necessary condition to be able to transform the environment—to continue transforming it—through design.

Having identified a kind of awareness as a condition of possibility of a particular variety of reflection, the question now is: How can this kind of awareness—transitional awareness —be achieved? According to theories of embodied and situated cognition, a particular variety of awareness, like every kind of so-called "mental" activity, arises out of a certain variety of organic, "bodily" activity, that is, a certain behavior of the individual who is aware in and with its surroundings—a certain conduct. This means that only through the realization of a specific kind of interaction with the environment can a particular variety of awareness be achieved.

The kind of conduct that enables us to be transitionally aware is characterized by two main traits. I already referred to the first one: *passivity*. Here, this term means basically a lessening of our will, and consequently of the target-oriented quality of our actions. In order to be transitionally aware, our actions should cease to be motivated and led by our own initiative. Instead we should let them be led by the activity of our environment. We should cease to act according to a fixation of goals and a voluntary mobilization of our acts in order to achieve them, and instead let ourselves be moved by the dynamics that we encounter. Without renouncing our agency, we should let ourselves *be driven* by the agency of our environment.

The second trait of this variety of conduct, facilitated by and complementary to the first, is an *open attentiveness*. Acting passively, we can let ourselves sense what is happening around us and with us. Without making any effort, without having any particular focus, without trying to make any differentiation—also not between ourselves and the environment—or any judgment, and instead just noticing it, revealing it, disclosing it—letting it be revealed, be disclosed as presence-for-us. We can just attend to what spontaneously arises in the current situation. This open attentiveness can be characterized, furthermore, as *intransitive*: there should not be any intention to transcend the attentiveness itself, there should be no aim to objectify or formalize the presences it enables. The intention should only be to become available to us-in-our-environment, to be open to the agency of both components of the shared system and to its constitutive dynamics. As a subsidiary, we should let this dynamics become evident— intuitively evident[23]—in the same way that photographic film allows the light to be seen in a different way, in a different medium.

A formulation coined by Kant in his third Critique laconically summarizes the fundamental traits of the kind of behavior I am trying to describe: *purposiveness without purpose*.[24] In the variety of action characterized by this apparently paradoxical formulation, the aim motivating the action is

22 I use the term "constellation" in a similar way to Dieter Mersch in: Mersch, D.: *Epistemologies of Aesthetics*, Zürich 2015. This book is an important reference for the development of the concept of aesthetic reflection that I am presenting here.

23 For the concept of "intuitive evidence" see: Varela, F. J.: Neurophenomenology. A Methodological Remedy for the Hard Problem, in: *Journal of Consciousness Studies*. 3, 4, 1996, pp. 330-349.

24 In his "Critique of Judgment," Kant delivers a first definition of his concept of "purposiveness without purpose" in relation to "will" (§ 10). Later on he presents a definition of beauty based on this paradoxical expression: "Beauty is the form of the purposiveness of an object, so far as this is perceived in it without any representation of a purpose" (§ 17). Nevertheless, the relation between beauty and "purposiveness without purpose" in relation to the "judgment of taste" is introduced already in §11. For my first interpretation see: Arteaga, A: Sensuous knowledge. Making sense through the skin, in: Elo, M. and Luoto, M. (eds.), *Senses of Embodiment. Art, Technics, Media*, New York 2014, pp. 85-96.

maintained. The action has an intention, a purpose. In the concrete case I am describing, the final intention is to reflect the environment, and the immediate intention is to become available to its agency in order to achieve transitional awareness as a condition of possibility to accomplish the final goal. On this base, I understand the negative formulation "without purpose" in a way that is similar to how I interpreted the term "passivity." Obviously "without purpose" does not express the absence of purpose—the whole formulation would be absurd—the same way "passivity" does not mean the absence of activity. Instead "without purpose" qualifies the purposiveness of the action. It qualifies its purpose. In my interpretation, "without purpose" expresses a *temporary suspension* of the established purpose: once defined, the purpose should be held in abeyance, should be "forgotten." It should neither be eliminated nor should it be explicitly present in the performance of the actions: it should not be in the focus of our attention. Instead, in order to achieve our purpose, the actions should be performed *as if* they would not have any purpose. The specific intentionality of the actions, once set, should be ignored in favor of the performance of the most generic, fundamental, and inevitable form of intentionality: the one that inexorably directs our awareness to something different from the awareness itself—in our case, the environment we aim to reflect.[25] Our intentionally determined goal, our premeditatedly defined intention—to reflect the environment—should slide into the background of our awareness and should not determine the flow of action, in order to allow the agency of the whole system, and especially of the environment, to become the leading force. Our volitional intention should be operatively suspended to let our operative intentionality—the most fundamental dynamics of connection with our surroundings—present the environment in its relational and processual nature. The purposiveness of the actions should be reduced to the intentionality that spontaneously emerges out of the coupling between its agent and her surroundings, and should not be determined—if this would ever be possible—exclusively by the first. The purposiveness of the variety of conduct able to induce transitional awareness is not configured by an individual, volitional, unidirectional purpose, but instead emerges spontaneously in a relational, dynamic field, due to the actualization of the embodiment of the one who is aware.

Following Kant, I consider purposiveness without purpose—here specified as passivity and open attentiveness—to be the most fundamental and defining factor, and the most indispensable condition of possibility, of what we call *aesthetics*. Consequently, I call the kind of conduct that allows the induction of transitional awareness, and furthermore allows us to reflect the environment in its emerging complexion, *aesthetic conduct*. I understand aesthetics to be primarily a kind of interaction, a particular *variety of conduct* able to operatively dispose our most fundamental dynamics of connectivity with our environment in a reflexive way. Acting aesthetically, being therefore transitionally aware, our perceptual world partially loses its stability and the clear contours of its objects. Their apparently incontestable obviousness, their ostensibly undeniable identity with the things they bring to expression, is provisionally suspended in favor of their relational constitution. Due to this variety of action, the presence of the

25 I use "intentionality" here in its phenomenological meaning of the *aboutness* of consciousness.

environment's transformative logic and the emergent nature of its objects coexist dynamically with their fully configured states. Their transformative manifestation makes them available for new configurations, for the emergence of new forms and meanings—better: for their emergence as new forms and meanings—and, beyond, for their transformative architectural design. This is the operative core of the transformative power of aesthetics.

On this basis, the term "aesthetic architecture"—a concept intimately related to "architecture of embodiment"—would point to a modality of architectural design practice understood as a process of environmental transformation necessarily grounded in the performance of an aesthetic conduct, and consequently endowed with its potentiality of radical transformation, rooted in the transformative nature of the environment it aims to transform.

I would like to summarize what I have elaborated thus far. The process of architectural design begins with the encounter between an architect and the circumstances that will be constituted as her environment. Due to the process of design, both entities co-emerge as their respective new specifications: as the object of design and its designer. Accordingly, the process of design can be understood as the coupling of two ongoing processes of embodiment, as the configuration and evolution of a dynamic and complex system by virtue of which its components co-emergence. The object of design is the emerging environment of the designer in and through the current process of design. This environment is present for her operatively, that is, implicitly in her conduct as the dynamics of coherence between the objects surrounding the designer, and between them and her. Since the object of design is the environment and the goal of the design process is its transformation, there is a need for a form of reflection that reveals the mutual transitions between the operative presence of the environment—the environment qua environment—and the perceptual presence of its components. Such a form of reflection would allow us to express the environment through a configuration of objectified presences—of singular phenomena. This variety of reflection can be developed on the basis of a specific kind of awareness—transitional awareness—which allows the simultaneous presence of the process of constitution and the constituted objects. This kind of awareness can be induced by a particular type of conduct—aesthetic conduct—characterized basically by passivity and open attentiveness. The process of design must be performed based on these varieties of conduct, awareness, and reflection in order to be a process of environmental transformation.

AUDITORY DIAGRAMMING

When hearing and listening acquire a certain preponderance among the activities performed by the architect in the process of reflective transformation of her co-emerging environment, this can be considered to be an *aural environment*. An aural environment, therefore, is not understood as pre-existing surroundings configured by sounds—a soundscape—but as a senseful milieu that emerges primarily, but not exclusively, conditioned by the performance of different practices of reflexive hearing and listening. An aural environment is not formed by sounds, but is predominantly co-constituted through hearing and listening. In other words, it is an environment that emerges strongly conditioned by different varieties of aural interaction. The phenomena that are present in an aural environment are not necessary acoustic ones—aural phenomena or phenomena related to sound—but modally non-specific ones that emerge as enabled by the performance of different varieties of hearing and listening, that is, phenomena that become present for the architect through hearing and listening. Consequently, hearing and listening are understood here as enabling conditions for the emergence of the environment, and not as procedures for its apprehension or mental representation. They are understood as particular forms of engagement with the environment, as distinctive ways to influence the dynamic coupling between the architect and the object of design. The specificities of these varieties of action enable the course of their co-emergence to evolve in a way that is different, for example, from what would happen if seeing and looking were the predominant sensory modalities. The aurally emerging environment thus becomes a possible other environment.[26] It is not "the same environment perceived in another way"—this formulation would imply that the environment is out there, being something in and for itself, to be discovered from different perspectives. Hearing and listening enable particular forms of transformation of the environment encountered by the architect into the environment that becomes her object of design. Furthermore, hearing and listening open fundamentally new possibilities for this environment to be transformed through design. To open up new basal possibilities of environmental constitution and transformation is the primary raison d'être of an auditive architecture.

An exhaustive description of the specificities of hearing and listening and of the particularities of aural environments would exceed the framework of this text. Nevertheless, I would like to point briefly to one basic characteristic of these modes of environmental engagement: their particular relationship with the process of objectification, that is, the process of constitution of perceptual objects in contact with their objective correlates. This feature is especially distinctive of hearing—the "simple nature" of the aural[27]—which makes this specific kind of activity particularly relevant for the reflective constitution of auditory environments. A comparison with the visual—accordingly, with seeing more than looking—can help to explain this issue. When we see, we always see something concrete, we always see some-thing. Even if we do not "know" what it is that we are seeing—if we do not have a name for it because, for example, we are seeing it for the first time—we see a clearly contoured entity that we can differentiate from its surroundings, and which we could describe: we see an object. To see always means to see differentiated singularities—to see objects.[28] To hear, on the other hand, does not mean necessarily to hear some-thing. Most of the time we hear without needing to configure the hearing experience as an aural object. Commonly, what we hear instantiates a fluid background rather than solid and singular presences—a background we can experience as such with no problem, an indifference we can smoothly coexist with.

[26] In direct reference to: Voegelin, S.: *Sonic Possible Worlds*, London 2014. [27] According to the expression of Jean-Luc Nancy, who, in contrast, denotes listening as the "tense, attentive, or anxious state" of the aural register" (Nancy, J.-L.: *Listening*, New York 2007, p. 5). [28] "There is, at least potentially, more isomorphism between the visual and the conceptual, even if only by virtue of the fact that the *morphē*, the 'form' implied in the idea of 'isomorphism,' is immediately thought or grasped on the visual plane. The sonorous, on the other hand, outweighs form. It does not dissolve it, but rather enlarges it; it gives it an amplitude, a density, and a vibration or an undulation whose outline never does anything but approach. The visual persists until its disappearance; the sonorous appears and fades away into its permanence" (Nancy, J.-L.: *Listening*, New York 2007, p. 2).

Hearing, therefore, spontaneously enables a dynamic, relational, non-objectual but operative presence of our environment that reveals its emerging nature. Consequently, the auditory presence of the environment—the presence of the environment as aural environment—provides a privileged condition for its reflection, and furthermore for its research/design, as emerging presence.

The practice of auditory diagramming that I am going to present in the following paragraphs has been developed in the course of the project "Klangumwelt Ernst-Reuter-Platz," on the basis of former practices conceived and performed in the context of other projects of the Auditory Architecture Research Unit.[29] The relationship between this practice and the conceptual framework I have outlined should not be understood according to two operations that are commonly used to describe the relations between so-called "theory" and "practice": "explanation" and "application."[30] The concepts I have described do not explain this practice, and this practice does not perform or apply these ideas. There is no such sequential series of "translations"—of transferences between stabilized language-based configurations and actions. Both the conceptual framework I have already described and the systematized forms of action I am going to present now were consolidated simultaneously in a relationship of mutual determination, and as a result of the interlacing of different practices performed in an iterative way, including field research, sound recordings, diagrammatic drawing, essayistic writing, conceptual analysis and generalization, literary research, and interdisciplinary dialogue, among others. According to the model of co-emergence underpinning my ideas about architectural design, a formalized practice or a conceptual framework are constructions emerging out of a specific dynamic connection between concrete varieties of action, which in turn are constrained by the arising artifacts they enable.

I understand diagramming as an experimental practice in a graphic medium, whose purpose is not to represent the subject matter to which it refers but to present its constitutive inner dynamic relationships, that is, the meshwork of forces that allows the components of the subject matter to cohere—to appear as an object. The practice of diagramming produces an image-like artifact that mediates between the one who creates it and the entity she intends by configuring an objectual analogy to a non-objectual presence—the processual structure of the entity at hand.[31]

VARIETIES OF AURAL ACTION

The conceptual underpinning for the realization of an auditory diagram is configured by a list of reciprocal varieties of aural action—modes of hearing or listening—and the intentional objects that can be constituted respectively through their performance. The fundamental idea here is that of a mutual dependence between both parties: certain objects can be constituted only through the performance of particular ways of hearing or listening, and, in turn, certain types of

[29] The most relevant of these practices was the "listening-protocol"—original German "Hörprotokoll"—developed in the framework of the project "long-term auditory observation Schlieren" (*auditive Langzeitbeobachtung Schlieren*). This practice helped us to identify the different varieties of aural activity and their respective objects of awareness.

[30] I consider the commonly accepted distinction between "theory" and "practice" to be neither conceptually correct nor operatively useful. Instead I prefer to distinguish between very precisely defined and performed practices like "to write a phenomenological description" or "to outline an auditory map," differentiating their respective degrees and modalities of reflection. The substitution of these established categories through concrete practices contributes to a focus on the specific actions performed in each practice, making it easier to establish clear relationships between them, and to clarify their respective cognitive functions.

[31] Notice that this procedure—the generation of an objectual configuration in contact with a non-objectual presence—is consistent with the function of transitional awareness. On this basis it is plausible to consider diagramming as a genuine aesthetic practice.

aural activities can be triggered by the spontaneous presence of a particular object.[32] This list, which was generated by, and is constantly developed through, the performance of this practice, is used as the underpinning for its realization.

We have defined four basic varieties of aural activity: analytical, emotional, imaginative, and associative. While the first is clearly a form of listening, the others are varieties of hearing. The aural activity we call *analytical listening* implies a very focused attention on those presences that define the experience as aural: the listener concentrates on what she is listening to, that is, on what emerges through listening as listened to—as sounds. The aural objects are the focus of awareness, and the act of listening is the predominant volitional action. On the contrary, in the case of *emotional, imaginative,* and *associative hearing,* the aural activity and the aural objects withdraw into the background, allowing concentration to focus on general aspects of the emerging environment. Although in practicing these varieties of aural activity the research/designer does not cease to hear attentively, she should not be focused on what she hears, but rather on the presences that emerge while hearing. The aural activity in these cases establishes a sensitive field of action that conditions the performance of other activities—reflecting, imagining, or associating. These other intentional acts are performed by hearing, while hearing, and thus conditioned through hearing, but are not determined by it.

I am now going to provide a detailed description of each variety of aural activity and the objects associated with each of them. To listen analytically means to actively attend to what can be heard, trying to establish precise differentiations between single units, between their components and properties, and between traits of their collective behavior. It is an activity, that is, a volitional and target-oriented form of aural action focused exclusively on the aural experience of the field. The listener acts as if she would use her ears the same way a speleologist uses her flashlight in an unknown cave. The realist idea of a listener exploring an existing environment configured by single objects is a useful metaphor in this case—a useful do-it-as-if. Through a recurrent performance of this analytical procedure, the intentional objects that can be constituted through this variety of aural action have been categorized and distributed in three sets, which relate to three fields of attention respectively: single sounds, general behavior of the single sound, and behavior of sounds as totality. Attending to the first group requires the sharpest concentration, the highest tension of listening, and the highest level of acoustical training and knowledge. These levels decrease the wider the focus of attention becomes, while attending to the second and the third sets.

The most basic and immediate result of listening analytically to single sounds is their identification: we hear cars, pedestrians, birds, and so on. This identification should be done as precisely as possible in order to not hear "cars," for example, but "an old car" or, even better, "an old Volkswagen Golf." In a second step, the identified single sounds can be aurally analyzed regarding their time structure—continuum, periodically or irregularly fragmented—their spatial structure—stable in a single location, moving along a line or within an area—and their parametric properties—the average, range, and time structure of their loudness, general

32 This relationship is nothing but an aural specification of the fundamental relationship between *noema* and varieties of *noesis.*

pitch, and inner pitch distribution. To listen to the general behavior of the single sounds means attending to their common ways of being present rather than their individual specificities. Listening with this focus, we can identify the level of differentiability between sound events (can singular events be distinguished from one another?) the level of their identifiability (can singular sounds be easily recognized?) the level of identifiability of the acoustic source[33] (can we recognize the vibrant body producing the sounds we are hearing?) the level of locatability (can the spatial position of the acoustic sources be identified?) the level of diversity of sounds, the level of diversity of time structures, and the level of diversity of spatial structures. Regarding the overall chronological and topological behavior of the sounds, it is possible to identify the general levels of steady, periodically and non-periodically changing sounds, and the levels of steady and dynamic distribution of the sounds. Each of these behaviors can be respectively differentiated with reference to close, mean, and far topological ranges.

The last focus of analytical listening is configured by the sounds as totality.[34] While in the former set of objects the listener attends to single sound events, considering their overall behavior, in this case she listens to the whole field that she is researching as an aural unit, trying to differentiate its global aural properties. The objects of attention that can be constituted according to this focus are similar to those included in the first set, listening to the single sounds. The parametric traits of the aural field—loudness and pitch—can be analyzed according to the same categories described for single sound events: the average, range, and time structure of its loudness, general pitch, and inner pitch distribution. Regarding its chronology, it is possible to identify the level of time density, that is, how many events occur per time unit—how "full" with sound the time is. Relating to its topology, it is possible to identify the spatial density and the spatial wideness—respectively, how high is the concentration of sounds in the research field, and how extensive is the field, according to what can possibly be heard. The last two parameters in this category aurally interlace time and space: the level of reverberation and the possible presence of echoes.

Hearing emotionally constitutes the most relevant part of auditory diagramming. This variety of hearing is the most specific aural implementation of the type of reflection I have described above. Consequently, in order to hear emotionally it is necessary to act aesthetically, and thus to be transitionally aware. The researcher/designer should reduce the tension that characterizes analytical listening to a minimum, while maintaining a clear aural connection with her surroundings. The aural presence of the environment must be sustained without being the focus of attention. According to the kind of open attentiveness I have described as a trait of aesthetic conduct, the focus of attention must be widened as much as possible beyond the limits of the aural. In other words, by experiencing against the background of a continuous but passive aural engagement with the environment, the hearer simply tries to identify the qualities currently emerging as (qualities of) the environment, as well as

33 Using the terminology of Pierre Schaffer, "identifiability" refers to the "*objet sonore,*" and "identifiability of the acoustic source" to the "*corp sonore.*" This clear conceptual distinction is commonly blurred, due to the use of the terms of the second to refer to the first: we say we hear a car, and not the sound produced by a car.

34 I use the word "totality" here in the way Henri Bortoft does, differentiating it from the concept of "wholeness," which I use to characterize the environment as emergent entity. While both terms refer to the complete group of elements that configure an entire entity, "totality" expresses a variety of entireness that is configured by a simple addition of components. "Wholeness" on the contrary designates a more complex relationship of mutual dependence between parts and whole. For an exhaustive explanation see: Bortoft, H.: *The Wholeness of Nature. Goethe's way of Science*, Edinburgh 1996, especially chapter 1, "Authentic and Counterfeit Wholeness."

those arising as (qualities of) her own emotional states. She tries to notice what moves her—her e-motions—and her environment, what keeps her and her environment in movement: towards each other, against each other, out of the current situation, deeper into it, expanding, compressing, etc. The differentiation between qualities of the environment and the state of the hearer is not considered relevant here. Both kinds of qualities emerge from the same system, configured by both parties, and cannot therefore be taken as "belonging" intrinsically and exclusively to one or the other. The differentiation between hearer and environment that underpins the attribution of qualities to one of them is facilitated by varieties of awareness that present both as categorically—and even ontologically—differentiated. Acting aesthetically, these categorical differentiations become blurred.

The metaphor I like to use in this case, in contrast to the speleologist I mentioned to illustrate analytical listening, is the enologist, trying to identify the qualities of a new wine. She would probably drink slowly, or at least take the time required by the process, perhaps temporarily closing her eyes, trying to "follow" the movements of the whole situation of tasting, the uncertain, vague sensuous presences, until she is able to objectify them: dry, mature, homogeneous, deep, mineral, lightly fruity, developing slowly, wide, expansive, etc. Although this can be considered a process of discernment—if, for example, the wine appears to be homogenous it is implicitly non-heterogeneous—the differentiations are not realized through the isolation and contraposition of components and aspects of a whole: it is not an analytic discernment. The differentiation here happens rather through a sensitive, open attention—an attention directed to the wholeness of events—and the passive intent to situate the subtle emergent presences adequately, coherently, in the semantic field, taking the sense of identity between both sensuous presences and concepts as criteria of truth. Due to the specificity of this procedure, it is not suitable to use pre-established qualities—as was the case for analytical listening—but rather to perform it as an open-ended process, as if every situation were new and unique, and as if we were hearing (it) for the first time. In contrast to the acoustic nature of the parameters in analytical listening, the emerging qualities objectified through emotional hearing are not acoustic properties. They are general environmental and subjective qualities—qualities of the current states of a self and its world—the constitution of which is conditioned by a specific variety of aural interaction.

The last two types of aural activity used to configure an exhaustive auditory diagram, imaginative and associative hearing, require a balance between active and passive action. Without renouncing the passivity necessary to hear emotionally—that is, keeping the aural experience in a present background, with the passive openness of an aesthetic action—the activity of the hearer must be reoriented according to two sets of questions. Regarding imagination, the questions are: What could sound here and now? And more relevantly: What could happen here and now? Concerning association: What does it sound like here and now? And more significantly: What it is like here? To imagine and to associate are the forms of intentional activity that substitute reflection on the background of the aural experience. Just like hearing emotionally, hearing imaginatively and associatively should be performed as open-ended processes, without relying on any pre-established category or object.

To imagine and to associate does not mean here to "escape reality," or to be oriented towards presences other than the ones arising from the field of research. On the contrary, imagining and associating—that is, (re)calling presences with different time and space coordinates—make possible the emergence of new phenomena of the present environment, since it is the imaginative and associative but inevitably perception-based interaction with this very environment in its actuality that makes it possible for them to arise.

DIAGRAMMING AURALLY

The realization of an auditory diagram takes these varieties of aural activities and possible intentional objects as a basis.[35] In order to diagram an environment aurally, it is necessary to conceive a spatiotemporal plan: a configuration of adequate positions in the time and space of the researched field. This plan can be configured by a single point, a series of points, a linear trajectory, or a random path into a more or less limited area, respectively in time and space. These choices must be made in a preliminary research phase, during which different zones of the environment to be researched/designed should be provisionally delimited by the performance of a simplified type of emotional hearing that allows for the detection of general differences between areas, that is, chrono-topological borders in which the environment becomes "different"—in which we begin to "be somewhere else." The extent and specific particularities of the identified zones will provide the base for elaborating a spatiotemporal plan.

Researching the field according to this plan, the aural architect performs the different varieties of aural actions, adopting the respective modalities of awareness. The sequence in which the different varieties of aural activity are performed is a personal choice based on individual experience of diagramming. The criterion to determine this sequence is the ease of transition from one to the other. I usually prefer to begin listening analytically as a way to establish a strong link of attention with the field, and then move to hearing emotionally, reducing the tension of my aural engagement while keeping the established connection. Later, maintaining my aesthetic attitude, I start to hear imaginatively, and then associatively, perhaps moving back and forth between these varieties of hearing and emotional hearing in order to finely reflect environmental qualities that might have emerged through imagination and association.

During this process, the researcher/designer writes down the emerging objects on a tablet using different colors or color variations for each variety of aural activity. Although paper can also be used, the possibility of manipulating the notated objects in an easy, intuitive, and (apparently) immediate way on a touch screen provides the necessary flexibility to adapt the diagramming to the emergence of environmental presences. This becomes evident once a few words have been written, when two operations are applied to them: changing their size and modifying their relative position on the surface. The first operation relates in a direct way to the level of presence of each object: the more

35 The description that follows refers to the process of diagramming performed on the tangible field in and with which the diagrammed environment emerges. Nevertheless, the same process of diagramming can be realized exclusively based on imagination.

present, the bigger the word that expresses it. The second refers to the relationship between the emerging objects: the stronger the connection between them, the closer they are moved together on the tablet screen. The nature of this connection can be diverse and more or less explicit or vague. The words on the surface should be moved towards or away from each other neither as a result of a logical deduction nor due to the establishment of a causal relation between them. Their proximity on the screen should exclusively reflect the commonality with which they appear, their "belonging together." Both the size of the single words and their relative position on the screen should be fixed intuitively, according to one single criterion: the *sense of spontaneous coherence*—or *Stimmigkeit*[36]—between what is arising on the surface and what is emerging as the environment.

The diagram begins to arise when the written words acquire dynamic and relational qualities through these simple operation; it thus begins to appear as a processual and relational whole. When this happens, the aural architect achieves a very rich and precise awareness of the environment qua environment—that is, as a co-emerging operative all-over presence—which reveals its inner logic of constitution—its transformational logic—as well as adequate ways to intervene in these processes of environmental transformation through architectural interventions. To diagram aurally does not mean to represent existing objects around the architect, but to reflect a dynamic and relational whole in its process of emergence, providing operative conditions for the appearance of its *analogon*, an equivalent network of objects expressed in a sign-based medium. The diagram is understood therefore not as a representational entity but as a non-reductive instrument of *cognitive mediation* between the one who is diagramming and the diagrammed. Through the reflective practice of auditory diagramming, both the current state of the environment and possible future states manifest for the researcher/designer in a clear, explicit, and intimate relationship of reciprocal continuity. Reflecting the emerging of the environment, the auditory diagram also mediates between its current and possible future states.

CONCLUSION

As conclusion, I would like to explain briefly the potential contributions of auditory architecture to the general field of architectural design. These contributions refer to the concept of architectural design, as well as its performance. The practice of auditory architecture provides an operative framework within which to conceive architectural design as the participation in a process of environmental transformation, instead of as the formalization and production of isolated large-scale objects. The performance of auditory-architectural practices thus mediates between the enactivist concept of environment and the architectural design practice, contributing to the development of an embodied and situated architecture—an *architecture of embodiment*.[37] Due to the operative presence of the environment, this kind of architectural design can only be instantiated on the base of practices of aesthetic reflection. Auditory architecture configures a framework in which this kind of practice can be conceived and performed,

36 The German noun "Stimmigkeit" derives from the verb "stimmen," which in a musical context means "to tune," and in a general context "to be adequate or coherent." The transformations of the words written on the tablet can be understood as a process of "tuning," that is, as a process of bringing them—as a player does with the strings of an instrument—into a mutual relationship of coherence, which in turn makes them cohere with the way their counterparts appear in the environment. As a consequence, the field of relationships that gradually comes into view on the surface—the diagram as a whole—will appear as coherent—"stimmig," tuned—with the environment as relational whole. 37 My research project "Architecture of Embodiment," begun in 2013, provides a wider background to develop my concept and practices of auditory architecture. In turn, I consider auditory architecture to constitute the aural perspective from which to conceive and practice an architecture of embodiment. For a description of this project: http://www.architecture-embodiment.org/

contributing, therefore, to the development of radically aesthetics-based architectural design processes. Due to the particular relationship between the activities of listening and hearing and the constitution of perceptual objects, the aural-aesthetic reflection of the environment can contribute to the reinforcement of its dynamic and relational manifestation, counterbalancing the tendency to objectification spontaneously induced by an exclusively vision-based reflection. In summary, the practice of auditory architecture can be understood as a germinal model of an exhaustively aesthetics-based practice of architectural design that enhances the process in which it is fundamentally embedded: the common process of sense-making.

sound

discre

movement p
balance between singular sound and cloud-so

medium, variable temporal der
medium

somewhat opp

dynamic　　　*empty*
medium to lo

high, variable spatial d

of me

cycles   steps
                    voices
ingle vehicles

ant
                middle frequencies
affic   medium loudness
d-sounds

variable loudness

e
        open
            medium to small width
ous
            medium to high differentiability
sity   medium to low diversity
                high locatability

sou

dis
movement pred

cloud-sounds predominan

low temporal density
mediur
distanc
empty
monoto

medium to lo
low spatial density

in front of me

steps

voices

single vehicles

middle frequencies
medium loudness

raffic

ud-sounds

variable loudness

eparation

large width

sity

medium to high differentiability
medium to low diversity
high locatability

low

observato

wi

minimal reverberation

half-open

retreat

space behind me

good differentiability only at close range

only single vehicles

good identifiability only at close range

good identifiability only at close range

autono

sparrows

blackbirds

voices

steps

m

(b

homogeneous d

layers
space in between
distance
density

emporally dense only in traffic circle

patterns just because of the birds

place

urban
variable
movement predominant

hard
nce between temporal typologies
functional
balanced

ty

traffic in mid-distance

ness

udness,
medium-quiet traffic
single vehicles

encies + high
s)

uencies + patterns (birds)

wide
cut off on the left

very lo
here b
traffic

p
t

low differentiability
low locatability
low identifiability

extremely low diversity

distanced

i

in

not involved

isolated

r

just movement
hardly any discrete sounds

**not motivate
to be here**

l density
r in

quite temporally dense
2 vague phases: entry and exit

re against
ner

low reverberation

hade

single vehicles
near the traffic
circle + entry
and exit

place

medium to high, variable loudness

in phases, consistent loudness (no patterns)

traffic close
to the circle +
entry and exit

stable distribution of frequencies

cut off on the left

wide

medium differentiability
low locatability
medium identifiability

no diversity

at the central ci

no

low reverberation

just movement
few discrete sounds

b

quite temporally dense
2 vague phases: entry and exit

er spatial
sity here and
 in traffic circle

posed

e activity

traffic close to the
circle + entry and exit

almost in the circulation
of pedestrians and bicycles

(medium to) high, variable loudness

s

single vehicles near
the traffic circle +
entry and exit

in phases but consistent
loudness (no patterns)

middle (low) frequencies

stable distribution of frequencies

medium temporal density

2 vague phases: entry +
circle / exit: pattern

3 phases of loudness: entry,   reg
exit, and in between

space
low diversity   just movem
low differentiability
good locatability only at close range
low identifiability

voices   mediu
bicycles

steps   pred

2 vague phases: lo

wide towards the east

pleasantly open

very low spatial density

empty

nothing behind me   hardly any reverberation

rculation

traffic

long sounds predominant

single vehicles

equencies

th more traffic

low diversit

low spatial density
low diffe
low id
lo
oriented towards the north
pressure ag
spatialy dense   cut-off circle
e
at the mercy of traffic

traffic p

space of circulation: parallel lines

voices
air ve

bicycles

middle (low) frequencies

medium (to high), variable loudness

minimal regularity

medium temporal density

just movement

predominantly discrete sounds and wavelike sounds

single vehicles

entry bismarkstr.

t gaps in between

ase 2: vehicles stopped in the circle

raffic phase 3: running circle

traffic

hardly any reverberation

sound only in

discrete

movement predo

balance between singular sound and cloud-sounds

medium, variable temporal density

somewhat oppressiv

dynamic   *empty*

medium to low diversity

high, variable spatial density

e

bicycles   steps

single vehicles   voices

middle frequencies

traffic   medium loudness

cloud-sounds

m to high, variable loudness

open

otonous   medium to small width

medium to high differentiability

medium to low diversity

high locatability

medium

large width
very low spatial density

full circl

in front

space of circulation: parallel l

voices

bicycles

middle (low) frequencies

medium (to high), variable loudness
minimal regularity
medium temporal density

fferentiability
tifiability
atability

just movement
predominantly discrete sounds and wavelike sounds

(observatory)

square

single vehicles

traffic phase 1: entry bismarkstr.
short gaps in between
traffic phase 2: vehicles stopped in the circle
traffic phase 3: running circle

traffic

hardly any reverberation

low dive

low
low
lo

very narrow

pressu

spatially dense

full circle with "weird perspe

space of circulation: corner

a

voices

bicycles

middle (low) frequencies

medium (to high), variable loudness

minimal regularity

medium temporal density

t the corner   just movement

predominantly discrete sounds and wavelike sounds

narrow

gray   single vehicles

traffic   traffic phase 1: entry bismarkstr.

short gaps in between

traffic phase 2: vehicles stopped in the circle

traffic phase 3: running circle

traffic

hardly any reverberation

Model 1

Gunnar Green

Boris Hassenstein

There are different kinds of models. Scale models are a magnification or a miniaturization of an object and often reproduce certain qualities of the original. Analogue models present structures, processes, systems, or networks of relations in a different medium. In scientific contexts we find theoretical models that are often based on assumptions "as if" elements fit into a strict logic. Model 1 is none of these kinds, but it operates between all of them.

Model 1 was built into a seminar room of the University of Arts and Design Linz as part of "Campus Exhibition 2012 Universität der Künste/Sound Studies: Lebensräume" at the Ars Electronica Festival. The seminar room measured about 18 meters in length, 8 meters in width, 3 meters in height, and had one door in the middle of one of the lengthy sides. It was spatially divided into three parts.

One — A montage of field recordings from Ernst-Reuter-Platz played in one side of the room. The essential qualities that this montage tried to present were homogeneity, stress, and non-differentiability. These characteristics of today's Ernst-Reuter-Platz were identified through methods of the Auditory Architecture Research Unit (AARU).

Two — The other side of the room was dedicated to possible and not-yet-present Ernst-Reuter-Plätze (plural). A single speaker played readings of design proposals, thoughts, and ideas that had evolved from previous research of the AARU, accompanied with multiple slide projections of past, present, and fictitious situations of Ernst-Reuter-Platz. Each slide projector rotated in its own interval. Speakers and projectors played continuously.

Three — The third part was a structure in the middle of the room. It consisted of ten tilted panels arranged in two rows. Separating part one from part two, this structure defined a space on its own. The panels were tilted at three different angles and slightly rotated away from each other. They also overlapped from 30 to 50 centimeters. Each panel had a weight of 8 kilograms per square meter. In this specific arrangement, the structure filtered out certain ranges of sound frequency. As such it did not form a solid border but a semi-permeable membrane, which allowed certain frequencies as well as people to pass through.

Model 1 did not exhibit designs. Instead, it created interwoven conditions for experienced-based access to their underlying thoughts. On this basis, active participation was required to realize other possible presences of Ernst-Reuter-Platz.

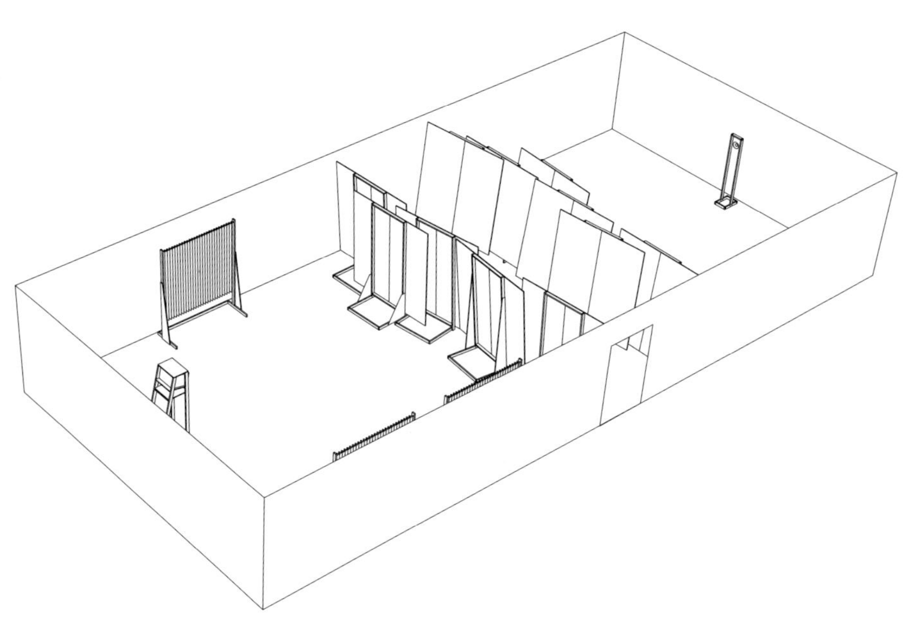

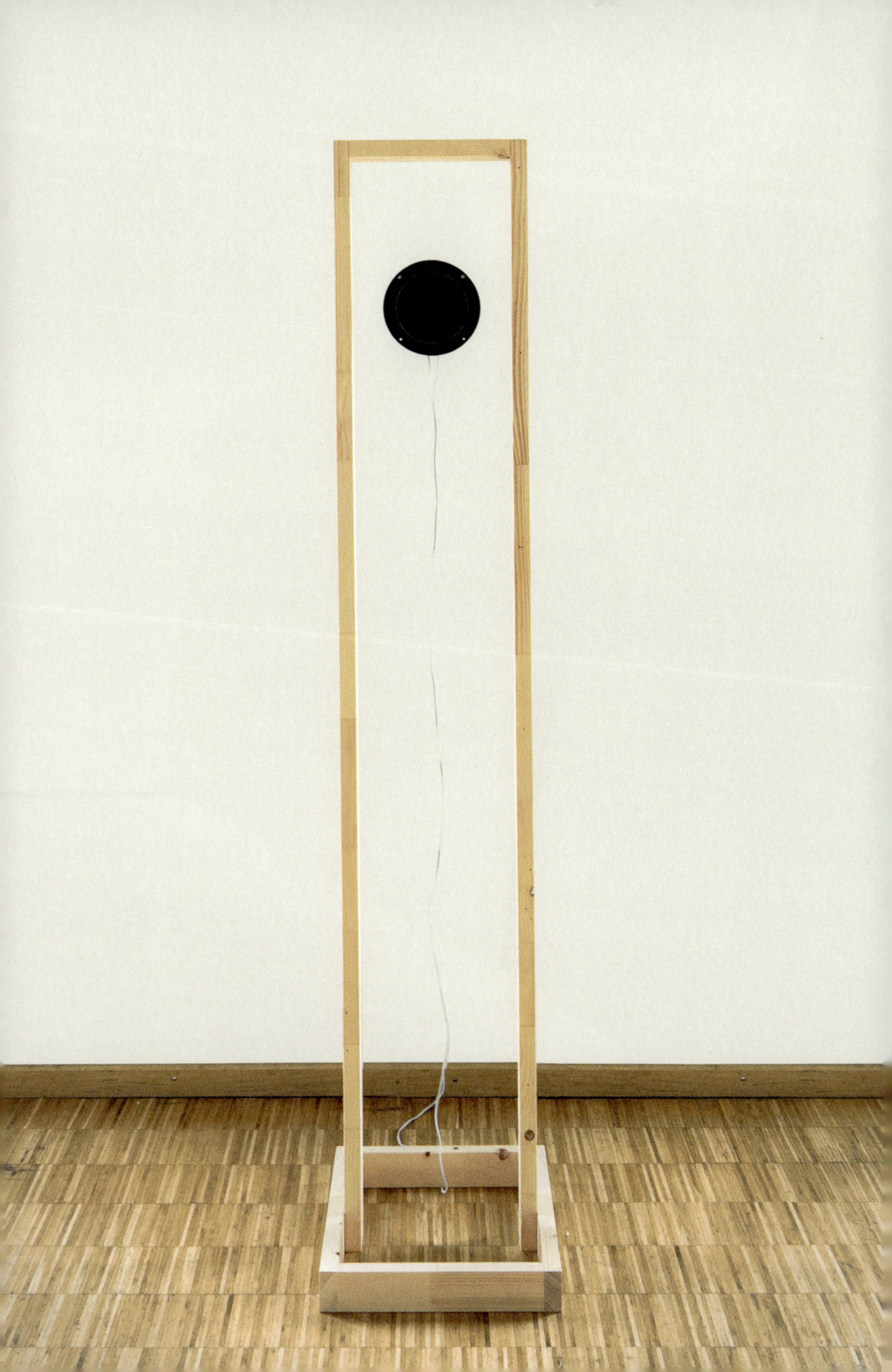

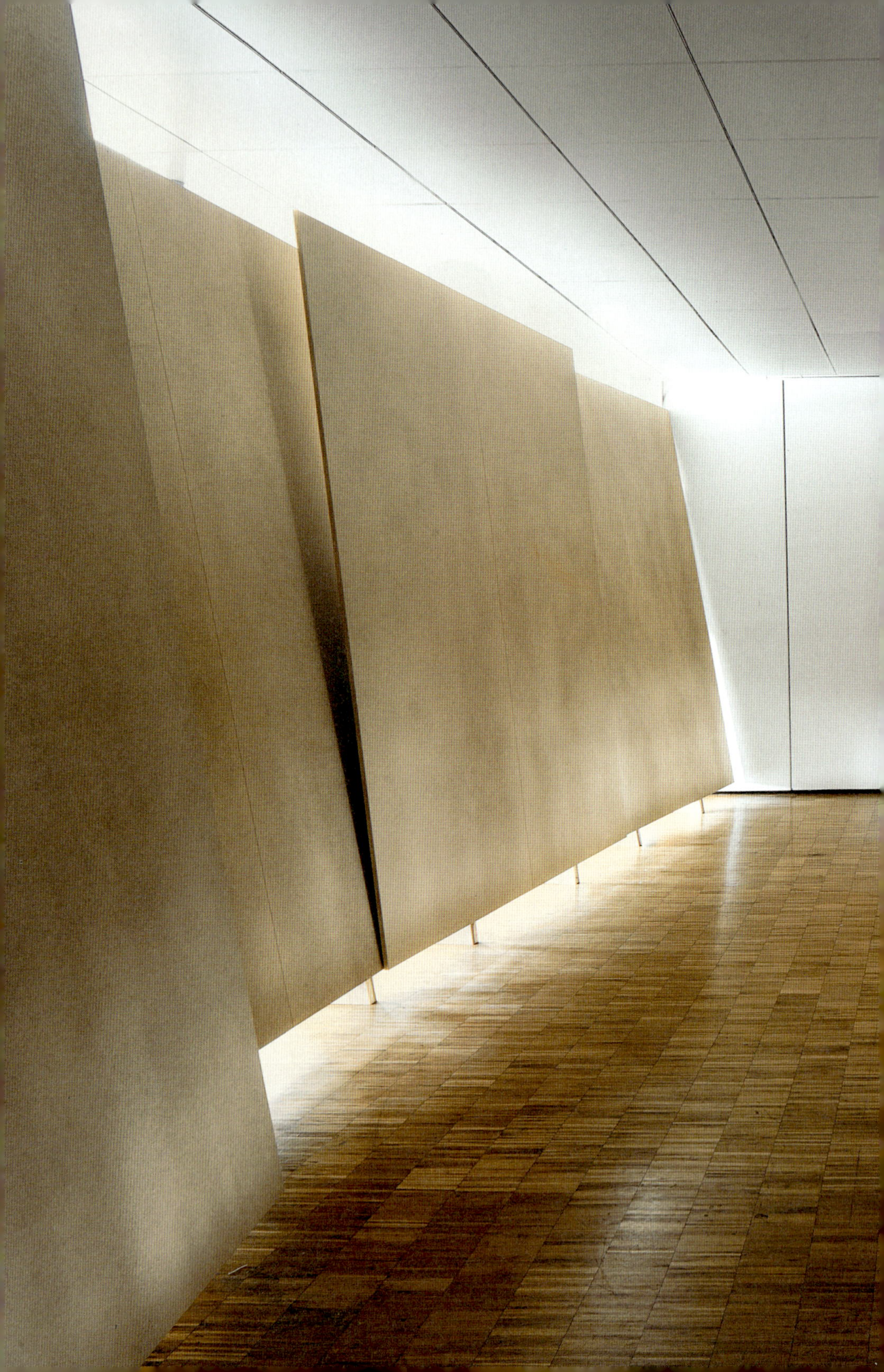

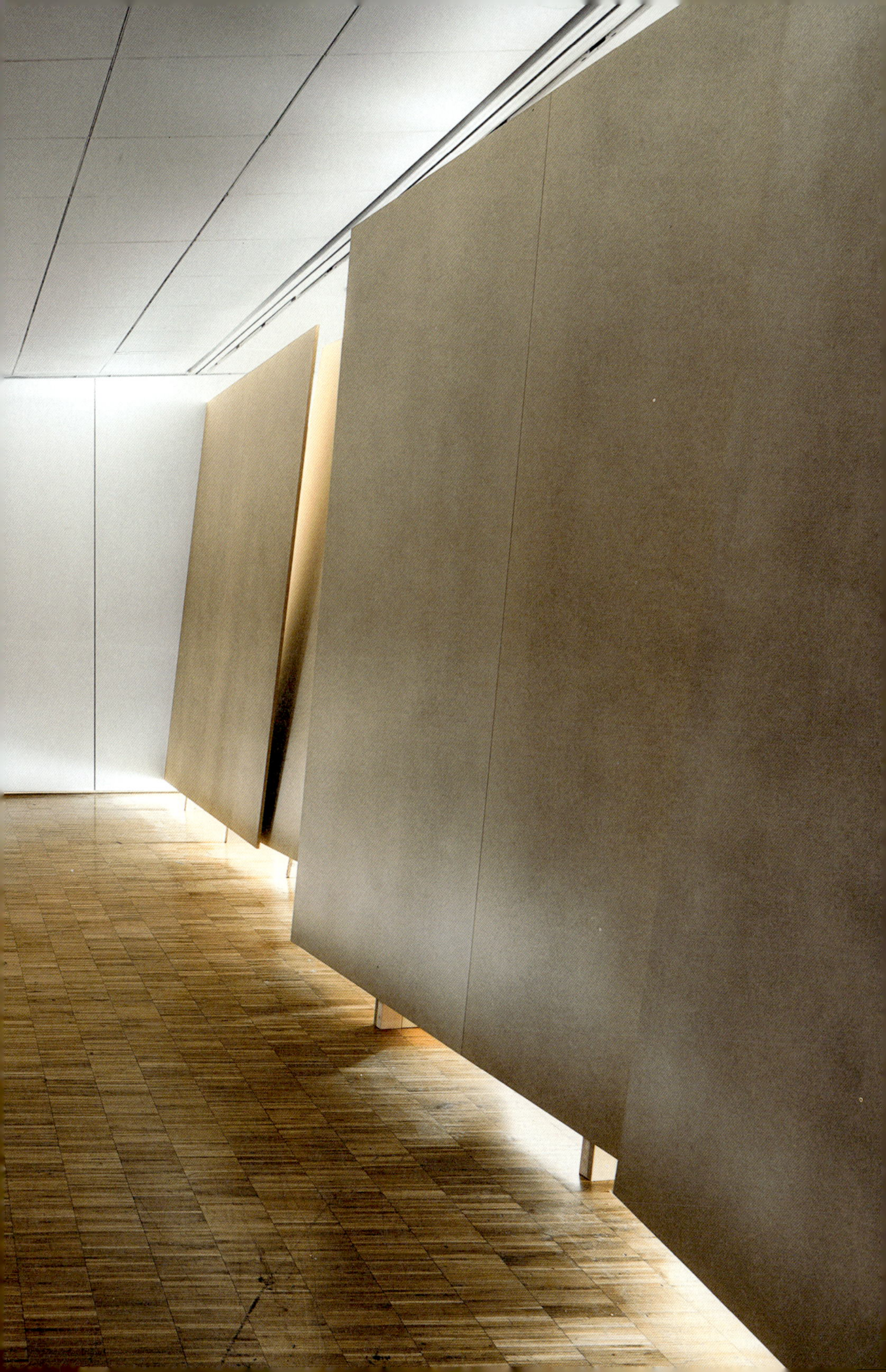

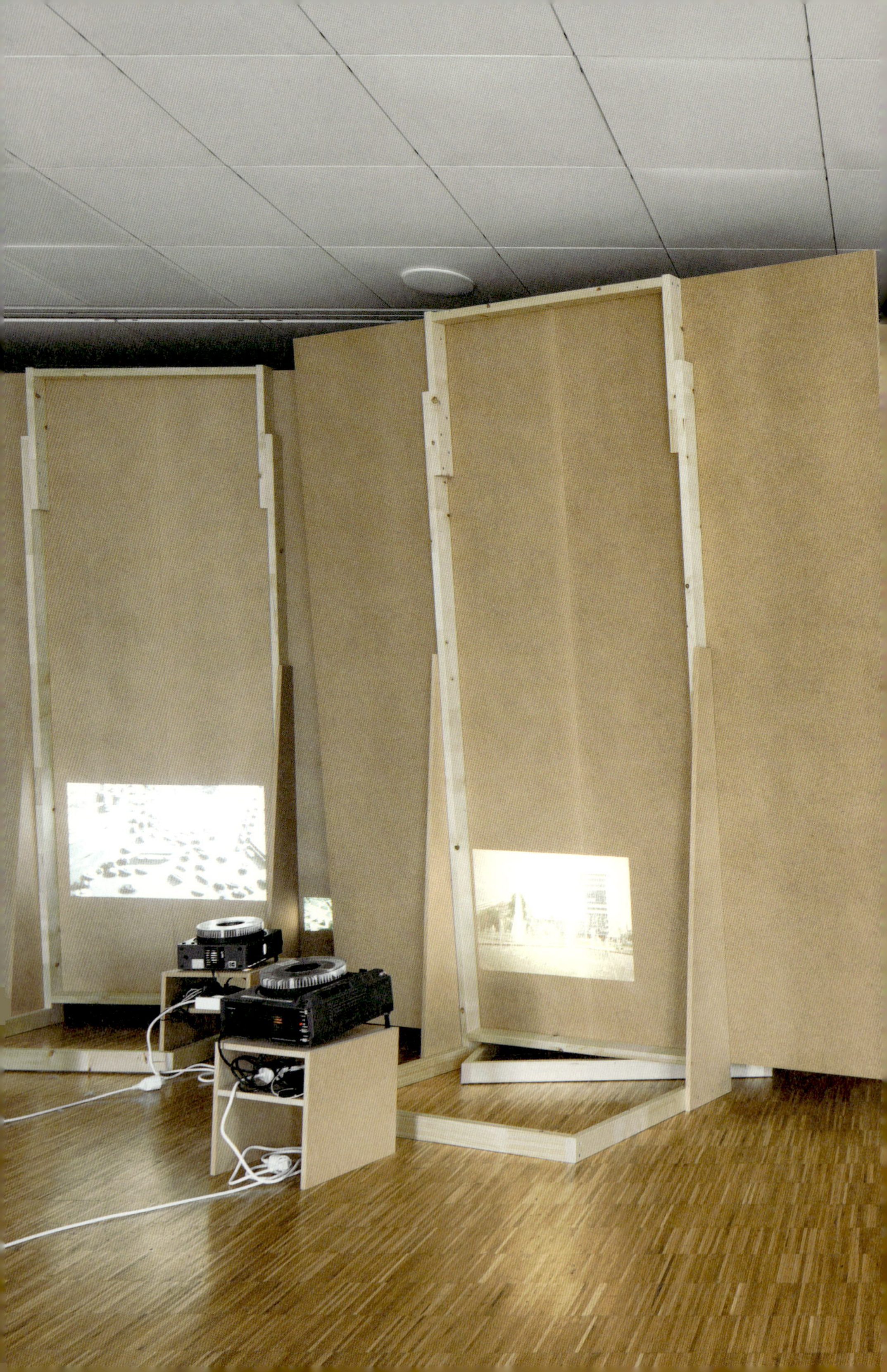

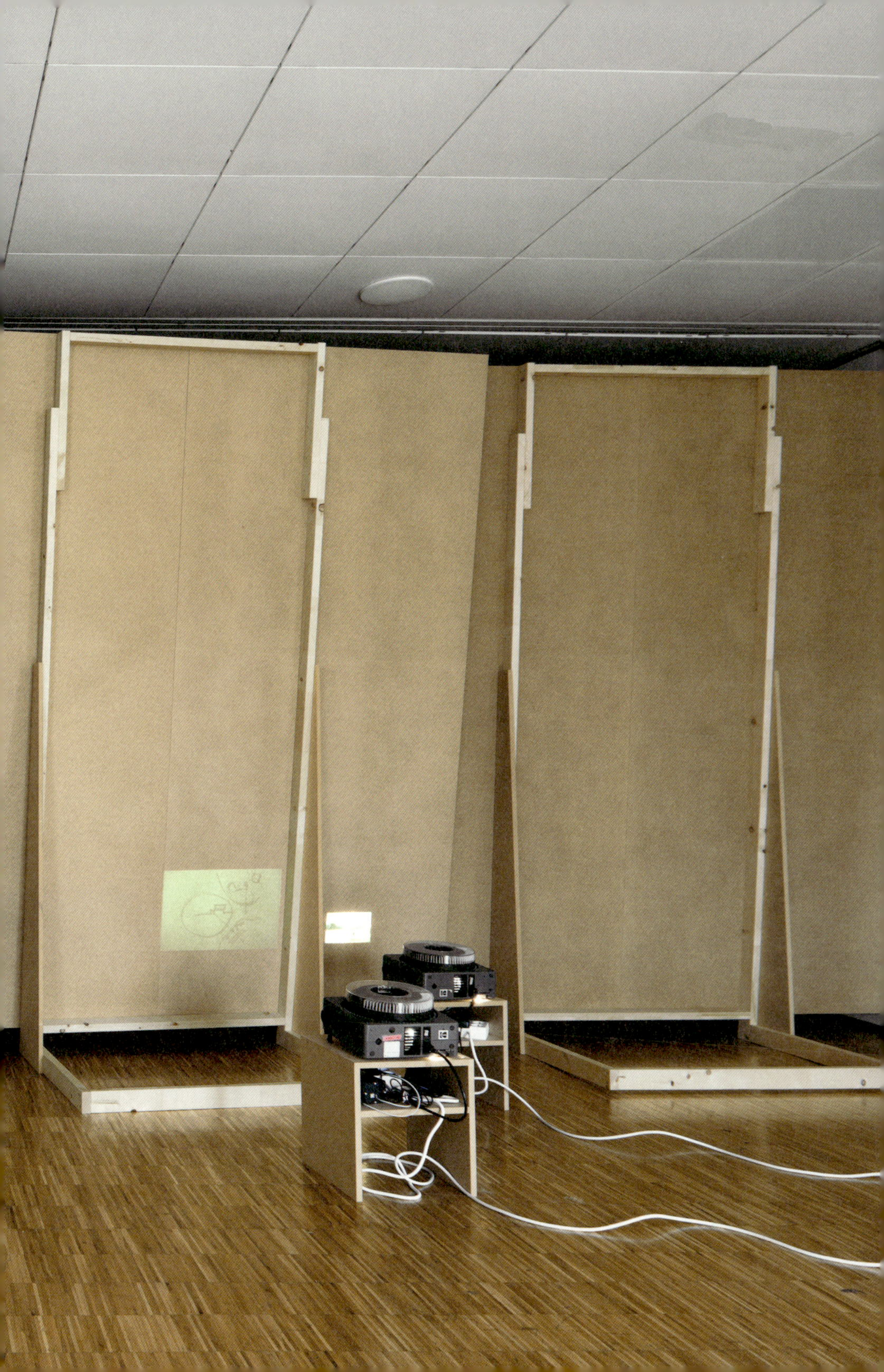

69

This section consists of three dialogues focused on different subject matters crucial to the development of this project. They do not comprehensively thematize Ernst-Reuter-Platz but address specific and fundamental issues.

In the first, held on October 29, 2013, Saskia Hebert, Stephan Günzel, Boris Hassenstein, and Alex Arteaga debated possible connections between architecture and phenomenology, with phenomenology understood not so much as a philosophical theory but rather as a methodological reflective practice. The question of the relationship between phenomenology and architecture was not raised from the perspective of the implementation of theory into practice, as is usually the case, but rather in relation to commonalities and differences between both domains of practice and, further, possibilities of their mutual influence or even hybridization.

The second dialogue, conducted on October 30, 2013, focused on the tension between protection and renewal of urban spaces. Gabriele Dolff-Bonekämper, Oliver Bormann, Boris Hassenstein, and Alex Arteaga talked about the concept of *access* as the basis for an alternative, integrative approach.

The first two dialogues took place in the so called "vitreous brain" of the former IBM-Building at Ernst-Reuter-Platz. The third, conceived by Thomas Kusitzky and with the participation of Frank Eckardt and Boris Hassenstein, was held on December 12, 2013, while visiting outside and inside spaces of Ernst-Reuter-Platz, mostly by foot but also by car. During this urban trip, participants reflected on the square's sociological history. The fragments of this dialogue presented here correspond to different stages of this parcours.

These three dialogues decisively contributed to the clarification of essential aspects of our object of design and the possibilities of its coherent, viable, and sustainable transformation.

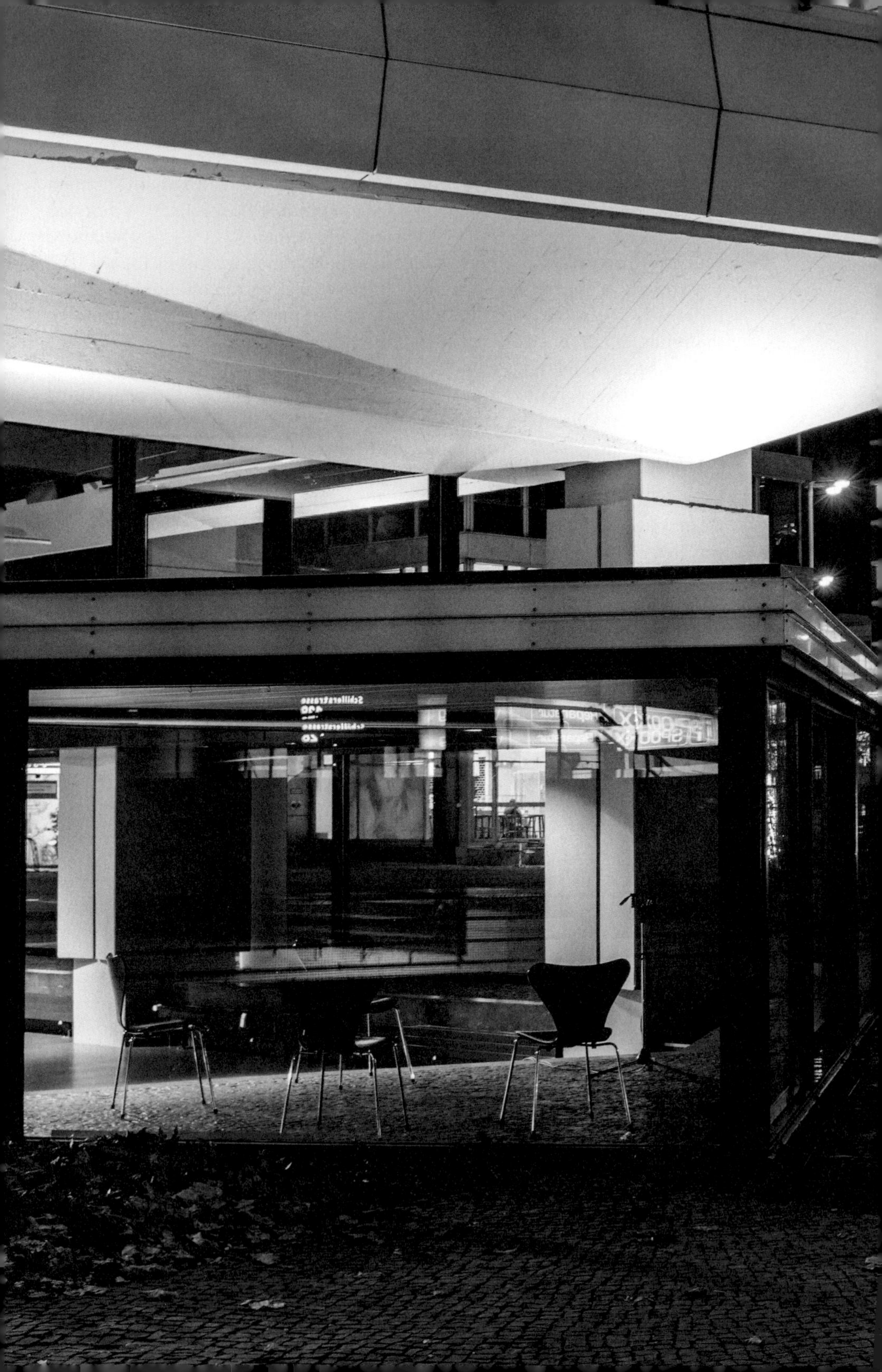

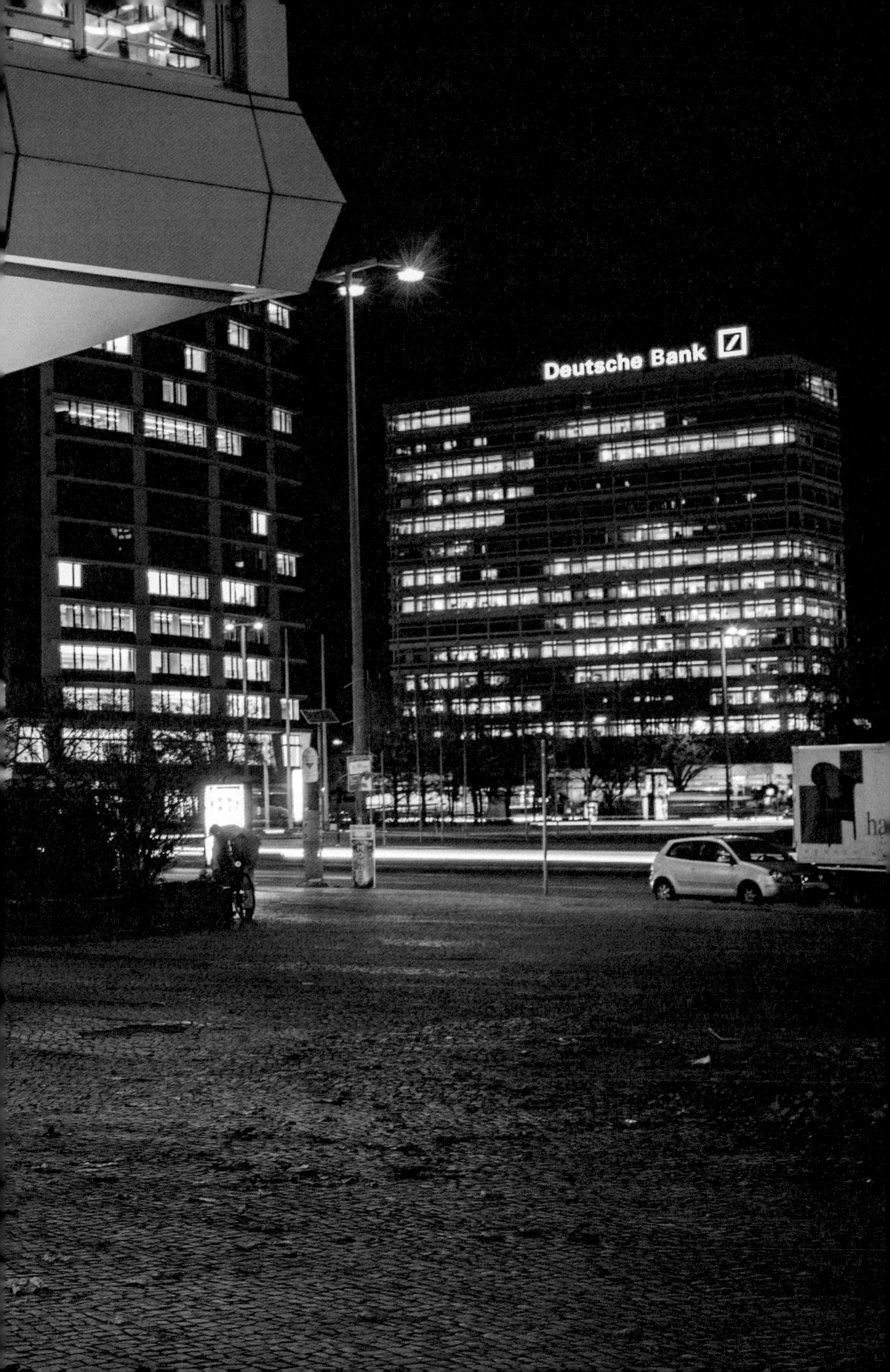

Deutsche Bank

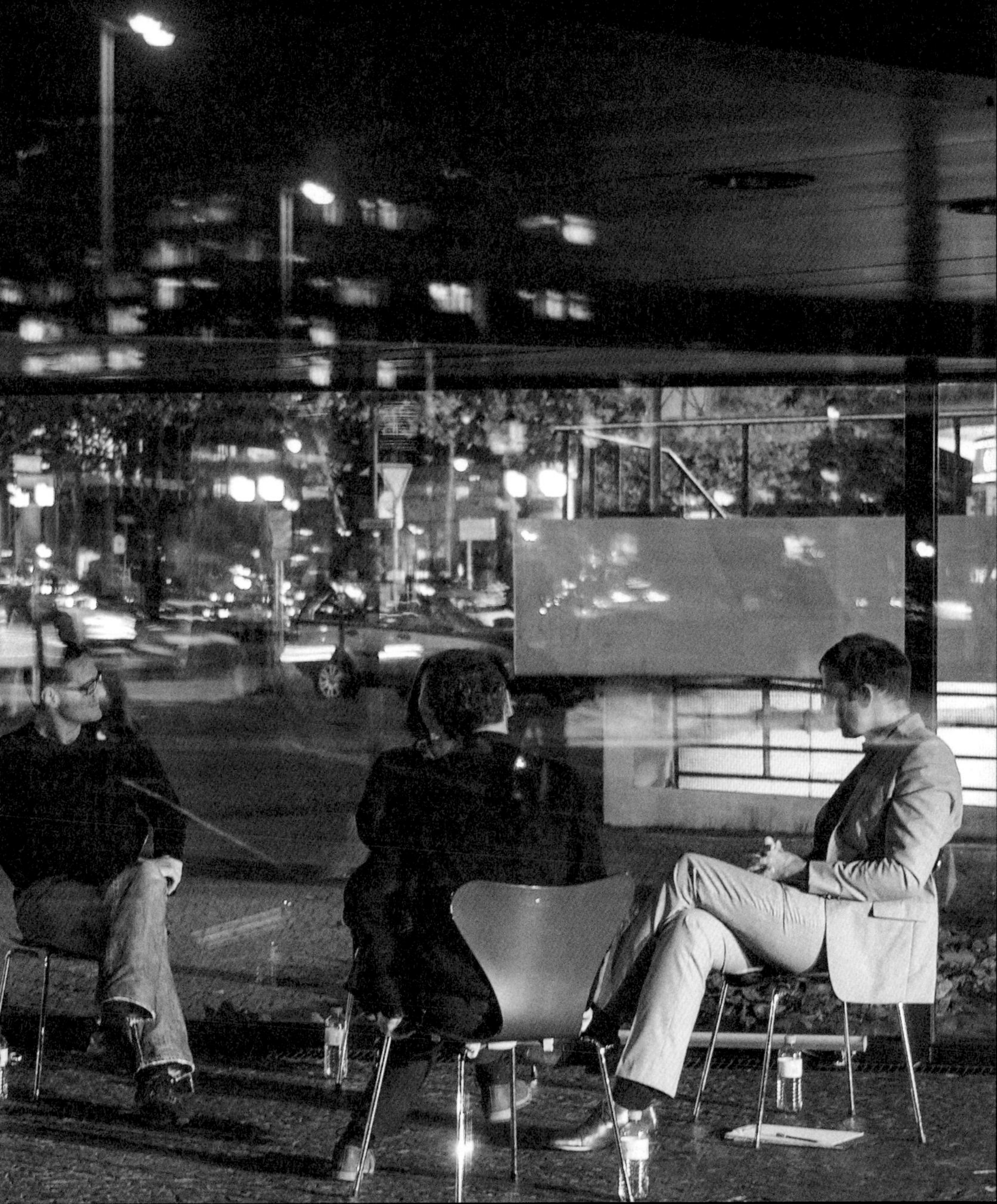

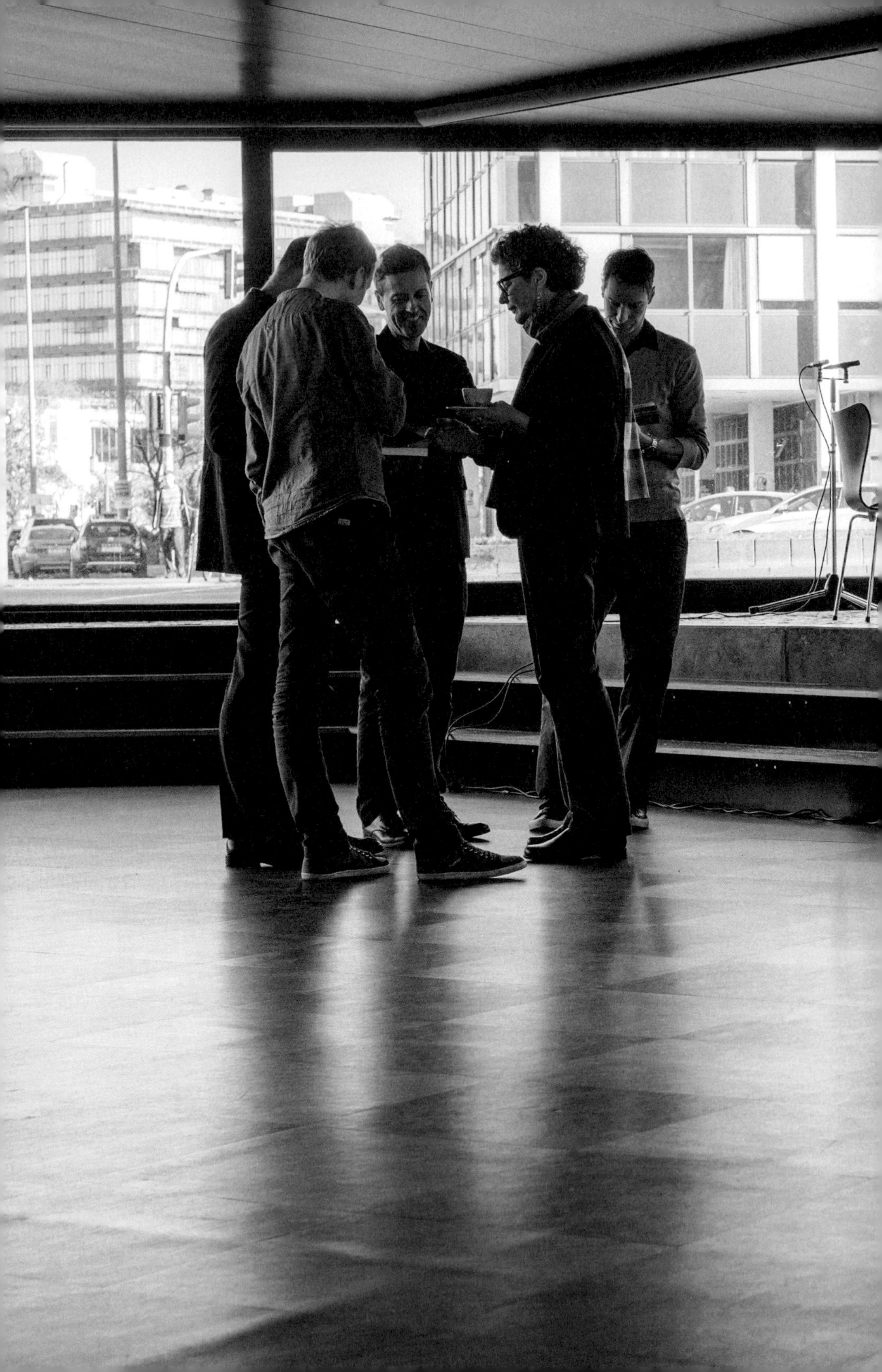

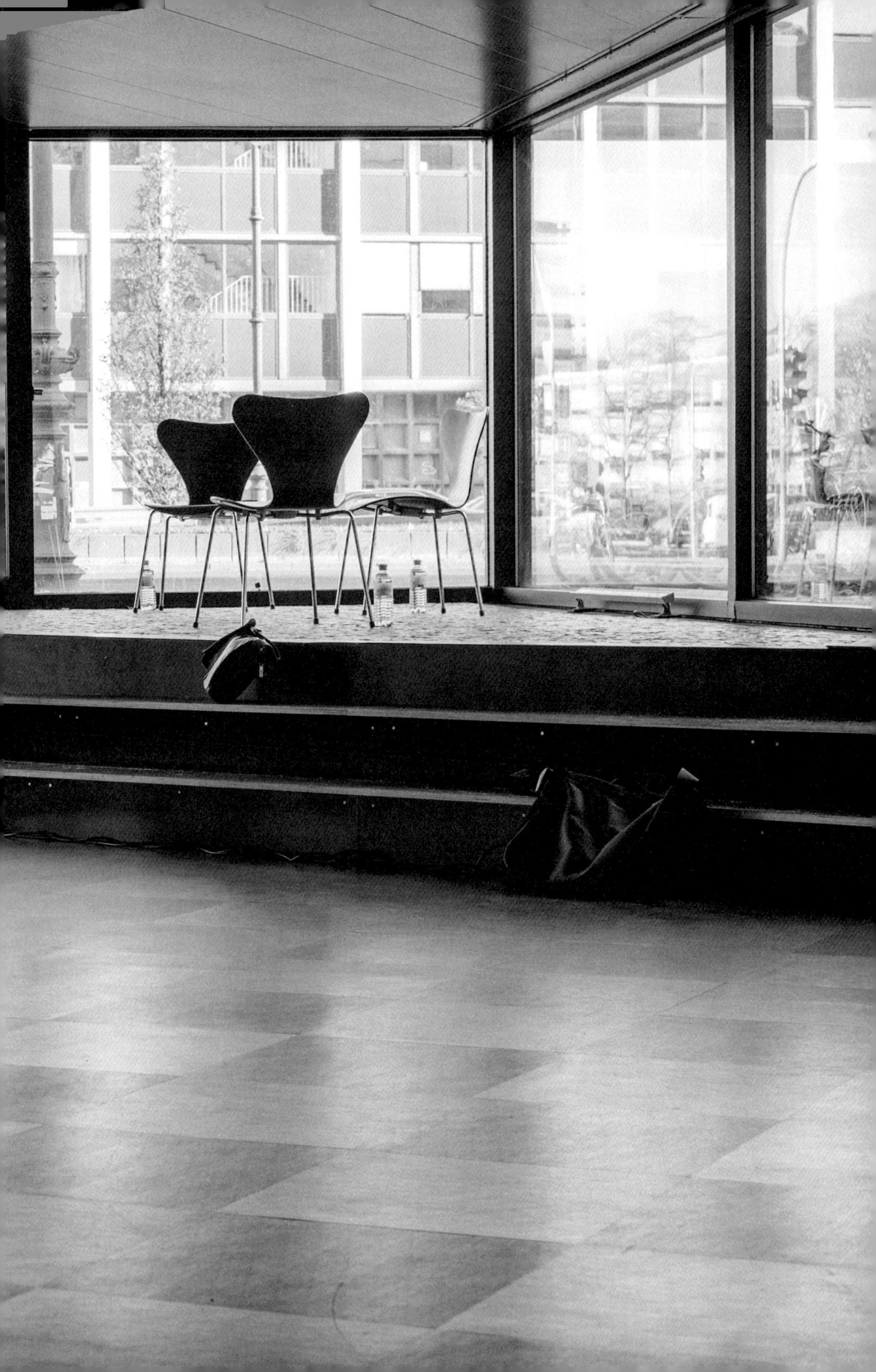

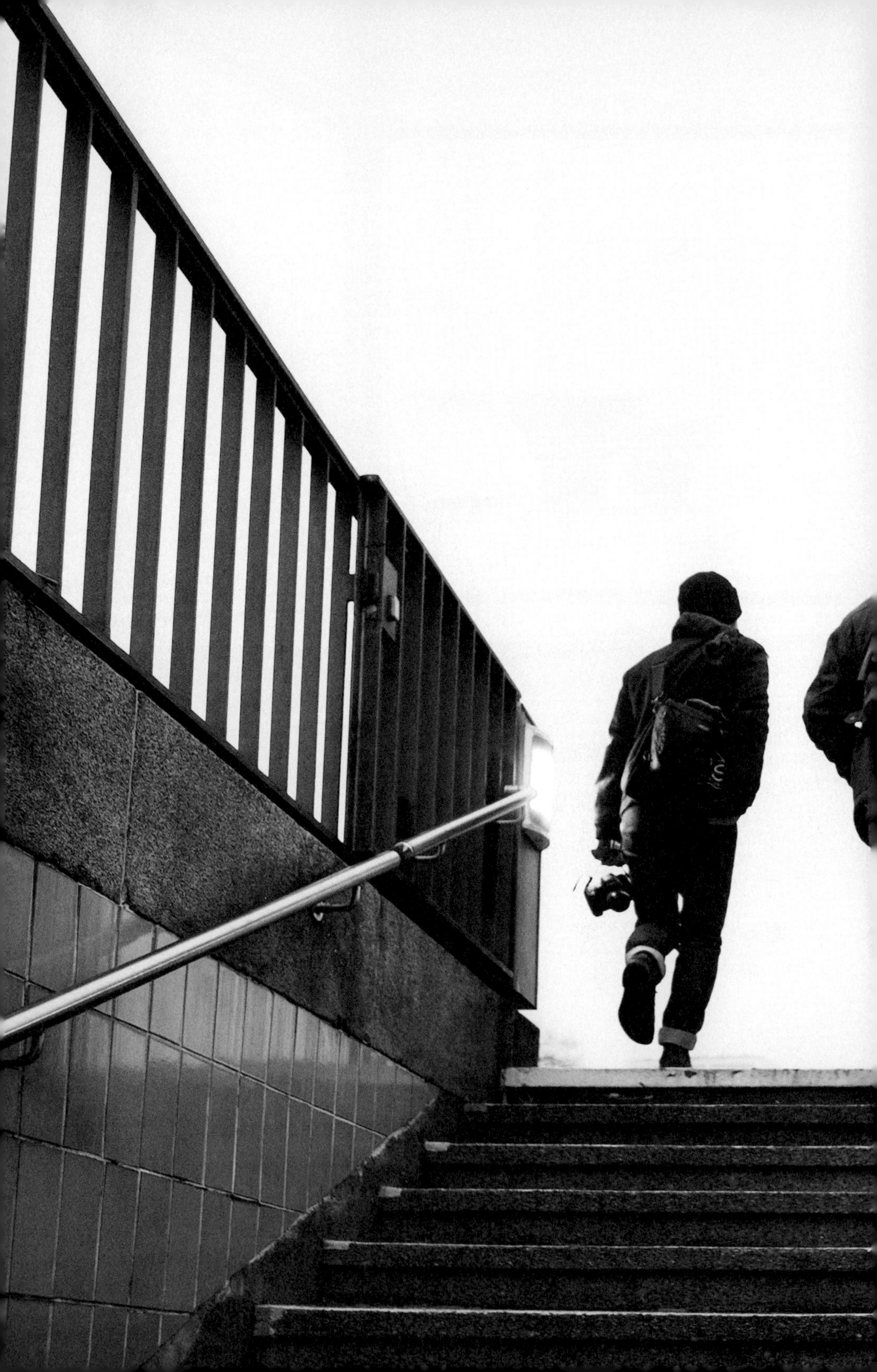

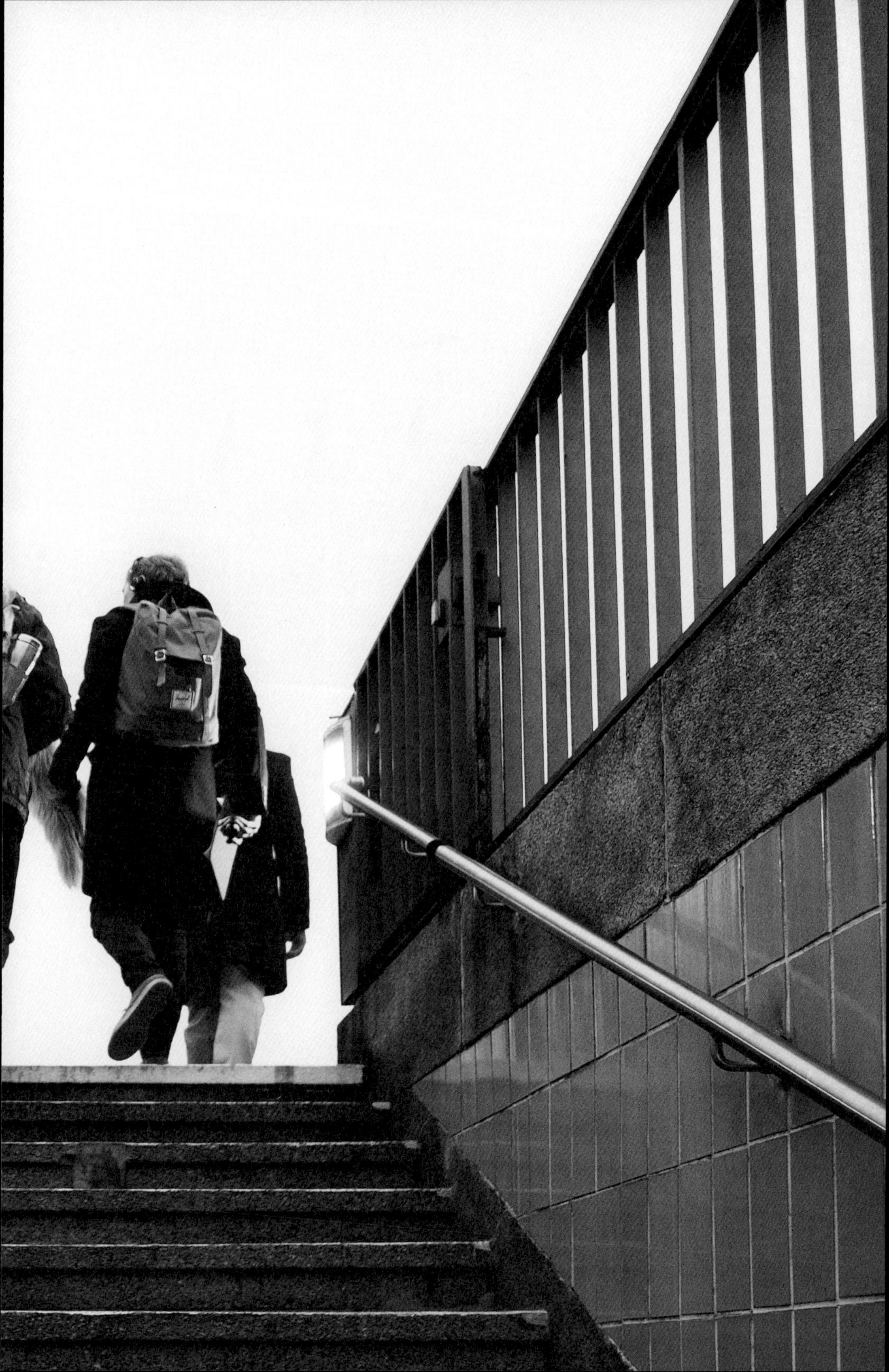

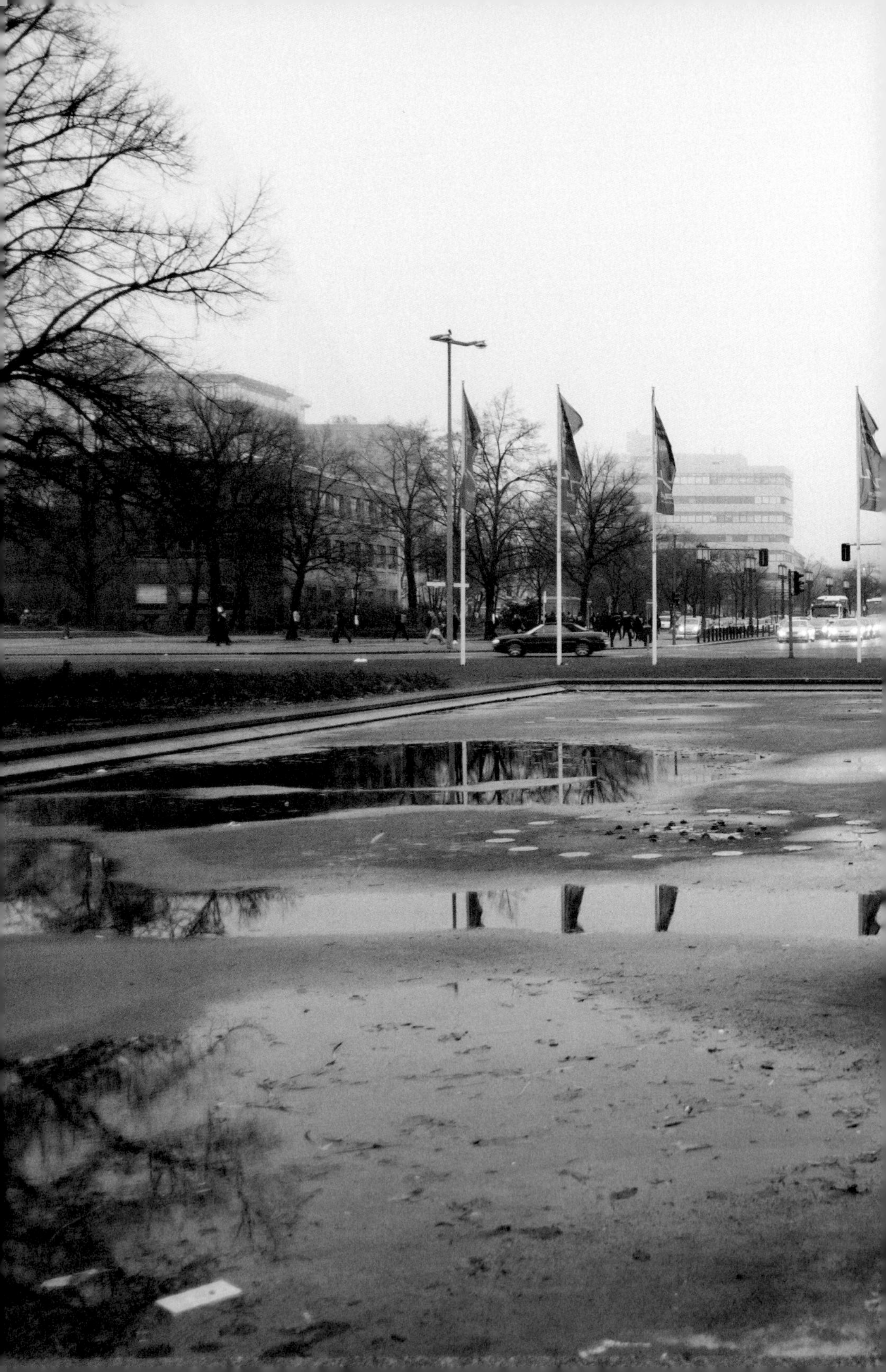

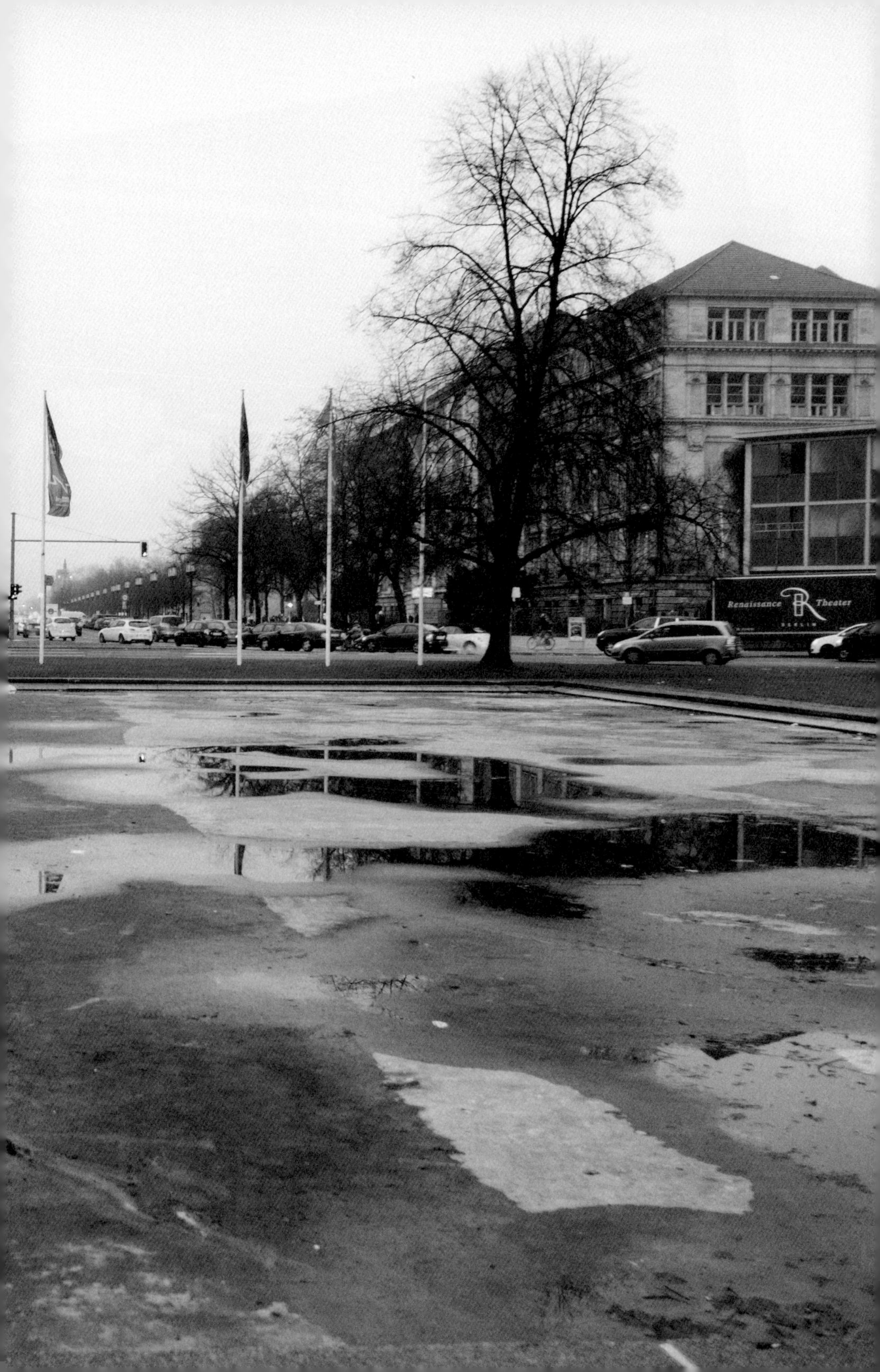
Renaissance Theater
BERLIN

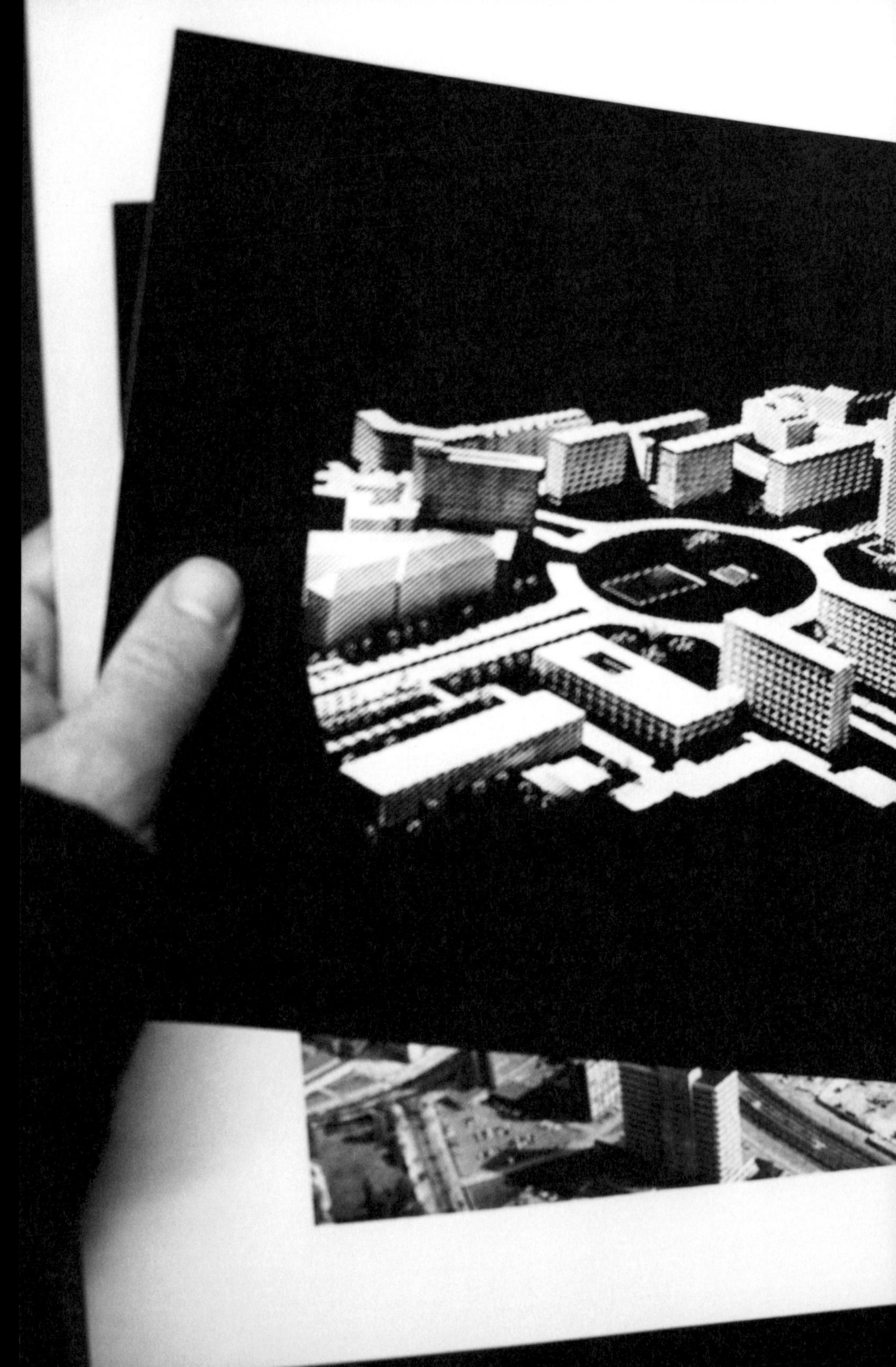

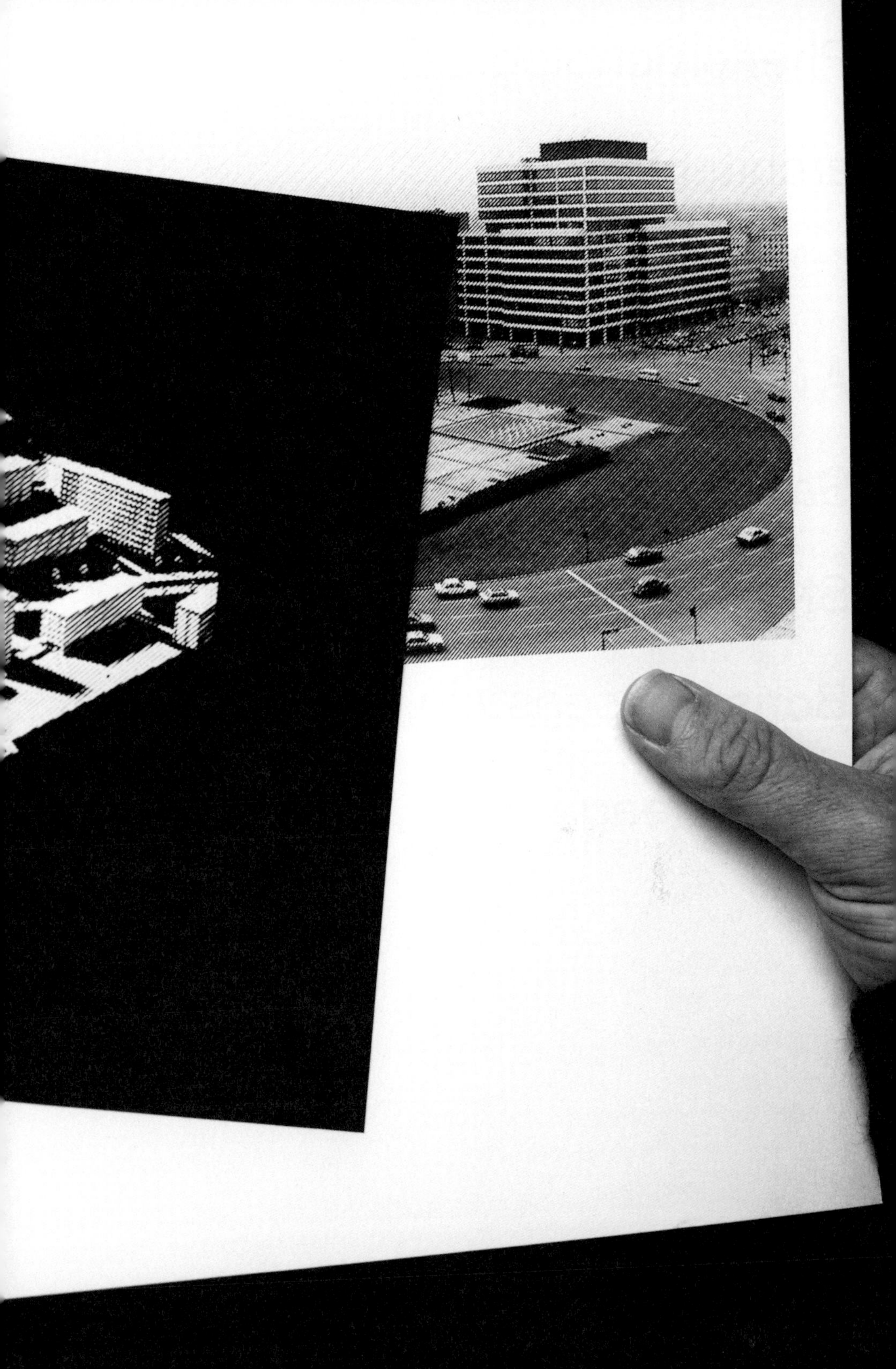

Phenomenological architecture?

A dialogue with Saskia Hebert, Stephan Günzel, Boris Hassenstein, Alex Arteaga

AA: There are several possible approaches to this dialogue. Two concrete points of departure could be your publications. Phenomenology is always present in your texts. It plays an important role in your work in many different ways. When we spoke during the forum,[1] Stephan, you made a distinction that was crucial for the discussion: not everything that is concerned with phenomena can be labeled phenomenology. Not every kind of work with the senses, or all work concerned with perception, can be called phenomenological. Phenomenology is first and foremost a methodical approach to dealing with phenomena. In my opinion, phenomenology is primarily method. Phenomenology is not the content or the explanation; it aims to provide explanations, but it is above all method. Method as the defining element of a practice. In this light, I would be interested in talking about practices and fields of practice. I think it would be interesting to first look at these two fields of practice—architecture and phenomenology—side by side, to see what kind of relationship exists between them and what kind of relationship could potentially be developed. So, as the starting point for this discussion, an open question: Phenomenological architecture? This doesn't mean the application of phenomenology in architecture. Instead, what happens when these networks of practices are positioned side by side?

SG: I find the basic idea very appealing, to talk about phenomenology as practice. In truth, the intention of phenomenology is to be a philosophical activity, which does not primarily advise people on how to improve their lives (as in what is often understood these days under "philosophical praxis"). This may be a side effect at the end of the day, but philosophical activity primarily undertakes an analysis of the environment in which we live. For phenomenologists, the phenomenon comes first—that is, perception. This "active" idea of phenomenology is the conscious act of observing. Not, as is often claimed, with the goal of sensing one's own body or becoming attuned to one's environment, but with the goal of learning something else about the world, something more than what can be gleaned from the usual ways we measure the world. To communicate these observations, and in doing so to maybe change the way we see the world, is the reason I find this idea of phenomenology as practice so appealing. Writing has to be preceded by something else: active concern with the world. To this end, we have to develop methods of recording that can register what is being perceived as immediately as possible. This is of course extremely difficult. Maybe today it would be possible to develop a phenomenological recording apparatus. The founder of phenomenology, Edmund Husserl, tried using stenography to describe the structures of perception while he was perceiving. As difficult and therefore problematic as this undertaking is, the basic idea of phenomenology remains that it is one practice, which might lend itself to operating in parallel with other practices, like architecture.

SH: I think that architecture—if I can adopt the position of

1 In the third part of the project "Klangumwelt Ernst-Reuter-Platz"—Lab ERP—five forums took place. They were conceived as open discussions between researchers from the Auditory Architecture Research Unit, students and professors from the Department of Landscape Architecture and Environmental Planning (Technische Universität Berlin), and the master program Sound Studies and Sonic Arts (Berlin University of the Arts). Stephan Günzel and Saskia Hebert, together with the sociologist Peter Fischer, were guests at the 3rd forum, held on May 23, 2013 under the title "Lived Space."

"making architecture"—is above all concerned with the transformation of the built environment. Meaning those spaces in which we all spend time, in which we live, perceive, act. What is interesting about phenomenology, as I understand it, is that it implies a critique of abstract science, or the attempt to make the world in which we live describable, measurable, countable, and representable. In doing so, it neglects essential aspects that are specific to space—the lived spaces. This happens in both science and in many practices. Is it important for architecture and those who make it to say, "There is more there than what you can measure, than you can represent, than you can draw, and you have to first put yourself in a situation in which you can perceive and understand this." And this is where the method begins: How does one do that, exactly? And how do we find a way to communicate that which we discovered? It's not easy.

AA: I think that the need for a phenomenological method—a methodical practice—originates in the idea that every phenomenon has its subjective correlation. Every phenomenon is also subjectively constituted. So when we investigate phenomena, we need to clarify the structure of their subjective constitution, and this demands that we see the world differently from the way we do on a daily basis. To observe the world in a different way, "without participating." And every practice is performed on the assumption of a particular world. Every practice occurs with and within one world. You mentioned the built world. Architects, to greater or lesser degrees, want to change the world. But which world? An already existing one? Which concept of "world" are they using?

BH: This becomes more difficult once we begin to observe how architects work. At least in the tradition of modernism, including post-war modernism, architects actually do have a secure framework to tell them how architecture is made. You analyze, you develop a concept, and then you execute that concept. But in doing so, it is easy to forget that we are dealing with a reality whose access has not been methodically investigated. This is where engagement with phenomenology poses a challenge, to be able to ask: Which processes are occurring, are they occurring simultaneously, can they be separated from one another?

SG: For one, that would be the inclusion of your own body, your own lived body, or your own perception, which is simultaneously being observed—and from which, to a certain extent, a universalization takes place. This is not to suggest a radical subjectivity, in which everyone sees the world differently. Instead it's about general subjectivity: how we are as subjects in the world, and how we interact together with the things in it. The phenomenological standpoint is simultaneously within and without—and this is precisely what makes phenomenological work so difficult. But maybe it is possible to set it up in parallel to architectural practice, insofar as architecture is itself always part of a certain lifeworld and certain needs. Not necessarily the needs of residents or users, or even the lifeworld of the architects themselves: their design practice and the structural requirements imposed on architects.

SH: I think that if this is to be done seriously, a lot more has to be abandoned than just the usual methods. I see a fundamental problem of architecture in the fact that no one involved acknowledges how deeply they are influenced by culture, how much they carry with them, and consequently how this determines what they see. That is a tiny portion on the surface, because you only look as long as you need in order to confirm your own ideas or even prejudices. But to avoid this requires some effort: you have to confront a situation, maybe for a longer period, and—this is something we did in our projects at the UdK[2]—you actually have to talk to people, different people, who bring in different perspectives, different knowledge, different expertise.

SG: It's not for nothing that phenomenology gave rise to hermeneutics, which emphasizes even more the dimensions of sense or horizons of sense in order to generate descriptions of the lifeworld. These can be descriptions of what is or is not variable in building and dwelling. Phenomenology is concerned with showing irreducible moments of the practice of the lifeworld. These moments could be identified by means of experiments, which might investigate whether it is possible to dwell without the classic structure of ceiling, wall, and floor. What is it like to expose oneself to a completely different dwelling, what changes if you live in a mobile house, or on a glass floor? This can actually be an element of research, alongside discussions with the users of this architecture: to expose them to this kind of unusual experience of architecture in order to find out more about one's own basic needs. Something that has been lost in pure functionalism. In modern architecture, the emphasis has tended to be more on the basic needs of the building than those of the people.

SH: The concept of "function" that can be unequivocally assigned is in principle a contradiction of what phenomenology calls the "field of activity," which deals with the following: What does the space make possible? What range or scope for action do I have? How can I use it differently, variously, together with others? For me, spatially speaking, those are the exciting questions when we look at architecture phenomenologically. What does a structure enable me to do? What else can I do with it? To what extent is it flexible, not only in the sense that it can be used for potentially different functions today, but also in the sense that it can react to the "shifting baselines" in society, so that in the future we may be able to use it for something completely different?

SG: But wouldn't that then be the phenomenological method in architecture, which suspends prior certainties? It's about not just building the architect's dream house, but instead dealing with a given situation and making discoveries within that situation.

AA: It's always—at least as I understand what you both are saying—about a release. The release of an unreflected, assumed concept, whether it be about dwelling, building, or designing. It's about the release of a concept that appears to be *the* concept. And I think that these apparatus, these various possibilities of realizing these releases—whether they are bodily experiments or collective forms or experimentation—have one thing in common: they are all

2 Student research and design projects, under the direction of Saskia Hebert, were part of LIVED/ SPACE/LAB at the College of Archive, Media and Design of the Berlin University of the Arts.

organized forms of action that facilitate this openness, this *eidetic varia-tion*. But the thing I find interesting is how you do it so that it doesn't just happen at the desk or in a purely verbal form—that is my main criticism of classic phenomenology—but instead through a variety of resources: bodily, collective, social, medial.

SH: Another important point in this context—and I don't know to what extent phenomenology has anticipated it—is that everything that we experience is not only a contemporary segment of space and time, but also finds itself in a process of transition. In this way we bring a particular history along with us, and the built world also embodies the historicity of its construction or usage. But we need to think about this further. Then we won't be developing objects anymore, instead we will become part of the process. And, from the standpoint that we take within that process, we can only oversee a certain framework: the present, a little bit before it and a little bit after it. As I see it, this means not exactly the overcoming of all concepts, but at least a respite from the very architecturally aligned idea of absolute order. I believe we have to open ourselves to the process that we are accompanying, and maybe influencing. Yet as an architect you don't interfere quite as absolutely as some might think. And those architects who do act in such an "absolutist" way are subjected to vehement criticism these days, and rightly so. It's a question of degree and also a question of horizon, in the spatial as well as temporal sense.

AA: With the release of concepts, what I mean—and I think I see here a strong similarity to what you were saying—is that the primacy lies not with the object, but with the process, and that the object is simply a temporary stabilization of the process. Processes, however, which do not end in objects, such that the object is and remains process-immanent. That is what I mean by release: the questioning of the validity of the object in favor of a radical dynamization.

SG: When one thinks about processes, one is forced to combine phenomenology with dialectics, which relates to the architectural thinking of Henri Lefebvre: at least concerning space, his idea was to combine the subjective side of perception as the field of phenomenology with the design-related conception of life-spaces and their collective implementation. Dialectic here means a passage through the process. Even if one departs from phenomenal structures, that still does not justify the primacy of perception. We may have the phenomenological primacy of access to the lifeworld, in which cultural symbolic structures and underpinning History will be disclosed later, but each of these aspects has already influenced perception. This can be understood as an extension of phenomenology, from which standpoint the conception of space on the level of design is also a form of perception; it is precisely this phenomenological reflection on architectonic design as part of the process of spatial production that is an essential component of architectural phenomenology.

SH: There is a nice quotation from Chipperfield. Before he received all these amazing commissions, he had written a little book called "Theoretical

Practice." There he argues that architecture has this big advantage over philosophy—architecture cannot only describe the space but also *make* it. And he describes this as the interplay of material and light and space (as volume)—so for him the "material" of architecture goes far beyond material things, objects, or constructive elements. And then he writes that the problem is that the majority of the entities we are dealing with cannot be described with the tools that we architects use. By making these drawings and abstract representations of facades, floor plans, and so on, we don't really address the sensuous experience, the being-within, the being-able-to-be-within spaces that have been drawn on the paper. We like to delude ourselves into thinking that the abstraction is sufficient to have an overview, and ultimately we can send the construction firm off to work with these artifacts, very practical. But in reality, the conventions of how we talk about space and how we describe it are pretty rudimentary in architecture.

BH: As architects we have a problem when confronted with our working equipment that is similar to the problem described by Husserl. In the instant in which something is written down, or an attempt is being made to capture it in whatever medium, you make a full stop. The flow of observation or perception—including self-perception—is interrupted and reduced to a single moment: held tight, one could say, or frozen. That is what we architects do in our professional daily praxis. When something is created on the construction site, it acquires a monolithic massiveness. During the design process we are heading towards this moment, so that this flow can't be maintained forever, even if we would like it to be.

SG: The elements to which the architect should devote his attention, for example, in the design practice, the optical dimension—the drawing, the sketching, the modeling, the rendering—are emphasized, whereby other sensory qualities would not be as present, such as the temperature, the humidity of the building, what does it feel like to sit in one of these dry office rooms. Or even the acoustic dimension: How does sound behave in the building? Those are things that are often only considered at a later point; for example, if it turns out that a conference room is too reverberant and it's not possible to communicate over a certain distance. Ways have to be found to experience the sound of a room beforehand. And how will it feel, in the sense of temperature and humidity?

AA: One can rely on calculations, but I don't believe one can calculate that. Of course one can calculate values referring to these fields—when it comes to sound we can measure intensity, but intensity is not the same as loudness. There is a correlation. There is a relationship between objective correlates and the phenomenon, but the phenomenon is a dynamic in-between. If I may, I'd like to pick up the thread of your processual turn, and say that it is always about a constant process in which we intervene. This approach implies another big turn as well: the turn towards a way of thinking in which the sensuous—because it is processual—is not opposed to knowledge and construction. And going beyond this, it also implies breaking the primacy of the visual—and, on this basis, developing new approaches to design that are not exclusively visual, not fixated on forms.

SH: At the moment, there is a tendency in architecture to tell stories. Meaning not presenting your concepts so much as finished pictures, forms with defined contours, or objects that at some time will be standing somewhere, but instead as narratives, as relationships of events and experiences. In this way the temporal aspect that characterizes the process can be integrated, at least as a suggestion, into the design. Of course this isn't entirely new, but maybe that's not what is expected here, rather that we use familiar media and tools to approach other things.

AA: I don't see these media as representational media, but rather as constitutional media. For example, we work with "auditory diagrams." In doing so, we're not concerned with representing sound, but with using this technique to think about a place aurally. The turn towards the bodily-processual requires a fundamental critique of these practices, and also the development of new ones: a fundamental critique of these practices as representational practices.

SG: What is crucial is not the reduction to sight, but to a particular kind of visual representation, which then becomes dominant and leads to absurd statements. Phenomenology has tried using terms like "atmosphere" and "Stimmung" to resist this.[3] Unfortunately these terms are loaded with esoteric connotations, but once you begin to grasp them more seriously, they indicate other spaces and other modalities of how space can be perceived. "Stimmung" is an acoustic metaphor (the tuning of an instrument): the moment of "Stimmung" has a lot to do with the sound of a space and the perception of the sound. Atmosphere refers to a more chemical space, if you like, not to "hard" physical or geometric transitions, but to "soft" transitions from warm to cold or from damp to dry. The challenge here is to find ways to represent that don't just fall back on geometric plans. "Diagrammatic" is, I think, a suitable key term: it would refer to descriptions of structures or relations in spatial contexts that can be characterized qualitatively. So how do you describe something like that? It can be in a narrative form, using brief sketches that are not geometric but rather topological. Consider Fernand Deligny's drawings, for example.

AA: What I consider to be problematic is to base this discourse on the concept of representation. The concept of re-presentation implies a duplication and therefore a reinforcement of a particular concept of reality. Reality *is* not: it becomes. If that is true, can we still talk about re-presentation?

SH: We use the instrument of notation in our work: holding on to one aspect, one spatial quality, not a quantity. Qualitative spatial experiences can refer to any one of the three levels of "lived-space," as Elisabeth Ströker describes it: mood space (gestimmter Raum), space of action (Handlungsraum), and perceptual space (Wahrnehmungsraum). These three levels are of course interdependent and cannot be separated from one another—but they also cannot

3 The German term "Stimmung" means "mood" or "atmosphere" as well as "tune" or "tuning".

be separated from either their spatial setting or the perspectives of the individuals embedded within that setting. This must be clear when one intervenes. And when one alters built structures, the purpose of one's intervention only reaches to a certain extent: I can decide if a space appears narrower or wider, more or less filtered, more or less visible. Yet at the same time, I will also always be altering the possibilities of action, the space for action, and the performative potential within this area. I will be influencing the atmosphere, I will be manipulating the possibilities of experiencing this space, without being able to control all of this myself, or even being able to imagine these effects in their entirety. This, by the way, has been a major point in the criticism of modern architecture: just because you don't consider atmosphere while producing places, it doesn't mean that there won't be any. And it may even be that atmospheres have been created that nobody wanted in the first place, that show up without being wanted. Phenomenologically speaking, spaces can never be empty, and they are never without an atmosphere, but a lot of architects don't understand this. When they see an unbuilt site, they say: "That's so empty, we can fill that!" But this is also due in part to the fact that many of them only look at the plans and don't go to the supposedly empty locations, because if they did, they would see that they are not *empty*, they are just *unbuilt*. That is not the same thing. This is where I often miss the necessary precision in architectonic discourse.

AA: Before we can have precision, I think, it has to be perceived. Cage comes to mind here: When do we have sound? When do we have music? First there's nothing there. Then the concert begins and then the music is there. I know that there are different interpretations of 4'33"... What I find interesting about this piece is that—exclusively using a temporal framing—it can be shown that sound is there, that sound was always there. But we continue to think that nothing sounds in the concert hall before the musicians start to play. I see here a commonality with the idea that space only exists when the architect has positioned something there—when something has been built.

BH: I must say, for as long as I've been having this discussion with Alex, I have been increasingly fascinated by blank sheets. If we have just established that a plan is not the representation of a reality lying somewhere behind it, but instead first of all a plan, then we have to ask the question: What does the practice of drawing mean? If we notate something by drawing, then it has a power of its own. It can be the image or the thought or the concept of something that leads to another action, or gives reason to other actions. So now we can find new uses for a tool of our very own. I think that, maybe, many such small acts of taking a step back and reexamining that will bring us to a point in our activity as architects from which we can begin a new kind of discussion. It may require many, very small activities that then head off in unexpected directions. For example, describing Ernst-Reuter-Platz using listening protocols: these are not representations, they are bound to specific activity at that place itself.

AA: I think we have arrived at this very radical actuality of phenomenology: "Tell me what you see, now!" The phenomenological description: I stand in front of something and try to perceive what I currently perceive instead of perceiving what I usually perceive. That's why, in my e-mail, I asked the following question in preparation: What happens to the architect when the validity of the world is suspended? I find your work very strong in this respect. That's why I asked at the beginning: What exactly is the object of architecture? If I answer this very boldly, and apply it to my own work, then I would say that it is absolutely not the built space, but rather the lived-space.

SH: Sure. But that is harder to quantify and also can't be produced in a targeted manner, because of course it only begins to exist in the relation between people and space, and it has many different facets and many interpretations. And it's this differentiation and contingency that we architects find so hard to bear. We like to be in control. But you can only have this sense of control if you in turn suspend life, that is, if you say something like, "We have no influence over what happens in the spaces we build: life will somehow find a way to arrange itself within these spaces." If you acknowledge that spaces are never empty and are never without atmosphere and will always be in use, then you can't seriously make a statement like that. Unless you really do reduce architecture to the building of houses and say, "I am a creator of buildings or a planner for stacking bricks or artifacts ready to be used." But seeing it in a more complex way opens up new possibilities for architecture, because then a lot of different activities can become architecture that previously would not have been considered as such. This might also be another "shifting baseline." For example, I could temporarily transform this space here with a happening, a flash mob, a gardening project, or a nice little roadblock—maybe even more fundamentally, intensively, or sensibly than with architecture. There are tools we already have and we can use them in new ways. And there are tools we have let other people use so far, and we can employ them and do something different with them. I think the most important thing is to not withdraw from this cognitive process, saying, "OK, now I've solved this problem and been paid, I'm off." Instead we have to take seriously the fact that it's always just an intervention in a segment of time, and maybe it will develop in a direction you may have anticipated, but then again maybe not.

SG: But then we also have to take this radical step of saying, "Architects should also intervene when they aren't asked to."

SH: Exactly! They have to.

SG: That would be a kind of proactive architecture.

SH: Right! Many do this already. Because basically it's about the question of what is actually important in designing and changing a city, and what is marginal. But of course it's also tempting to play around with forms, with designing objects. Large objects, things that cost a lot of money, and you can control their appearance and form. That normally stops at the façade, though.

AA: Yes. I can also see these shifts. I think it's good that you mention control.

You can control objects. They have clear contours and are therefore controllable. We act on their contours, on their shapes. But what it is possible when it's not about objects, but about processes? I think that this substitution implies a new behavior based much more on adaptation, on transformative intervention, than on control.

SH: Fine, but the dilemma is that we are paid for exactly this simulation of controlling knowledge. Clients and constructors, even societies, demand forms and images, not processes. For example, look at the City Palace in Berlin (Stadtschloss): that would have been a wonderful opportunity to develop opinions democratically, in a process, about what people want there—because it was not necessarily the palace that was missed. But everyone just wanted to know what it would look like, even when it wasn't at all clear what should happen inside. I find it puzzling that people think architects should be responsible for solving problems like that.

SG: Now that space is being treated differently as a topic, these tasks fall to the architects: this cannot be avoided. If architects are seen by society as the ones who fulfill this function, then of course one architect can say, "OK, that's not my job," but it's a part of the process that architecture in this way becomes the central focus.

SH: The question of what should be done with the Berlin city center is entirely legitimate; it's fine for us to be asked about this. What I think is fatal here, though, is that we are not allowed to ask questions in return, because we are supposed to be supplying the answers. Even to questions that are not fully formulated, and consequently can't be solved or answered. In the formats in which we work—for example in competition procedures, where everyone already knows exactly how much money is there, how many square meters you need, how big the site is—we simply are not allowed to get behind these firmly established parameters.

AA: I understand that you would like to be asked, but you want to be asked differently. The question is: How would you like to be asked? This is basically the question: What is the function of architecture? Or: What should the function of architecture be in this new context?

SH: I think we should first ask the architect what he thinks the problem is, not define the problem and then go to the architect and say: "Can you please fix this?", when in reality maybe it would have been better to ask the hairdresser. That's what I mean. It would be nice to be integrated into the process of defining the questions. With the City Palace, for example, the Parliament decided that we need a palace. So that really was one case where I don't think we were at all to blame for any lack of results.

BH: But designs were handed in, despite that.

SH: Yes... of course... That's the argument: "If I don't do it, someone else will."

AA: The whole thing raises the question of architecture as a form of thought. By this I mean that there are certain practices that create certain worlds. For me, thinking means creating worlds, co-creating worlds, or, even better, co-constituting them. So I think that it makes sense to ask an architect about the question and not about the answer; that is, to integrate the architect in the process of constituting worlds from the very beginning.

SH: That might be architectonic phenomenology...

SG: It is certainly a philosophical architecture, because in philosophy it's never about finding answers, but rather posing the right questions.

BH: Isn't it true that if we try to more narrowly describe an architectonic praxis in dialogue with phenomenology, we can then rely on these methods? If we find methods that are up to the task, indeed we have to rely on them. Eventually we will be confronted with questions to which we can't respond, because the methods we use can't help us.

SH: I'd be much more afraid that we would once again have the feeling that we have answers on hand that offer no alternative. That would be the bigger danger, producing a new -ism and thinking, "That's how we'll fix it, that's how we'll get everything right."

BH: The -ism relates first to the reproduction of answers. And my question is aimed at this: whether we want to get to the point where maybe our praxis has to be defined a little more narrowly, because we realize that we can limit certain issues from various sides but not from the one side where we can really fix it.

SG: There are at least two sides. One is—where our discussion began—the question of what a phenomenological investigation or a phenomenological experiment looks like, and how it relates to the description. The other has to do with the epoché method, or the suspension of judgment: a philosophical attitude or phenomenological ethics that should be disclosed to a contractor. There are these two sides. Maybe it's a slightly paradoxical undertaking, but we can hold ourselves to a method that we have devised; at the same time we can approach the task at hand with this attitude, and then project this attitude outwards.

SH: There's an old saying: if you ask an apple tree for the solution to a problem, it will give you an apple, and if you ask an architect, then of course he will suggest a house. And I think that is beneath us, and we really should be able to say: "Take an apple. Or ask the apple tree, don't ask me." But really, at the end of the day, that has to do with an ethos, the professional ethos.

BH: Isn't this ethos also a very personal affair? The hope for achieving a communal ethos that is socially recognized, in a world that is increasingly atomized: Isn't that a completely futile and even horrifying vision?

AA: It doesn't necessarily have to come to that. In the praxis of phenomenology one always takes a step back, but one remains engaged with the topic. It's no paradox: you take a step back to create space where you were standing. Space for examination, space for insight and for opening. This is why I'm not at all scared of talking about ethos. Ethos as attitude, not a normative ethos. I'm thinking about, for example, taking a step back from control, taking a step back when it comes to providing an answer, a step towards formulating the question.

SH: Yes, exactly, it would be going too far to see it as a normative project.

Our responsibility is constantly growing, and our chance to control things is continuously receding. I think that can be proved with relative certainty. The conclusions we draw from this are going to differ from individual to individual. Some will try to tighten the control screws and others will try to reduce their responsibility, but at the end of the day, that is the state of tension in which architectural creativity resides: society has incredible demands, and at the same time it's increasingly difficult to remain productive using this old catalogue of tasks that we have. Also with an eye to the fact that we may want to make a living somehow.

SG: We have to see the opportunity, of course, that we are talking, thinking, and working in the context of a university—and see that as a space for experimentation, where an attitude in the literal sense can be developed, so that at the end no one is standing there alone as the only person who is trying to do it. Of course I agree that the level of isolation with such a project is very frustrating. Nevertheless, there is no alternative to experiencing for oneself how neighborhood can be configured. An architect who removes himself from all this, and maybe isn't even in the city, on-site, that would be a contradiction, an ethical contradiction.

BH: I wouldn't restrict this to professional education, because architecture is constantly being generated afresh in discourse—at least if we're talking about architecture that is built, not necessarily the architecture that we architects anticipate. This discourse in turn affects reality. In this sense it's important to find an argumentation within the discourse that doesn't get stuck in some kind of -isms proclaiming, "something must now be like that," but maybe also encompasses forms of access that allow for deeper investigation, for fascination. This would be something that could very intensively flourish in discourse.

AA: In discourse and in practices: reflected and reflecting practices. This attitude and this behavior are reflexive. Critically reflexive. There is an enormous transformative potential here if we address it as an open-ended process. I see phenomenology as an open-ended process. I understand it fundamentally as an approach that, by necessity, has become a methodical practice.

A dialogue with

Gabriele Dolff-Bonekämper,

Oliver Bormann,

Boris Hassenstein,

Alex Arteaga

95

AA: The idea for this discussion arose in two forums. The first was concerned with the workshop process, and the second dealt with monument preservation.[1] In the latter you [Gabriele Dolff-Bonekämper] said something that seemed to me to be particularly relevant. You said, and I'm paraphrasing: "Ernst-Reuter-Platz is a work of art, and monument preservation has to make it possible to perceive it as such." I thought: "OK, if we accept that as departing point, then we can think differently about monument preservation." That is where the idea for "access as a principle of preservation" came from. This idea implies—one would think—a certain paradox, because of the relationship between preservation and access. If I'm trying to preserve something, then I could be tempted to block access to it. So what could this preservational access, or accessible preservation, look like? While I was thinking about this, I thought of your [Oliver Bormann's] work, specifically your ideas about the remodeling of Ernst-Reuter-Platz, but also your architectural concept: an architecture that doesn't draw attention to itself. Not, as you call it, an architecture of spectacle, but an architecture that allows access to the place where architecture is built. Architecture is always built in a place, it creates a place, but it also transforms the place in which it is built. Based on these two approaches, we can imagine an architecture that would not necessarily stand in opposition to monument preservation. I would like to offer this idea as a starting point for the discussion.

GDB: Protecting and concealing, and protecting and displaying, are two different possibilities. If something is valuable, then you can maybe preserve its value by concealing it, or you can maintain its value and maybe even enhance it by displaying it, because the more people can see it, the more valuable it could become. That is the reverse perspective, so to speak. The one is: I conceal it and restrict access, and thereby raise the value of the object, like in a treasure chest that is only opened once a year. The other is: I think something is precious and valuable, I want to ensure that as many people as possible get to see it; in this way it doesn't lose any of its value, but instead increases in value, because for me the concealment itself should not be a strategy. Certainly not in monument preservation, because monuments are not part of a treasure hoard, they are situated in public space. So for me it's clear that if I want to observe something as a work of art, and maybe as a landmarked monument, then of course I'm not going to be at all interested in hiding it from view. Instead I want to draw attention to it. Because many people use Ernst-Reuter-Platz—people who walk around and occasionally wait at the traffic lights, or complain about how it's so windy here—they rarely make the effort to look more closely. Looking closely is the first access to a work of art, but if it isn't being looked at, then it is not socially realized. That is my point of access to this question of value and visibility. The question then arises, of course, if I say: "Ernst-Reuter-Platz is a work of urbanistic art," which I have said and will continue to say, then you could say that the work is complete, and that any addition or excision would damage

1 During the project "Lab ERP," there were five forums, conceived as open discussions between researchers from the Auditory Architecture Research Unit, students and professors from the Department of Landscape Architecture and Environmental Planning (Technische Universität Berlin), and the MA Sound Studies (Berlin University of the Arts). Oliver Bormann and Andreas Quednau participated in the first forum on "City Planning Workshop Process Ernst-Reuter-Platz" on May 2, 2013. Gabriele Dolff-Bonekämper, Philipp Oswalt, and Klaus Lingenauber were guests at the "Monument Preservation/Temporary Spaces" forum on May 30, 2013.

the work. I've made that point myself on occasion, and I would repeat it, depending on what plans are being made, what kind of architecture is being considered, what changes or developments are proposed for Ernst-Reuter-Platz.

OB: Might I ask if you followed the workshop process,[2] in which five teams investigated the area, including the square itself, in order to conceptually redefine it?

It just occurs to me because it was interesting that none of the teams who investigated the site really questioned it intensively. I was actually expecting that the whole Berlin debate about inner city planning under Hans Stimmann, and the related paradigm shift in Berlin's cityscape that occurred in the 1990s, would be an influence here, but this was absolutely not the case. That came as something of a surprise. But there was nevertheless a latent discontent among the teams and their client concerning the situation at Ernst-Reuter-Platz, maybe due to the ambivalence it carries these days. Almost everyone values the site itself as an ensemble and as an urbanistic highlight, which really was outstanding at the time of its construction. Yet at the same time, there seems to be this need to adapt it to today's social requirements, or to make it more useful, more open for appropriation. The usefulness of the site seems to be unsatisfactory, and there was also a sense of aesthetic unease. On this basis it makes sense to talk about the idea of "Ernst-Reuter-Platz as a work of art." I wouldn't want to contradict this from the outset, but I do have the impression that in saying so, we withdraw from a number of arguments. If one says, "It's finished, it's a work of art and has to be viewed as such," then that eliminates other aspects of the site in the cityscape.

GDB: I see what you mean. I meant what I said differently. Because unlike a painting, which you shouldn't touch and which no one else should continue painting—not even the artist himself, because it's a fixed work and it's finished—unlike that, this is an ensemble of buildings that are in use, and a square with traffic and pedestrians and a central island with living, thriving plant life, and so there is something like a rhythm here, there is something like breathing, and there is what I've called the choreography, the sequences of movement on this square. Thus I could call the square as it is in this choreography, with all its buildings, a scenographic ensemble. And if the movement and the scenography are supposed to be coherent, then everything would change if I were to alter one factor. And that is where we get to the issue of accessibility. Accessibility is also something mental, so first of all it has to be conceivable that something like Ernst-Reuter-Platz can be a work of art, that it can be a monument with all of the consequences that I just mentioned. The other thing is of course visual accessibility and literal accessibility—on foot, with a bicycle, by car, you could call it the "enterability" (*Zufahrlichkeit*)—that is, how is the square organized. Is there any way that the flow of traffic and the treatment of various road-users around this circle can be influenced? And if so, if it can be influenced, then how, and what would change in this square?

2 City Planning Workshop Process "Ernst-Reuter-Platz," coordinated by the Berlin Senate Department for City Planning and the Environment (November 2012–March 2013).

AA: The idea that accessibility is mental means that we are talking about the experience of the site. We are no longer just referring to its materiality, although we will not be neglecting that aspect.

GDB: Of course, otherwise there would be nothing there.

AA: Exactly. We need this materiality. The mental is not something happening in the brain, instead it's something happening in and with the world.

GDB: Exactly.

AA: The problem comes from the use of the term "work of art." I would question whether any work of art is ever finished. But there is a difference. You mentioned three types of artistic discipline: painting, choreography, and scenography. Let's start with the "simplest" example, as it were: painting. A painting may be finished, but of course—leaving aside Duchamp-esque interventions for the time being—nobody intends to change the painting itself. The painting will however always be observed in an "apparatus of accessibility," as in museums or galleries.

GDB: That is an excellent term, I can only agree. Because the work as an artifact may be finished, but the work in perception and in presentation, in connotation, in contextualization, in all possible variables of interpretation and presentation will always be newly appropriated and changed without anyone actually laying a finger on it; although of course it will be touched, because paintings need to be restored.

AA: For example. Or also if it is lit in a new and different way.

GDB: That too.

AA: When we talk about colors in painting, our statements are based on the foundation of our experiences with particular lighting conditions. There is always a whole apparatus, in the Foucaultian sense, of the way discursive and non-discursive practices work together, which conditions accessibility and, through it, the painting as phenomenon. But here we are dealing with an urbanistic work of art. And regardless of whether or not the site is finished, here as well we should make sure that it is accessible as a work of art. I do think that with respect to the apparatus of visibility—of perception— thought could be given to architectonic interventions.

GDB: Absolutely. Again, I can only agree, because the apparatuses can be temporary actions. They can be little interventions. If however they are supposed to be more massive interventions, having to do with regulating traffic, speed limits, and the rhythm of traffic, then there is a greater responsibility for the extent and duration of the intervention, and the demands are raised as well. This is clear. This means that whoever intervenes here had better be good, because any other option is just fiddling around...

BH: I'd like to get back to the concept of art, because a work of art demands autonomy, and it also demands that the viewer withstand this. In the world of architecture we have great difficulty with that. As an architect I have to be clear about the serving role of my work.

GDB: Sure, someone should also be paying for you, and it is also supposed to be useful.

BH: That's a fact. But when post-war modern architecture is the subject, the challenge is bigger. Each generation have to define this course for themselves. Just like each individual has to find a way to access a work of art, a generation have to newly appropriate a historical period, a piece of architecture, or a public space. Today we are dealing with a Zeitgeist and a generation that like to occupy, to appropriate, to emancipate themselves, and to take direct action. Now we want to explain to them that Ernst-Reuter-Platz is a settled, autonomous work of art, and as such, every detail of its structure, including for example the pavement, is protected. Are we taking this idea too far, or do we actually have to put up with it?

GDB: Are you asking me, or everyone?

BH: It's a central question for the contemporary user and also for me as an architect. We have been concerning ourselves for over a year now with the question of what to do with this square, in the sense of interventions or actions to undertake here. For me this has been a constant one step forward, one step back. One idea to do something arises, and then the next moment this idea has been withdrawn and we start thinking about something like freeing up park benches, like a restorer would. Or making random observations like, "There's a bench over there with no seat anymore, look, isn't it a crying shame about those concrete feet just standing around, they're really very nicely designed…"

GDB: Someone really does need to put a plank on top of them.

BH: Yes, there are moments like this, and then there are the other moments, as in: "It can't go on like this, we have to do something, change something." The will of forming begins again. And in this conflict I ask myself: Are we caught in this conflict, or can we bring the debate a step further?

OB: We also have to sharpen our attitude towards this square. The issue of how to deal with it, or how to transform this site, was a very difficult one. During the course of the workshop process, which carried on for weeks, we became increasingly scrupulous. Eventually we had to say: either we have to largely accept the square as it is, spatially and as far as the construction is concerned—and in that case I also wouldn't try to transform it in any major way—or, alternately, we begin to radically break it down and redefine it. One of the teams suggested basically digging underground levels beneath the central island and rebuilding the surface area with questionable conservational aspects. Through this intervention they proposed to make the underground space useful as part of new and intense programming. If you were to look out the window from here, maybe you wouldn't have noticed much of a change, unless you really knew what you were looking for. This approach would have been an attempt to introduce an intensive new usage to the square, which at the same time would have provided new stimulus for the surface.

GDB: Uh, then the garden monument conservators would have been up in arms, because that would change the entire surface design of the site.

OB: Yes, it would.

GDB: Because then, where now there are very few people, there would be a great many, and that would mean having to change all the paths and access…

AA: But they were all beneath the square...

GDB: Sure, but I mean, when you go in there and you're supposed to only walk through tunnels—I don't believe that for a second. So I think it would have meant enormous changes above ground...

OB: Maybe it wouldn't have changed very much above ground, but that was just an example of a proposed new permanent plan for the square.

GDB: It does raise logistical questions, but... instead of that, someone could have had the idea of raising a 25-story cylindrical high-rise on the central island...

OB: I think at some point one of the other teams did come up with something like that.

GDB: Yes... well I think that's just about the stupidest idea...

OB: The square makes a lot of sense when you look at its history. You do get the impression, though, that it's suffering to a certain extent from loss of significance, that its status as a work of art is also less recognized now, and that it has problems being acknowledged as such, because—and this is often a problem with modern architecture—while educated observers may see the quality of the buildings at a glance, for most people it's just "modern building blocks." That may be a cultural problem, maybe even a German problem, because architecture and city planning are in part handled differently in other European countries. And this connects to the question of how to establish mental access to Ernst-Reuter-Platz, and how to make this access wide enough to welcome more than just students of architecture and small art elites. Also, can we prescribe a specific usage or another kind of programming without structurally transforming the site to a large degree? We had a lot of trouble with this question.

GDB: Well, we have two very different positions here, and I think that is quite exciting. And it raises some very different thoughts for me. Referring to your first point, when I look at the site, it was built during an era in which new was good. There was also absolutely no alternative to this, because what was old was largely broken—broken in many different ways, not just physically but fundamentally. Besides, here we were on the East-West axis, so all these pro- and contra-Speer arguments are also involved. But even more fundamentally, the site comes from an era in which new was good and old was worthless. Unless of course we're talking really old, but not 19th century. That is why these rounded fronts on the historical buildings, which these days are so admired and loved, in the past nobody cared about them. So it's clear that the transformation comes thanks to a period of rejection, deep-seated rejection of historicism, and intensive focus on the future: modernity, newness, openness, speed, movement, all these positive terms... By now, this period is itself historical. That new is good, there was no alternative to this back then.

OB: Not only that. It has actually been reversed: today the former "good" is ostensibly "evil"...

GDB: Yes, exactly, that is exactly this paradoxical reversal of perception and also of orientation towards the future, towards, "We will master the world" and all of that. It's all there, so to speak, in Hermkes's plans for the square, and every single client who raised a building here, it's also in their plans, down to that now vacant post or administration building—or whatever it used to be. This is the built message. And now, when we transfer from monument theory the paired concepts of what was wanted (das Gewollte) and what has become (das Gewordene), from the theories of Alois Riegl, then it's about the monument that was planned and the monument that has become real, the one that was conceived with a specific message, and the other one, which with time becomes historical or old, and then exists as a monument for new contemporaries. But when we are talking about urbanism and architecture, then we have the planning intentions—what is wanted—and we have the present—that is, what has become. If you oppose these two and say, "Nothing turned out the way it was supposed to," then that can devalue the currently existing object. Or you can say, "They built it wrong back then," and invalidate it like that. Or you can also say, "What it has become is so shabby now that we don't want it anymore." This means there are various possibilities for approaching these two poles, with critical or affirmative intent. Some could say, "Because it was wanted back then, we have to accept it now," and others say, "Because it has become what it is, we now have to accept it." And between these two—the poles of what was wanted and what has become—there is a growing tension, which with increased distance in time and also due to changes in society and perception manifests again and again. And in stages, you might think, this "being wanted" and this "having become" should be newly questioned and reexamined.

AA: Yes, but we can view these two poles either as fully autonomous, or as two forces within a situation: the situation of becoming.

GDB: And also the situation of—what should I call it—you can continue to draw on it, and so I want to tell it to the end: narrativity. That means which story is being told here, and which story do you want to continue to have told, which story is no longer being told and has been lost, which story is currently being sidelined because other interests predominate. And to what extent can we possibly also—and I am intensely familiar with this from the context of communicating about monuments—not reproduce what was originally wanted by telling a story in a new way, but rather develop a feeling for what it has become; this does not entail a purely affirmative relationship, but rather only in the sense of providing access.

AA: Exactly, that's what I meant. Both poles condition one another constantly in the context of the current becoming.

GDB: Absolutely. That is progressive contemporaneity... Because these are always new presents. And every new present must be thought anew. The current present not only allows us, it challenges us to investigate this tension between what was wanted in the past, which you had better appreciate. This is a matter of research and knowledge and if you refuse it then you're stupid. Research and knowledge are essential, otherwise you don't understand yourself in your own present moment, but please, no awestruck veneration for what has been researched and the resulting knowledge. What is needed is a critical and maybe also empathetic distance. If no distance can be established, then you have become a part of the whole, and therefore you are no longer able to intervene. A monument-preservationist evaluation inherently involves gaining distance from the object, otherwise I would be unable to evaluate. With artistic evaluation, and the exploration of options for artistic interventions—that is where I would approach you, as architects, as possible creators of artistic interventions. You can only conceive and position your ideas once you have gained some distance, without forgetting the closeness within this distance. That is quite a complex dialectic effort, because without closeness you can't get the distance, and without the distance there is no closeness. That has been my experience with monuments. I have to gain some distance between myself and the object, otherwise I wouldn't be able to see. And I need the closeness—and to be able to touch it, and these kinds of identification—otherwise I would have no feel for the object.

AA: Exactly. If we can now return to the topic of accessibility, my question would be: What exactly is the object of this accessibility? When we observe these dynamic aspects of the site, all of which occur simultaneously, then shouldn't precisely that be the object of accessibility? Without negating the generative function of the materiality of the site, we are talking about something else here. What it's really about is the accessibility of the process of becoming-the-site. In reference to the object, I see constructive intervention—not just temporary intervention—as a possibility. Accessibility always means seeing something and not seeing something. Accessibility is always also a blockade.

GDB: OK... by selecting one option, you can't keep the other one as well.

AA: Yes, that is why, when you formulated the theses of "monument conservation as access" during the forum, I asked the representative of the Berlin Monument Authority (Landesdenkmalamt): "If we accept this thesis, what then should be protected and conserved?" The answer was: "Everything." But that can't be the case, because this "everything" would obstruct all movement.

GDB: No, that's not at all possible.

AA: But then the intervention that you [Oliver Bormann] mentioned would be possible. It would mean material sacrifice in favor of access to the processes of becoming-the-site. Precisely on this basis, I see monument preservation and new architecture as practices that could flow into one another. So not only a new approach to programming, but also constructive intervention. Not that I would prefer this, but we have the option of considering it, even if it would entail a material alteration of the site.

BH: This site represents a difference. In the process of working with Ernst-Reuter-Platz this insight became more and more important. Over time I began to like the place because of it being so different. In the idea of the European city and European public, urban squares, which actually are all used in pretty much the same way from Lisbon to Helsinki. Now I have to put this aside and let the site begin to speak as architecture. This would mean that I will allow for this difference, that this public square is not primarily a place to spend time. The fact is that people spending time here are more or less tolerated. Then I have to accept that it is not the traffic that is a problem, but—to exaggerate the point—the problem is the other way around: me, when I sit around here, maybe I am the one disturbing the traffic. I have to accept this contradiction when I say, "There are squares, and there are other squares..."

GDB: Yes, Ernst-Reuter-Platz is not a failed Savignyplatz.

OB: Absolutely. At some point we also thought, "Modernism was not able to create public squares," at least not in the sense of what we might now expect from a public square. But we do have to recognize that this square plays a very different role in the city when compared with classic Gründerzeit squares. I think that it's more interesting to ask: How does Ernst-Reuter-Platz function in urban context in comparison with other city squares, and also in comparison with its own specific surroundings? What kind of relationship is there between the site and its urban hinterland? And once again on the topic of "constructive change" of Ernst-Reuter-Platz: our concept became increasingly far removed from this question, it really didn't interest us very much anymore. We began to concentrate more on temporary measures, although we could not yet identify any concrete examples. On the contrary, we thought this would be a project that could be developed together with people from monument preservation (perhaps as a design project at a university), and then further explored in negotiations and processes in order to determine what monument preservation would allow, and how much of a range of tolerance exists. Who moves where and in which position, all of this would eventually have to be fixed in the concrete plan.

AA: I think it's interesting that criteria can be established for this. The answer to the question, "Are we allowed to build here or not?" can't simply be, "No." New criteria can be developed, based on the concept of accessibility and a complex definition of the object of this accessibility. We could start by defining what possible interventions are supposed to accomplish. Not only in terms of programmatic usage, but in the sense of perceptual apparatus.

OB: But would that be an idea or a concept that would be newly and permanently applied to the square?

AA: Not necessarily. It's also a matter of the duration of the intervention. A constructive intervention need not be a monument for the ages— ephemeral architecture.

GDB: That would certainly be interesting. But the question of course is if it should or could be something really captivating. I think the latter would be more appropriate, because if on the one hand I say modest, and then on the other hand I say here the standard is very high, then of course with each and every intervention the aesthetic standard has to be equally high, or it will all collapse in on itself. And that can't happen.

AA: I don't think that the criterion can be the fitting together of new and old, as in I see object A and I see objects B, C, D, and E standing around and say, "Yes, they belong together somehow." Much more interesting, I think, is what happens to objects B, C, D, and E when you introduce object A. How does this new object intervene in the processes you mentioned? How does it contribute to the accessibility of these processes? Of course, that is all phrased in a very abstract way...

GDB: Yes, but I like it!

AA: With this approach, I'm not making any one form concrete. I phrase it openly because I think it's appropriate to keep the process of finding the form open, because basically, we can't know...

GDB: No, we can't know if it's going to be round or angular, or black or white... But we can say, "OK, let's have a look at the buildings that are already here and the stakeholders associated with these buildings, and let's start with the architects—who exactly *is* Willy Kreuer?" Who are the people, what kind of architectures, styles, purposes, interpretations are associated with each of the individual components? The more abstractly we consider it, the more appealing the idea becomes. Also the idea here on-site, at Ernst-Reuter-Platz, in real, existing spaces and not in spaces that have yet to be cleared, so this could be the edges of the square or the center. Whether the central island means the greatest freedom, because it looks so available, or whether when you look at it and see a laid-out garden, in particular when you look from above you can see it very clearly, when we look from here—we can see that there's not nothing there, there is something. Even if it doesn't look like some Baroque garden, where anybody would immediately recognize that it's a horticultural work of art, I think we can also view it as an example of horticultural art. And to say, "It's just green, it's available," is also a bit cheap. In that sense all areas are occupied and allocated, and yet we still have to approach this situation of being occupied and allocated and say, "OK, then maybe we'll build something here," without ruining the rest. But what can you build there on the central island at a site like Ernst-Reuter-Platz?

OB: The approach should be that by hindering perception, perception first becomes possible. And of course one can very well imagine similar or slightly altered concepts. At the end of the day, it's always interesting that it happens over a period of time that has yet to be defined, and that it doesn't become a permanent intervention.

AA: We need difference. Perception requires difference. This refers to the dialectic between seeing and not-seeing, between blocking and opening. There's a kind of irritation and confusion that can also facilitate the accessibility we're talking about.

BH: I needed quite a long time to understand how subtle this access really is. In the first steps of the analysis and in the early stages of the design process it felt like an obstacle. This applies to the physical access but also access as a process of understanding. This kind of access already inherently incorporates a mental instant. The actual access to the square presupposes an effort on your part: taking a step back from the impulse to just walk across the square, instead going down into the subway, then finding the path, going through the tunnel and entering this area that seems so isolated and lonely. And only then is there this sudden and intense opening of the space.

GDB: By walking up into the light. That is a very strong effect.

BH: Yes, it's almost a kind of allegorical situation, albeit one made with the simplest of means. There is this same old, apparently trivial handrail, outside in the entrance to the subway as well as over there on the central island, the same simple materials. It took me a moment before I realized how consciously these instruments have been put to work.

AA: When I hear that, I have to think of Tadao Ando's conference pavilion for the Vitra. A conference pavilion is a building in which many people meet. So one would initially imagine that the access would have to be wide. On the contrary, Ando designed a narrow door. Leading up to the door is a relatively narrow, long path, with a concrete wall running along one side of it. If you want to enter the pavilion for a conference, you have to walk by yourself for a while, and walk alone through the door. And only then are you able to start talking. In our case that means: if you want to get to the central island, you first have to go down, find the way, and then arrive at the island. That combines these two strategies, which you [Gabriele Dolff-Bonekämper] mentioned at the beginning: concealment and display.

BH: It means to work with a double approach. This is increasingly developed as a design method. It had to provide the concealment, and then again the opening. In doing so, I came to the question of whether this model could provide a way to free ourselves from the debate about scale. The question of scale is lethal for the discussion. These widths, these huge dimensions, they diminish every intervention, and demand an unachievable scale.

AA: But if this visibility is what is being aspired to, then that could easily result in what you [Oliver Bormann] call architecture of spectacle. It has to be something visible that does not draw attention to itself, but rather directs attention to the square.

GDB: The eye-catcher, that's like the staffage figure in Gilly's drawing of the Marienburg. The observing figures are supposed to direct whoever is looking at the picture to observe the object. That is the double distancing. This pointing gesture, that is a fundamental issue. The pointing figure, the architectonic pointing figure, has to function differently than a literal pointing finger. But ultimately the idea of the pointing figure brings back this idea of correspondence with the surrounding buildings, like Hermkes already said... it's like a conversation.

OB: Consequently new architecture could be included in this "conversation circle." I think an architectural intervention here could function as a pointing finger when viewed from outside, and yet at the same time, from close range, enable perception.

AA: The pointing figure should direct attention. But one should not—as the Chinese proverb says—look at the finger when the finger is pointing to the moon.

GDB: You should be looking at the moon. Yes, but of course it does depend on what the finger looks like. Because it can't be invisible.

AA: Exactly. And now we've arrived at the question of form. This is where the discourse as discourse has to come to an end...

BH: The discourse about the finger as attention guide again presents the square as concept. This could be the basis for a strategy: the introduction of a repetition, of this concept of finger, of this intervention genuinely conceived as something temporary, as something temporary and recurring.

GDB: Something recurring, changeable, always new and different, which always has the function of showing, pointing. That would be a wonderful motto. Because this way you wouldn't be thinking about what kind of support would get how many cubic meters onto the central island, how many square meters, and how would it be heated? How would it be constructed? And this in a way that would please everyone afterwards.

OB: A nice standard would be if you always had to position yourself in relation to the square.

GDB: Yes, but that means of course that if this is what you want, and if you could actually imagine that this could be something, then it's something that doesn't earn money, it costs money instead. I think this is an important point to add, that ultimately it has to be a collective of supporters of the buildings surrounding Ernst-Reuter-Platz who have to gather the funds, and I'm not talking about just a couple of Euros, it has to be a little more than that, in order to increase the current value. If we could manage this together, a long-lasting campaign of "pointing-architecture" then this will become a top location. But I think that without a concept for sponsorship, this kind of design concept just collapses immediately. And this sends a double message, I think, because the planning of an intervention is a plan for increasing value, not decreasing value. It's an expression of esteem and appreciation, not an expression of finding something inferior and wanting to get rid of its flaws. I think this is a fundamental question. If you say this is all flawed and we're going to correct it, or if you say this is actually pretty interesting and good, and we could add something so that we can also help shape it. And so that this square remains in the present, in which form can also be invented.

AA: Or so that it can be perceived.

GDB: Yes.

A dialogue with

Frank Eckardt

and

Boris Hassenstein

FE: As an urban sociologist, what I find interesting about this square is of course the way it mirrors the functional model of Berlin, which has developed and changed in various ways during the last, let's say 150 years. I think Ernst-Reuter-Platz is very emblematic; it represents a paradigm within which to study exactly that. On the one hand it shows something that expresses the functionality of modernity, and on the other hand it clearly shows how this functionality doesn't always work the way it was intended. It was the division of West Berlin from East Berlin that prevented this idea of a growth model linked to a functional site from ever being fully realized. Now, when the opportunity is there for Berlin to sprawl, a completely different growth model is being implemented. And Ernst-Reuter-Platz is kind of stuck in the middle. On the one hand it's manifesting this growth model in such a clichéd manner, and on the other hand it no longer fits into it at all. If we look at what is happening here, it's an increasing growth in density, a development inwards, multi-functionality and the overlapping of functions. That's what I find so interesting about this square from an urban-historical perspective: that it is on the one hand an anachronism in the growth model of today's Berlin, and yet on the other hand it still serves that old growth model, what we would call the Fordist model—that is, maintaining the separation of functions, even though it no longer has any meaning in this form. Upgrading the square is actually part of a process that we could call aestheticization, which embodies a completely different growth model, or development model, for the city. So the question is whether Berlin is pursuing one of these models more than the other, as it were. Whether this functionality and the separation of functions prevails, or instead the newly aestheticized development of the city. The whole model for Berlin as a metropolis began in the middle of the 1920s with the construction of this mobility infrastructure, the S-Bahn and the motorway. But it was never fully realized; it was continued under conditions that made the whole endeavor just absurd. That is why Berlin, for many people, was a place of alienation, of estrangement, because this functionality hadn't legitimated itself. Why would you need such huge infrastructural projects if there could be no horizontal growth? In this sense, Ernst-Reuter-Platz was a kind of caricature of that growth model. And now it partially fulfills this function alongside a development that is at the same time rendering it obsolete.

FE: Bauhaus, or the movement in the 1920s, was set on creating or distilling an aesthetic of modernity. In this sense, monument preservation is justified. If this aestheticizing urban growth logic asserts itself, then this kind of aesthetic will cease to exist. I believe that this aestheticizing urban development model is a form of retro-perspective. I believe that we will continue to return to this form of aesthetic, but it will not survive as a fundamental model. We will want a kind of patchwork aesthetic, even though the square is designed to reflect precisely that, while at the same time leaving space for other possible interpretations. I don't believe that a pure return to the aesthetic of modernity will be accepted in the long run. And if it is, then only intermedially, or sensualized, with other ways to approach and experience it. But if we actually did want to return it to how it was in the 1920s, let's say in the period of aesthetic modernity, then that would certainly not be accepted in the long run. "Freezing" the experience of a location via aesthetics simply doesn't work. That has been the experience in the field of monument preservation in general. We may wish for it, and the purists amongst the monument preservationists wish for it too, but without an intermediation and the option to constantly reappropriate it, to interpret it afresh, it cannot really exist.

FE: The usage of the site is no longer subordinate. In functional logic, the square had a beautifying aesthetic, so to speak: consequently, it should be made even more beautiful. But it is no longer going to be possible, because this site is not going to be a distributary hub for mobility in the long run. With the central train station and other locations in the city, we have a completely different distribution logic for traffic streams. The appropriation of the inner city also means taming these streams, reducing and slowing them. For that reason I cannot imagine that in the long run this massive orientation towards car circulation will last. So the surroundings are going to slowly dry up and slow down; certainly when you look at the nearer inner city districts, Kreuzberg, Mitte and, Wedding are going to contribute less and less to the traffic flowing towards this site. In that respect, this square is no longer going to be able to survive with this functionality. This means it's going to have to adopt a different functionality, and that includes experiential and perceptual qualities that people will be looking for here. Which in turn will accelerate the process of acquiring a new functionality. We have to constantly pose the question, "Traffic from where, to where?" The classic course of traffic was from one functional unit to another. That is, from residence to workplace. The industrial age is long gone in Berlin, which means that what we are now seeing is a kind of mobility concentrated more closely on one's own living situation, hardly any of the kind of mobility that moves in one direction to one location. There is an island-like mobility; one visits various locations throughout the city, but there are no longer these coordinated movements. That's why I don't think that traffic investment or volume is going to grow strongly enough to justify a square like this. On the contrary, I think it's more likely to diminish and become more strongly oriented towards public infrastructure. Public local traffic—that will continue. But not that you will want to travel quickly from one part of the city to another. I think that will be less and less the case. The daily commute to work will shift to the outer districts. This can really only be good news for City West. The quality of life will increase.

FE: The question is: What is modernity, or what did it want? I think that modernity was not primarily interested in arranging specific organizational forms of urban development, but rather in enabling, improving, and accelerating further development of the city, increasing efficiency and rationality, making it easier to plan. And that, now as then, is what citizens expect from urban planning and urban development. Only the needs will change, and the need to travel distances quickly, which is the need served by this kind of infrastructure, will no longer be so pressing. Once your most urgent needs can and should be met in the immediate vicinity, then you are certainly not going to want to get into a car and travel long distances. Instead, you'll want to have whatever it is in your immediate surroundings. And it is precisely the groups currently driving the gentrification process who are going to push this through as well. They push it through with ideas and demands made on urban planning, as well as with their political and social weight. So I rather think that this is a question of social positioning, whether or not Ernst-Reuter-Platz should be maintained: I think that people will point to the fact that those who still have to commute long distances need it as it is, and those who want to settle here in the inner city with a work-home-lifestyle are more likely to reject it. That is why I think that squares like Ernst-Reuter-Platz are going to become contested sites. Those who want to keep them as they are will be those who still want a very, how can I put it, Fordist-modern lifestyle, or those who have to live that way. And the others, who relocate here because they have everything in their immediate vicinity, will only need connections to the train stations and local supplies. And for these people, a square like this is really more of an eyesore than anything else. If this site were to indeed lose its functionality—which of course it won't for the foreseeable future—but if it is redesigned, then there will of course be an effect, it will produce a degree of uncertainty. This doesn't have to be a bad thing per se, but it could lead to calling the whole concept into question and saying, "Fine, let's rebuild this site as a residential area." The pressure on the real estate market is going to be intense enough that at some point, there will begin to be discussion about closing down the square entirely and building something completely different in its place.

BH: This site is also a prominent location for office space, which is coming more into focus with the reevaluation of the City West. Property owners are increasing economic pressure. This will likely be in opposition to a possible appropriation of the site from the perspective of the residents. On the contrary, it will more likely be the economic usage as a location for office space, possibly also including the generation of more traffic, which will initially be pushed forward.

FE: If you look at the first plans made following German reunification, you can see where residential areas are marked and where office space is supposed to go; you can see that none of it turned out as it was intended, it didn't work. There is this one map that I believe can still be found on the Internet, where you can see that the wish was that the big global companies and businesses settle here. None of that happened. I think it is rather implausible that more office space will be developed here. That would have to arise from a specific dynamic, a clustering of particular branches, and I don't see this happening. I think people still want certain high-end service industry offices to set up here, but I think it's not really happening. So I do not think that the development of things is going to lead to a situation like, "We want more big offices here now, like in the American central business districts, skyscrapers and so on." I can't see that happening. Only if and when the traffic can be slowed down, so to speak, will this become an attractive location for luxury residential offers.

BH: This square is strongly characterized by two functions, university and office space. These two functions absolutely dominate the immediate area; there are no others that are even remotely as important. We can see this in how the square is used, how the ground-level zones are used, how the pedestrian flows organize themselves around the square. All of this precisely points to these two usages.

FE: At the moment that is the case, yes. But I don't think it will stay like this. On the one hand, I think that classic office work will continue to be scaled back. The number of people who work in banking has decreased rapidly over the past 20 years. Large office locations like Frankfurt have begun to transform office blocks into residential blocks: Niederrath is an example. I don't think there is a need now for large office blocks. I don't think there will be companies—although there may be, you can never completely discount it—who will say, "OK, we want to invest here, we want to set something up." But as I see it, this era of high-rise culture and the office block is pretty much over and done. They are no longer the pioneers of urban development. That is also the current trend in university culture, to live closer to the campus, to integrate it into living and working; and the people who work for Deutsche Bank, et cetera, also want to be able to live closer to where they work. All this, I think, will certainly lead to more demand from within the branch, if there were the possibility of living here. That may seem utopian at the moment, given the traffic, but once that has diminished somewhat there will almost certainly be opportunities to design and arrange things, to force this issue. That's one possible perspective.

BH: Ernst-Reuter-Platz is a listed monument. We posed the question: Do we also have to place the traffic under a preservation order if we understand the square to be a historic monument? Because the traffic forms and constitutes this site, and an entirely new developmental perspective would be opened if the traffic were to diminish or be largely redirected elsewhere. This brings us to the next line of conflict, because the conflicts about approach and usage of the square are growing. They are acquiring an aesthetic dimension.

FE: I think we have to simply say that the square has not achieved the functionality we usually expect of locations like this. We still have to consider that right over there used to be the end. I can remember that in the 1980s, it was often possible to be alone driving from the Wall to here. This function, pulsing, accelerating, distributing the traffic, it never actually had worked at all in West Berlin, only in an extremely reduced form, not at all comparable with what it's like today. There was a kind of race to catch up after reunification, and it should really be a part of the history of Ernst-Reuter-Platz that this paradox existed. In a way they staged a modernity here that was no longer necessary. West Berlin didn't have a growth model. It simply couldn't grow. But they tried to imitate and introduce it, and this imitation is part of the history. Trying to block that out, saying, "It always had this function," that's just nonsense. It didn't have it for over 50 years. And exactly this would be part of what in my opinion should somehow be expressed in monument preservation, that there was a development concept that was supposed to be realized here that made absolutely no sense. That is, not the sense it should have made in a classic city, which would be to disperse and distribute traffic. You could drive somewhere else from here, but it was a pretty limited choice, and this acceleration was completely unnecessary. Why accelerate traffic when there was nowhere to go? That, I think, is also a part of the history of Ernst-Reuter-Platz, and it just doesn't surface anywhere in the considerations about monument preservation. Really, only the form and the aesthetic of the site are being looked at. But I think that what is special about this location in particular is how major elements in West Berlin city planning were set on initiating or simulating a growth model as if the city were not divided. After reunification, Ernst-Reuter-Platz suddenly had a completely new significance, and the city developed in a way that was very different from how the West Berlin city planners had envisioned it in their growth models up until 1989. They had planned it like this: Ernst-Reuter-Platz will at some point mobilize the entire city.

BH: Of course, it was always staged as a symbol. They wanted to show that their own development model was superior—here's the parallel to Strausberger Platz—and so they created a site that maybe didn't function too well, also in its implementation as traffic planning, and indeed it couldn't function. But it is symbolically very valuable with its circular form, which picks up on Strausberger Platz and also the Großer Stern, and it proposes a kind of alternative design to the axis plans of the Nazis. The main emphasis was subtly shifted and a series of significant motifs introduced; for example, the square is not exactly laid out along the central axis. They tried to create an aesthetic alternative, firstly to the Nazi plans, and secondly of course a symbol had to be generated in the competition between the two opposed systems. This also belongs to the discourse about monument preservation. The question now is how we deal with this, how can we view the square today, in concrete terms?

FE: Yes, but at this point we can see that monument preservation cannot be reduced to reconstructing a site such as it once was. Because the meaning it may once have had cannot simply be visualized. It must be made accessible at some point, so that it can be understood and experienced. And a physical-material reconstruction is just not sufficient to provide this.

BH: Now we have a situation here in which not much would have to be reconstructed, because the square is—materially—almost completely preserved as it was, right down to the paving stones, the benches, et cetera. We can actually see the first construction phase; we're standing on what was historically built. We don't have to reconstruct all that much, but we can of course see that the square has been intensively modified. There are a lot of small changes, but also a few larger ones that obscure our view of the original form. These are subtle changes, but in total they do radically change the appearance of the square.

BH: If we look down closely at the gable wall of this house, then we can see that the grid on the surface of the square ends precisely at this gable wall. So the square completely contains the Telefunken high-rise, it belongs in its entirety to the square. The architectonic design also tells us that this building has a ground level façade to the back, towards the petrol station, which is no less carefully designed than the side of the house on display towards the square. The buildings were intended to be positioned as modern objects in a tableau. Ernst-Reuter-Platz is actually more than what we initially perceive, that is the traffic circle. The square is much more deeply involved in its environment. This thought certainly played an important role in the original conception of the square. And this also has to play a role in our discussion about of how the square should develop.

FE: The interlocking of the square with its environment is already present in the old metropolis plans for the city's squares in the 1920s—that is, Alexanderplatz, Potsdamer Platz—which were also not implemented. They were only begun, most strongly at Alexanderplatz, but they also included exactly this kind of interlocking. They were also conceived to be able to organize these traffic flows, but they were also meant to be a part of urban life, integrated into their environment. And I think that this thought may have continued, more than a very strict classic modernity. Anyway that's what I think about when you point out that this integration into the neighborhood was also in effect here. To an extent, the square also has to be understood in the context of its immediate environment. Of course the Technische Universität, that's obvious, but I also think we would have to look more closely at this detail you drew attention to earlier, to what degree this site might still have a functionality for local residents. It becomes apparent in all the studies and investigations that this has been completely blanked out. In the classic manner, there is an exclusive focus on this one functionality, traffic, and no attention is paid to the issue of what the square means for those who still live around here. Even if it's just work, being employed somewhere around here, or just living here, which is still the case for some. It's relatively densely populated, you could say. If we look at the Arc de Triumph, for example, you don't see this there at all any more. To try again to explain the way this was implemented according to Haussmann's theory, which somehow underpins it, we could look at it as a classical division between inside and outside. That, I would say, has never been realized in Berlin. Based on metropolis planning for the city's squares, it also was not meant to be realized in this way. The planning always aimed for a certain vitality, integration with housing, with the residential environment. The discussion was also criticized during the redevelopment of Potsdamer Platz. And that, we can honestly say, was realized in exactly this way. It's as hermetically sealed off as it was actually intended to be in functional modernity. The realization of a place—an island, basically—that was also criticized and never actually the goal of planning.

BH: I also have to ask myself whether the identity that Ernst-Reuter-Platz offers against these enormously contradictory backgrounds is something special, which would afford us special access to the square: that we needn't grasp this site as a normal city square, because maybe it also cannot be that.

But it is a square that has indeed drawn its peculiarity from the history of post-war modernity. How can we further develop it without negating this idiosyncratic nature, without staging "cappucino-culture" all over the place?

FE: I think that is exactly what has not been done. The specific spatial qualities of this location have never been investigated, because the perception of the location as a transit space is assumed. But I don't think this was actually realized. Maybe there is a history of the usage and the appropriation that has happened instead, and that is invisible. It's probably in the heads of the people who lived there, but otherwise it has vanished. The other question is always whose past is being preserved and whose is not. I don't know what significance Ernst-Reuter-Platz had for many people. I do think that one would have to do a kind of oral history here, in a way. It would be difficult and laborious, but I'm sure that old West Berliners would like to have something to say about it. The quality of this location, this emotional significance, these things are not in opposition to functionality. It is instead actually the promise of modernity, an optimistic perspective on urban development. It was planned on such a large scale; for a lot of people this also means hope, hope that the city will eventually develop in such a way that it manifests also here. This emotionality, it's intrinsically linked to the functionality, it's an optimistic view of the world. I think precisely this is what stirs the emotions, emotions that want to stop this cappuccino-culture from growing here now, when there is no longer any real perspective. Where something like, "The city is developing, improving, growing faster, more modern"—that doesn't show up here any more. That's the final stage, that's the end of the road. So I can well understand the people who say, "That's a pity, something is dying here."

BH: Now we reach a point that Gabriele Dolff-Bonekämper brought up in our discussion. She said—I'm paraphrasing—"Ernst-Reuter-Platz is a kind of museum of modernity." Here we have a showcase of all the various phases of post-war modernity, as well as all the major forms, all essential figures of city-planning that were used by modernity. They're all collected here. And that is the basis for her insistence that Ernst-Reuter-Platz is a piece of art, that it has the inherent qualities of a work of art. This might be controversial...

FE: I would indeed challenge that statement. A work of art in classic modernity is in fact not public, not external. It is instead an individual expression. And this here, this really is the expression of a social design for space, where precisely the individual is not supposed to be expressed, where it's removed. The term "work of art" in my view always implies that someone has the opportunity to somehow form his or her own personal and subjective viewpoint, and that is not what was supposed to happen here. This space was instead conceived as modern and functional, for the non-subjective, for the pedestrian who cannot settle on one viewpoint, but rather as indistinct as possible, to enable passing through, passing by, or using the space. To declare all that to be a work of art—I do have problems with that.

BH: This highlights another interesting line of conflict. That this site, almost like a hermaphrodite, carries inside the spirit of modernity, but at the same time it is charged with symbols and artistic gestures that are very specific to this location. And also specific to an era, a political situation, not only to the social discussion but also to the status of the divided city as a staging of, and symbol for, free Western democracy. Here it suddenly becomes apparent that two parallel courses of development actually led to the specific design of this site.

FE: No doubt. My criticism is directed more at describing it as a "work of art." That's exactly what I meant at the beginning when I talked about an aestheticized understanding of the city, something that wants to stand in opposition to the functional and even replace it. And that involves calling all of this art—comprehensive urban construction, urban planning, all of it. That is indeed an important aspect for many people nowadays, but in this phase that was absolutely not the case. In classical functionality, aesthetics were subordinated. What was of paramount importance was that it must, or should, function well.

BH: It did at least have to be convincingly staged as an image, and a lot of effort went into that.

FE: Yes, exactly. It was a staging of a whole society. It was not laid out as a work of art. That is a kind of retrospective interpretation, but the intention back then was certainly not to present this site as a work of art. The intention was rather to show, as we talked about, that we are better—ideologically, economically, politically—and we can build something here that may be completely unnecessary when it comes to functionality, but if we wanted to, we could develop the city until we had a real metropolis, like other major cities. This was all staged, it was at times completely over the top and exaggerated; this was the situation in which fissures appeared in these claims and demands, along with possibilities to operate within these fissures and introduce new interpretations. This happened on an individual level, with people occupying this space emotionally, but then also in the sense of an artistic-aesthetic praxis. But we would surely bypass the core or character of this place if we were to define it in sum as a work of art. This, I think, is what we're doing today, but I don't think that was the idea of the city planners back then. I would have to be very mistaken about that. Of course it is still interesting to see that many different forms of modernity can be found here. No question, that is fascinating. Yet this also implies that there was never anything like a uniform identity. That is important.

BH: But we can see that urban construction was much more strongly ordered and organized than it may seem today, and also staged in a much more unified manner. But we can also see that the modern repertoire of forms, which is present here, has been greatly expanded, and this has led to a diverse architectonic design that has left the very uniform image of the classic-modern urban vision far behind.

FE: The real history would be a history of diversity, and the multiplicity of modernity, and also the history of modernity, the historicity of modernity. A history that shows that modernity is not something timeless, but instead an urban praxis that grows and develops over decades, driven by various agents. Both by those who planned and built the houses, and by those who lived here. This history should be preserved, and not just, let's say, the founding idea, which was itself never fully realized except in fragments and isolated quotations that can still be found here. And so I believe that modernity has earned the right to be preserved in this way. Not in the sense of something static, but instead in all its diversity and dynamism and continued development. In other words, I would always be in favor of preserving these sites in a way that remains open to interpretation, not in a form that views the original idea of modernity as a reality that as such never existed, and probably never even wanted to exist. One would assume, let's say, that the final appearance, what is graphically represented here, is what was intended, and that it wasn't mainly a design meant to guide an intellectual approach as a thought-provoking impulse. We can find indications in many texts by architects that they didn't really want to build like this. And a lot of architects were shocked when it was actually built the way it finally was. There are also comments by Le Corbusier in that direction. In my view that's a misinterpretation of modernity's design. It's more an intellectual approach, the visualization of an idea that was not intended as a dictatorial command to implement it exactly thus. On the one hand that makes it harder to conserve this site, but on the other hand it makes it easier. Because if you allow for the dynamic, if you recognize that dynamic, then in a way it's easier to let it go and just trust that things will develop in their own way in this place. If you don't do that, then you either end up with an aestheticization, or the entire concept will fail and a completely different plan to use this space will assert itself. I don't think there is any viable alternative to dynamic, openly interpretable preservation. Because if you do not allow this, you will end up with a fight about "Who gets to say what things should look like here." And then either one single interpretation will take over, or there will be no more consideration, and someone will just plan something new and begin rearranging things in a new way.

The functionality of this space will change in one way or another, we can't say how. But artificially maintaining it in completely unchanged conditions, that doesn't even work with listed buildings, and of course not with such a dynamic place as this. Anyone who wants to take this approach is going to invest an awful lot of resources and eventually fail. In any case it will lack the dynamism that has been here consistently from the initial design up until today; it will instead be the attempt to freeze it. In doing so, you would contradict the entire endeavor. In doing so, you would make a museum of modernity. And modernity will not let that happen.

FE: Nowadays, in cities in Brazil where there was similar modernist construction, we can see very clearly that the entrance situations are completely inaccessible. There are no more ground level points of access, or if there are, they are very strictly controlled. That's always a clue that it is the tradition of modernity, a tradition of form, and we have to keep an eye out to see if it stays like this. The thesis would be: no, it won't remain like this. That is another thing that could be investigated here at Ernst-Reuter-Platz, and also conserved. To investigate precisely this dynamic, how this inner-outer situation has changed over the course of time. That would be really exciting, finding a way to represent that; it would also be an extremely important experience for modern architecture, which shouldn't repeat itself. If you say, "OK, we can go to a museum here—if we take it literally—we can learn something here."

If one really says that this should become a museum, then the question arises: What kind of museum pedagogy should underpin it? Because that too has changed. It used to be just about exhibiting objects, now it's more about enabling visitors to experience history. That would be a part of it: How did these various people—planners, designers, architects—deal with modernity through the years? How did they change themselves, how did they appropriate and design? This goes right up to the question of how was it experienced, how was it lived—how was it perceived in the most different ways? So if we do take this idea of a museum at all seriously, and we don't just want to produce some kind of white cube where there's an exhibition of whatever, but instead we actually say this entire location is a museum, then we would have to consider it as such. And then it would make sense. But making it a museum in the sense of, "We'll put it on display and preserve it for posterity," I think that approach is problematic. That would deny other interpretations, uses, perceptions, and it would also only be accessible for certain social groups.

BH: We're in a space that has been meticulously designed down to the last detail,[1] but which today seems—to me at least—like a landscape of ancient ruins, as if the cultural reference had been lost. What we're actually seeing here

1 This part of the dialogue took place in Herta Hammerbacher's lower garten (Tiefgarten) in the Hans Scharoun wing (low-rise) of the architecture building of the Technische Universität Berlin at Ernst-Reuter-Platz.

are many single moments of design motifs that have since become obsolete, because they provide responses to questions that are no longer relevant for us. As people living in a big city, we have largely already made our decisions about how we want the city to be. Necessarily, a demand arose for more individual access, for individual appropriation. This can be seen particularly clearly at locations that have eluded this individual appropriation, which derive from a social model that didn't actually want individual access. But isn't it precisely here where monument preservation is most needed? How can we preserve these testimonies of modernity without completely severing such sites from any practical usage, while still conserving both their intention and their material form? How can we keep them accessible for future generations? How can their development also be ensured? What options are available to us here?

FE:　The site should be preserved, I think. The problem is that it's hardly possible to preserve it. If we really did want to preserve it, clean it up, then what would develop would be precisely that which in my view could be the experience with this location: trying to carry over something in modernity, which is actually a very old idea. Unifying polar opposites, integrating nature, but tamed and shielded off and quieted down, this doesn't work. That's actually a kind of negative experience. And that is always problematic: How can we preserve the experience of failure? Because if we were to preserve it, we would be denying its present condition and saying, "OK, we'll pretend it still functions." A lot of people want this. They say, "Fine, it has to be prettied up a bit, cleaned up a bit, bit of paint here and there." But the lesson would actually be to say, "Well OK, this is how they imagined it, and that didn't really work out, and it still doesn't work today." This sort of negative learning is extremely problematic, extremely difficult. We have the same kind of problems with all other negative historical experiences. Just consider the Holocaust Memorial: How can we prevent something that is in reality a negative experience from becoming aestheticized and beautiful? This is precisely what could also be seen here. Modernity failed in some points, and that also has to be experienced if we don't want to repeat those mistakes. This is an extremely challenging pedagogy, but I think it would be worthwhile.

BH:　The failure of modernity is often emphasized these days, but modernity of course also had an unbelievable character of liberation, throwing overboard all the unnecessary social constrictions. Above and beyond this historical level, it also brought unquestionable spatial benefits, as well as a usability we can still experience today. I wonder whether there isn't a large portion of the promise of modernity that remains to us today, which we can evaluate positively?

FE:　I would also see it that way. I think that when we look at how urban development works in developing countries, we can see that it's no coincidence that modernity is of course the form in which cities are reorganized. There's always the hope that great tasks and problems can be solved that couldn't be tackled with more individualized ideas, let's say, or rather more diversified ideas for urban development. The high level of performance of modernity is unbroken, I think. There is no alternative model.

BH: This is even more astounding today. Because viewed globally, modernity is still a very potent model. It also dominates quantitatively. Urban development in developing countries largely follows the model of modernity. And there are very few other models in the developed nations...

FE: Well... New Urbanism concepts. That again is the only model where you could say it's even a little bit prominent compared to the modern city. But otherwise I would completely agree. New Urbanism, which focuses much more strongly on community-oriented approaches to construction, in extreme cases gated communities. But also this kind of settlement structure. Those are community-oriented construction approaches, and they're also increasingly common. But generally I would say that when you look at China, Brazil, India... Lagos would be glad to be following a modernist urban plan. That's the hope.

FE: Yes, and now maybe back to acoustics. I really think the main difference—well, there are two levels. On the one hand there is actually an acoustic of this square, and on the other hand there is of course noise, noise production. We can certainly say that has been drastically reduced. Since cars have become significantly quieter, the noise level across almost all cities has dropped so much during the past 20 years that the acoustic qualities of an urban location do indeed now play a greater role. That's one level. The second level is that cities organize themselves around sensory, acoustic, aesthetic, visual aspects; that is, they establish their identities—supported and of course influenced by information and communication technologies—and all of this combines to produce a different kind of city and urban society than the "city of noise." In my view the "city of noise" was a city that actually demanded relocation to the interior, to inner space. We would not have been able to wander around the square here so freely discussing things as we can now. Or else this was only possible in very limited forms, the piazza form for example. But as a rule noise was something that had to be fought. When it came to acoustics, the central theme of the city was really protection: protection from damaging influences on all sensory organs. But that doesn't mean that these places had no sensual aspects. Or that those aspects couldn't be constructed by individual people through their perceptions, conceptions, or based on architectural discourses. We can't do without sensory conception; every form of construction, spatial appropriation, spatial planning is always also sensual. But it was a kind of defensive sensuality. Getting back to Ernst-Reuter-Platz, that's how I would understand it: the attempt to reappropriate it, to win it back, does not seem so urgent today, because these perceptions that were so strongly conditioned by noise and pollution are no longer there. Instead we have a stronger, holistic sensory understanding of the city, which is perceived differently by different social groups who place different demands on it. There are some, I think, who demand this very intensively and actively. Typically, I would say, those who are better able to socialize themselves sensually, that is, to actually and intensively experience and shape their personal ability to perceive sensually. Typically it is those, I would say, working in the service sector, in the cultural and knowledge economies. And then of course there are others for whom it doesn't play such a large role, who continue to take a more defensive stance. And I think that is the fundamental conflict in urban societies today. Social inequality and social differences are no longer—or let's say, no longer exclusively—defined by factors like income gaps, but also in the question of which space I can experience sensually, and how and where I can appropriate this space. And so this quality of spaces—the quality recognized by perception, also acoustic perception—plays a very different role than it did 30 years ago. In addition, in the modern city, there has been of course the peculiarity of staging. The modern city was only partially realized here. It was a kind of pseudo-debate, but also pseudo-opposition. But I think what is more decisive is that Berlin has now arrived at a mode of normal metropolitan development, so now the questions are very real. That's a little bit of what I think about this place.

FE: The lack of interest in the use of the square—well of course, we could go to the metro station over there—is completely understandable.[2] I'd never do that. Nobody would go into the metro to get onto the square, to then do... what? It's the end of the line. So if the square really is considered the end of the line, then it wouldn't work, but if you went all the way across and through this place to the other side, then the dynamic of the square would produce something completely different. Then, I think, interest in it would grow. Pretty soon people would be coming here, saying, "Can't we set up our street food stand over there, can we sell coffee here?" Then the whole issue of monument preservation would come back to a central point in an extreme form. Can we do this? Would this be in the spirit of the architects who designed it? Do we want to do this? Is this the kind of dynamic we want to allow, is this a dynamic in the sense of modernity? Or is it alien to the spirit of modernity? Then we would begin the second phase of the debate.

BH: We didn't want to respond too hastily to this point in our design process. We notice during this process all too clearly that every response is a determination that shuts out other options. We could see that simple solutions or patent remedies or pre-designed models simply didn't help us at all. We need something that establishes a much broader basis for the discussion, more than a design idea of any kind. In my view it's much more important to start a dialogue and create the opportunity for future dialogues in order to better approach these situations.

FE: Yes, right, I see it that way too. Only the situation now is that it's limited. With the form it now has, with access so

2 Frank Eckardt is referring here to the traffic island (Mittelinsel), which is only accessible through the metro tunnel.

restricted that other possible forms of use are just excluded, basically any kind of use is unwelcome. And so the decisive, discursive issue is: Do we even want a use for this site? That shouldn't be decided via design projects, but instead via public discourse. Then we really have to ensure that differing ideas about how this square could be used are equally included in the discussion. Including the option to say, "No, nothing should be redesigned, it should stay the way it is." But all this has to be discussed in an open-ended way. I also see it that way. There is a lot in favor of leaving it as it is, but then there is also an argument for saying, "No, we're now going to rearrange it to allow for greater access." And accordingly we would open the door to the essential issue: "OK, if this should indeed become a transit site, from here to the other side of the street, what does that mean for a such a square?" That, I think, is a very complex question, and surely it should not be answered through a design project.

BH: The idea of just holding an architectural competition and then setting a definitive solution, that wouldn't do justice to the complexity of the issue, or to its social relevance.

That's why it is very important—and this picks up an idea that has repeatedly surfaced in many different discussions and conversations we've had on this topic—that we need a forum or a permanent framework in which we can discuss Ernst-Reuter-Platz.

FE: The traffic circle in general is a very interesting phenomenon. It's a kind of contradiction, one would think. Because linearity, getting from A to B, seems to exclude circular traffic motion or make it undesirable.

It is actually interesting that people tend to think about modernity as free of contradictions, but in reality it is extremely contradictory. This in turn has its own aesthetic, its own sensuality. This driving in circles— we all immediately know what it means, but what about how to describe it as a peculiar form of perception. Normally one would say that one overcomes space within modernity. Circularity leads to not leaving the space. One stays there, stands still, racing standstill. That's actually interesting for me. This probably goes way beyond what you want to do here, but it's a quality that is very rarely thematized.

BH: It's clear that this circular form is what was wanted. It wasn't about trying to find a way to organize traffic most efficiently in some kind of round form; instead the form of a circle definitely was wanted. I think that the symbolic form here was far more important than the function. The references were the Grosser Stern and Strausberger Platz, and the intention was to show what a modern city looked like when it was situated in a comparable location. One can recognize it again and again, that Hermkes's urban design actually was based on orthogonal structure that followed the classic images of modernity, but then the streets and the circular form of the square followed completely different ideas.

BH: My thesis remains: it was fundamentally a symbolic site. It was consciously staged as a symbolic site.

FE: The question then is whether or not modernity is conceivable without symbols. As a matter of course it seems to be so, taking as a basic reference, for example, the debate on ornament. There is only functionality, efficiency, and so on. But there is no architecture without symbolism. Because otherwise we wouldn't even understand architecture, we wouldn't know what is directly in front of us. It's a different kind of symbolism, but it is not devoid or free of symbols. That's why I believe that this square is very clearly a symbolic site. The question is, just what is it supposed to symbolize, what is it not supposed to symbolize. And I think it was meant to symbolize progressiveness, modernism, improvement, speed, and of course these ideological dimensions. The implementation, the appropriation, has introduced other symbolic languages. Ephemeral, rather fleeting. Someone who lies down here to read the newspaper at noon, that's a very different symbolic language, and it's not here, we only know that it remains somewhere in the collective consciousness, or only in the individual experience. But it is there. If we now say that every kind of memory is equally valued, or should be equally valued in a democracy, then this too must be represented somehow. The assumption would be that there is more of it than we would think. And of course, again, this question that modernity wanted or already had its own symbolic message, this, "Things are moving forward, things are getting better, liberation"—this should also be expressed. All of that is integrated into the symbolism of the place, but it has to be established. It should be established.

Projects

This chapter presents projects by Anna Bogner, Maria Horn, Lucas Hövelmann, and Marco Mattelig. These projects were realized in the framework of a constellation of simultaneous seminars—an introduction to auditory architecture, a design seminar, a reading seminar, and a seminar on the sociological aspects of urban auditory design—conceived and conducted by Alex Arteaga, Boris Hassenstein, Thomas Kusitzky, Laura Wahl, and Jürgen Weidinger. Although many of the student projects that were realized in this context reached a high reflective and creative quality, we selected those presented here due to the singularity and efficiency of their transformative proposals. Addressing the problem of redefining Ernst-Reuter-Platz from different departing points, elaborating approaches through multiple perspectives and practices, and coming up with diverse solutions or procedures, these four projects show a wide scope of inspiring possibilities to face the divergence between the current state of this urban space and the lives of its inhabitants—their needs and wishes, or even their dreams and hopes.

Anna Bogner's project *beyond erp* resolves the conflict between no intervention and material rebuilding by displacing the transformation of this urban space to the field of narrative-based imagination. Her periodically published magazine *Beyond Ernst-Reuter-Platz* operates as a platform to reimagine and reinvent this square. As Anna writes, it functions as a medium to "create new stories out of existing history, yet to come, or maybe not," and thus to reactivate this environment simultaneously as an agent and receptor of possible urban change. We present the magazine's first edition here.

Marco Mattelig's *360° ERP* is the most "constructive" of the four. He proposes to build an elevated conveyor belt over Ernst-Reuter-Platz that allows people while in movement to observe the dynamics of the square, without intervening physically in its development. This new element materializes one of the most fundamental principles of Hermkes's design—the perception of an urban space in movement—without altering the traffic circulation privileged by Hermkes, while providing a new and singular alternative for pedestrians. The photographs selected for publication show perspectives on Ernst-Reuter-Platz from different points along the conveyor belt.

The idea of redefining the square by intensifying sensuous access is a central aspect of Lucas Hövelmann's project *Studio ERP*. In this case, an artistic intervention in the central circle of Ernst-Reuter-Platz creates new conditions for its perception and thus its reconsideration as a contemporary urban environment. Lucas's intervention is conceived as the first in a series. Subsequent projects would be selected through a series of competitions (another element of AARU's design). The call for proposals for this competition has been defined by Lucas and it is printed here alongside his design.

Maria Horn created, as Anna did, a framework for imaginative transformation, but in a graphic medium. Performing one of the most basic aesthetic practices of architectural design—drawing—not as representational but rather as generative method, she turned her original design for Ernst-Reuter-Platz into a departing point for a self-generating process constituting infinite possible squares. A short story interacts with this expanding and expansive drawing field, producing fruitful mutual resonance. Besides this text we reproduce the complete drawing, and some details in 1:1 scale.

Beyond
Ernst Reuter Platz

Die Arbeit beyond erp ist ein Versuch, dem Ernst-Reuter-Platz näher zu kommen und zwar nicht im Rahmen einer materiellen Transformation. Was bedeutet hier beyond? • Beyond is the space, both actual and symbolic, that allows for the projection of reasonable doubt, the place of uncertainty that defindes the limitations of the self and goes in search of the other, the unknown, the unforseen, the yet to come.[2] • Es gibt heute keinen Konsens darüber, wie die Frage: »Was soll mit dem Ernst-Reuter-Platz geschehen?« geklärt werden kann. Er (der ERP) steht mitten in kontroversen Diskursen, welche zwei perspektivischen Polen unterworfen sind: Das historische soll behalten werden (selbst wenn es nicht zeitgemäß ist). Es soll ein neuer Platz entstehen, der zeitgemäßen Anforderungen entspricht und dabei die historische Substanz nicht erhält. • Diese zwei verhärteten Perspektiven lassen jedoch einen ergiebigen Diskurs nicht zu. In dieser Unentschiedenheit bleibt der Ernst-Reuter-Platz heute per defekt quasi ein Museum unter freiem Himmel. • Mit der Arbeit beyond erp soll der Rahmen gestellt werden, einen hybriden*, vielfachen Ernst-Reuter-Platz zu imaginieren. Die Arbeit soll durch die Umwandlung von bestehender Geschichte neue Geschichten — yet to come, or maybe not — schaffen. beyond erp bildet einen Beitrag gegen ein homogenisiertes Stadtbild, einem, welches die Stadt als Marke etabliert. Das imaginative Narrativ soll als Hilfsmittel dienen, um einer Komplexität, die es zu denken gilt, gerecht werden zu können. • die: berp ist eine Aufforderung zu Mut, und Waghalsigkeit, zu Fantasie und Leichtigkeit, zur nichtfunktionalen Lebensform, zu Freuden, und Experimenten, zum nicht-trivial sein. Sie will unkonventionell sein aber nicht an erster Stelle. Wir dürfen Sie nun einladen, liebe Leser, über die erste Ausgabe zu lachen, zu weinen, oder in ihr zu schwelgen. Lachen Sie, und lachen Sie laut!

1 Alpha 60, the fictional controlling computer of alphaville in Jean-Luc Godards Alphaville 2 Sophie Warren & Jonathan Mosley: beyond utopia
* hybrid: hybrid sind zwei Elemente, die ausgehend von ihrer Eigenart/Ungleichheit in sich selbst in ein neues Element transformiert werden, in dem die Ursprünglichkeit beider erkennbar bleibt, jedoch etwas neues entsteht. Konflikt ist ein zentraler Bestandteil dieses Prozesse [driving force].

Beyond Ernst Reuter Platz

6

I dreamt about you and your traffic lights last night.
It was dark, time to flee, we were all running.
Finally crossing and hiding in the warmth of your center.

Berlin, Kreuzberg, Germany.

1

Ich habe keinerlei Vorstellung von einem Ernst-Reuter-Platz. Es ist einer der vielen Nicht-Orte dieser Welt. • Manche Orte existieren in meinem Kopf, weil ich sie bereist habe, andere, weil ich sie erlesen habe. Los Angeles ist ein Ort, den ich nur durch Bukowski und Chandler kenne, ebenso wie Paris durch Henry Miller. • Der Ernst-Reuter Platz ist nicht dabei. Weder war ich jemals dort, noch habe ich etwas darüber gelesen. Hans Fallada ging soweit ich mich entsinne nie über den Ernst-Reuter-Platz. Franz Biberkopf war am Alexanderplatz. • Man sagt mir, es ist ein Platz in Berlin. Berlin war mir als Stadt immer zu kalt und viel zu schnell. Das Schönste was ich von Berlin kenne, ist eine Verfilmung. »Stadt der Engel« von Wim Wenders. War ich körperlich dort, so habe ich es immer im emotionalen Farbspektrum als Blau empfunden. Kein träumerisches Blau, ein kälteres, technoides Blau. • So stelle ich mir auch diesen Platz in der Mitte von Berlin vor, etwas zu kalt, um sich länger dort aufzuhalten. Es ist kein Platz von dem eine Revolution ausgehen würde. Viel Verkehr und hastige Menschen, die an einer Statue oder Gedenktafel vorbei huschen. Der Name Ernst-Reuter klingt nach einer großen Persönlichkeit, es klingt wie Willy Brandt, vermutlich war er

Three-legged cat rescued A cat was found in the middle of Ernst-Reuter-Platz, wednesday shortly after lunch hours. Overtaken by bravery it had stumbled onto the island in the middle of the roundabout, but was unable to gather courage to embark on the journey back. While approached by local onlookers, the three-legged cat started to sing russian folk songs, paying little or no attention to the growing crowd. The fire brigade was brought to the place, and after 3 hours successfully managed to return the cat to it's owners on the mainland. **Friedrichshain Berlin, Germany**

»ich kenne diesen Ort« said the old lady in her green shirt with white dots, that made her somehow something. She wore big glasses and owned one of those golden necklesses that many old ladies wear these days. We were just standing next to the gravis building, when she started to tell her story. • »man wies mich beim nächtlichen Durchfahren links und rechts auf die hohen Gebäude hin. Aber ich staunte nicht vor den Kolossen, die sich im Kreis um mich herum gruppierten, diese Sorte von Ungetümen aus Beton. Als ich durch die Straßen fuhr sah ich die Lichter aus den hunderten Fenstern blitzen. Die Licht-bespielten Bäume in ihrer geringfügigen Positionierung mitten auf der Insel. • Gefunkel der Filmtheater und Magazine. Ein wohltuendes und heimliches Bild. Keines dieser Gebäude konnte mir alleinstehend imponiern dacht' ich. Zu allen hatte ich sofort ein harmonisches Verhältnis. Sie waren nicht groß. Der Platz war nicht groß. Er war vollkommen. Es war ein neuer Stadttyp, der dem Stand der Moderne entspricht und zugleich alles mitbrachte, was die Ästhetik erforderte. Wir zirkulierten über den Platz für mindestens fünfzehn Minuten.« • The lady left as soon as she had finished her story. It was 5 pm. I then started to walk the place in circles for 7*15 minutes and wondered about the word »vollkommen«. **Neukölln Berlin, Deutschland**

Beyond
Ernst Reuter Platz

9 Als im 6 5 0 sten Jahr nach Manimani der Rat der Zirkologie das erste Mal zusammen traf, achtete zunächst niemand auf den jungen ernsten Reuter, der am rechten unteren Ende der Tafel saß und zaghaft an einem Öligen nippte. • Der Rat war berufen worden, weil von seltsamen Vorkommnissen berichtet wurde. • Überall im Land gab es Unruhen. Die Bauern aus sämtlichen Teilen des Reiches klagten über riesige leere Kreise auf ihren Feldern, die den Ernteertrag minimierten. Lediglich die Ecken der Felder blieben noch unversehrt. Das verlangen nach Verantwortlichen schwoll in pestialischem Ausmaß an. Und so verwunderte es niemanden, das bald käuterkundige demeterinhalierende Birkenstöckinnen als Ursache für den Ausfall von Wachstum und somit Ernte, verantwortlich gemacht wurden. • Daraufhin beschloss nun der Rat eine Experten Kommission zur Aufklärung der Vorkommnisse zusammen zu stellen. • Als der junge ernste Reuter zur Leitung eben dieser Aufgabe bestimmt wurde, war er noch ganz und gar mit der Verköstigung seines Öligen beschäftigt. Bis zu diesem Zeitpunkt hatte sich der ernste Jüngling lediglich den Studien der Quadratur verschrieben, und war nicht wenig überrascht nun mit der causa kornkreis betraut zu

schon zu ihrem Ursprung zurückgekehrt.

figer stießen die Bohrarbeiter auf Quellen von tiefschwarzer Flüssigkeit, die in zähen Fontänen aus dem lehmigem Erdinneren an die Oberfläche quoll. • Schon nach wenigen Wochen stellte man fest, dass einige der Arbeiter nach übermäßigem Konsum des schwarzen Goldes von Ratlosigkeit und enormen Tatendrang geplagt waren. • Auch der ernste Reuter, der dem Genuss des Öligen seit jeher äußerst zugetan war, labte sich zunehmend an dem zähen Spirit. Eines Abends trank er gar ein ganzes Barrel und trat zum Aufgang der Sonne am zweiten Tag des dritten Monats, durch eine Pforte. Die Nebel lichteten sich und er erblickte eine glänzende, fremde Welt mit Kutschen und Rössern aus reinem Stahl, schnell und von unbegreiflicher Eleganz. In den Lüften drehten sich die Derwische um die eigene Achse und lobpreisten den Fortschritt in ohrenbetäubenden Geschrei. Schneller und schneller und heftiger bewegt sich die Welt in hedonistischem Übermut in den Infarkt. Dunkle Wolken ziehen sich zusammen, Engel scheißen, Ruß und Metall kracht ineinander. Inmitten des donnernden Getöses, fand sich der ernste Reuter in schockierender Faszination für den apokalyptischen Wirbel. Als das Brausen und Tosen verstummte, blickte er in die Gesichter von sieben wunderschönen Schwestern, die ihm den ewigen Zyklus aushauchten. Und das erste mal in seinem Leben zeichnete sich ein Lächeln in sein Gesicht. **Berlin, Deutschland**

Berlin geht nicht mehr. Eines Tages lief ich von der Straße des 17. Juni, der geraden übersichtlichen und möglicherweise langen Balustrade entlang in Richtung Deutsche Oper in der … Straße. Denn ich wollte endlich inszeniert werden in dem großen Bunker mit der Steinfassade in dem schon ein Dirigent das Leben lassen musste, weil vermutlich die Anstrengung der Fantasie, die eigene Vorstellung dem Publikum näher zu bringen, sein Herz nicht mehr aushalten konnte [man sagt natürlicherweise sei er an einem Herzinfarkt gestorben]. • Ich ging also entlang der Balustrade und las auf dem Boden »Berlin geht nicht mehr.« — ein Stück Schablonen-Kunst. Und als ich mich so dem großen Kreisverkehr nähere, beginnt meine Wahrnehmung mir einen Strich durch die Rechnung zu machen. [War es meine Wahrnehmung?] Denn der sonst so recht unauffällige Platz war plötzlich ganz grau geworden. Ein Meer aus grauem Nebel hatte ihn erfasst. Wobei sich nicht ganz sagen ließ, ob dieses Meer wirklich als ein externer Nebel meiner Wahrnehmung entsprungen war oder ob sich die Farbe der Umgebung in der ich mich aufhielt dermaßen manifestiert hatte, dass ich logischerweise nur noch grau sah. • In dem grauen, sehr grauen Strom ließ ich mich besudeln. • Als ich wieder auftauchte, stand ich in der Mitte und nichts ging mehr. **Berlin, Deutschland**

EIN PLATZ,

ein ort, was kann es sein?

von weit gekommen

sich wähnend am ziel

erkennst du die täuschung?

erkennst du es nie?

das knie!

das einst geformt diesen platz,

das knie zum kreis sich gewandelt hat,

der kreis ob er bleibt wer weiß es genau wird morgen noch sein -

was heute beständig dir scheint?

vom kreise weg treibend

die fliehkraft zieht dich heute, morgen treibt dich die lust,

welchem fluss wirst du folgen,

welchen weg wirst du gehn

welchem winde nachfolgen

welchen verlockungen wirst du nicht widerstehn?

ein platz folgt dem andern welchen weg du auch wählst die fliehkraft zieht dich morgen übermorgen die lust,

welchen weg du auch gehst

welcher strömung dich mitzieht,

auch hier und an den anderen plätzen

die vor dir stehn,

kannst du mancher verlockung nicht widerstehn

erst wenn du erkannt hast die täuschung, hat so lange gebraucht dies zu sehn,

es sollte nie geschehn

ich hab dein knie gesehn.

Bamberg, Deutschland

10 Glocken und Eiskreme standen bereit. das karusell hatte schon angefangen sich zu drehen das karusell hatte angefangen schon sich zu drehen. kinder und hup-hupen der vorbeifahrenden autos stören das rumm--rummelige dasein nicht. mütter, mütter, mütter und kinder, 1, 2, 3, versammeln sich an essensständen und loosbuden um zu schießen wo sind die väter wenn geschossen wird? die sind im krieg. aber der krieg ist doch längst vorbei? ist er, er ist. aber wo sind die väter wenn die kinder planschen im pool unter der fontäne? unter der fontäne wenn die planschenden kinder im pool wo sind die väter? nebenbei singt die dame in blao und blao ist altdeutsch so wie ihr gesicht wenn sie plötzlich ihren mund öffnet und schreit: ... in dieser stadt bin ich zu haus in dieser stadt kenn ich mich aus ... und wenn sie dann ihre runden dreht im autokarusell auf dem platz lautet der text vom zerknüllten butterbrotpapier bis zu leeren zigarettenschachteln und auf der bank saß fritz der nicht küssen kann die altdeutsche dreht weiter ihre runden im karusell aber sie will doch weg weg von zu haus' ist der fritz und lutscht an seinem eis. und neben ihm tobt es weiter. die blaska-pelle trifft gleich ein sagt die junge im gelben kleid. da kommen sie schon. und alles ist still die blaskapelle schreitet mit hörnen und posaunen im kreis über den platz.

Berlin, Germany

7 Am Dienstag hatte die Firma ihren Generalunternehmervertrag für den Neubau der Akademie am Ernst-Reuter-Platz gekündigt. Der Ernst-Reuter-Platz wird leider ein Element der Uniformität werden. • Es mag Plätze geben, wo dies denkbar ist am Ernst-Reuter-Platz nicht. • Ein 25 Me-ter breiter Sicherheitsstreifen, Poller, Wachhäuser mit kugelsicherem Glas, versenkbare Barrieren und ein nicht überwindbarer Zaun — so wollen die USA ihre neuen Server am Ernst-Reuter-Platz schützen. • Ihre Behörde ist ja vor allem mit Rekonstruktionen aufgefallen, die einen scheinbar ver-schwundenen Zustand wiederherstellen: etwa am Ernst-Reuter-Platz oder in Klein-Glienicke. • Für das Büro XXXXX aus Boston gibt es weltweit »wenig leere Baugrundstücke von solch großer Bedeutung« wie das am Ernst-Reuter-Platz. • Während der Abschlussveranstaltung ab 18 Uhr auf dem Ernst-Reuter-Platz wird das Feuer dann in einer Schale lodern. • Im Streit um die US-Server am Ernst-Reuter-Platz verdichten sich die Hinweise auf eine mögliche Lösung. **Nürnberg, Germany**

11 **1.** es war null uhr als die zeit am ernst-reuter-platz angelangte um sich in ihrer größenwahnsinnigkeit zu präsentieren. immer an ihrem rockzpfel hängend die geschwindigkeit. die langsamkeit haben beide erstspäter entdeckt, nicht auf diesem platz zu dieser zeit. **2.** zeit war untergegangen in der veränderung und der logik des in ihrer erscheinung auftretenden duplikats. **3.** die gegenwart nimmt den charakter der vermuteten vergangenheit einer noch kommenden zukunft an.[2] **4.** es war null uhr als sich die drei davonschlichen. **Berlin, Deutschland**

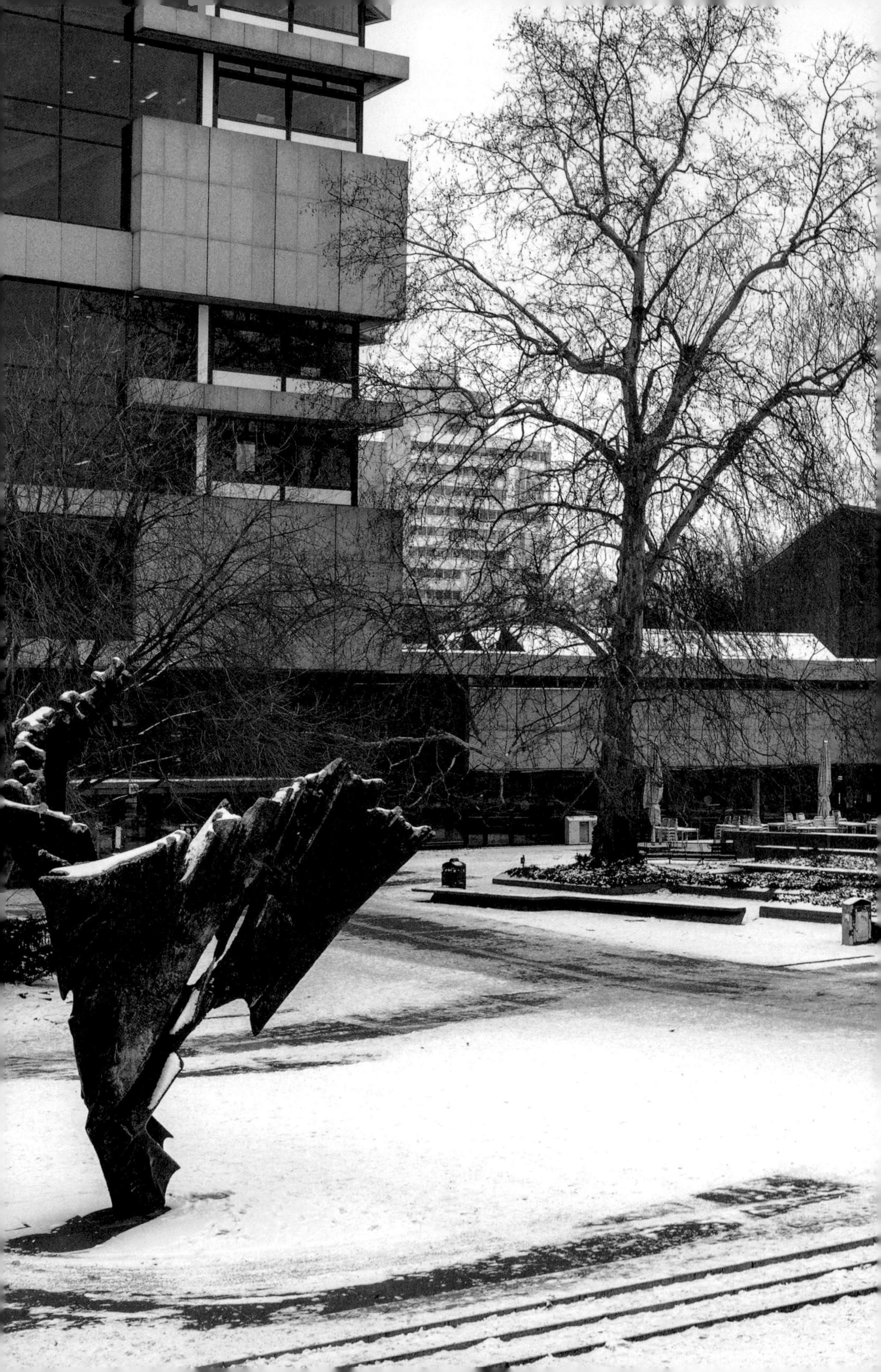

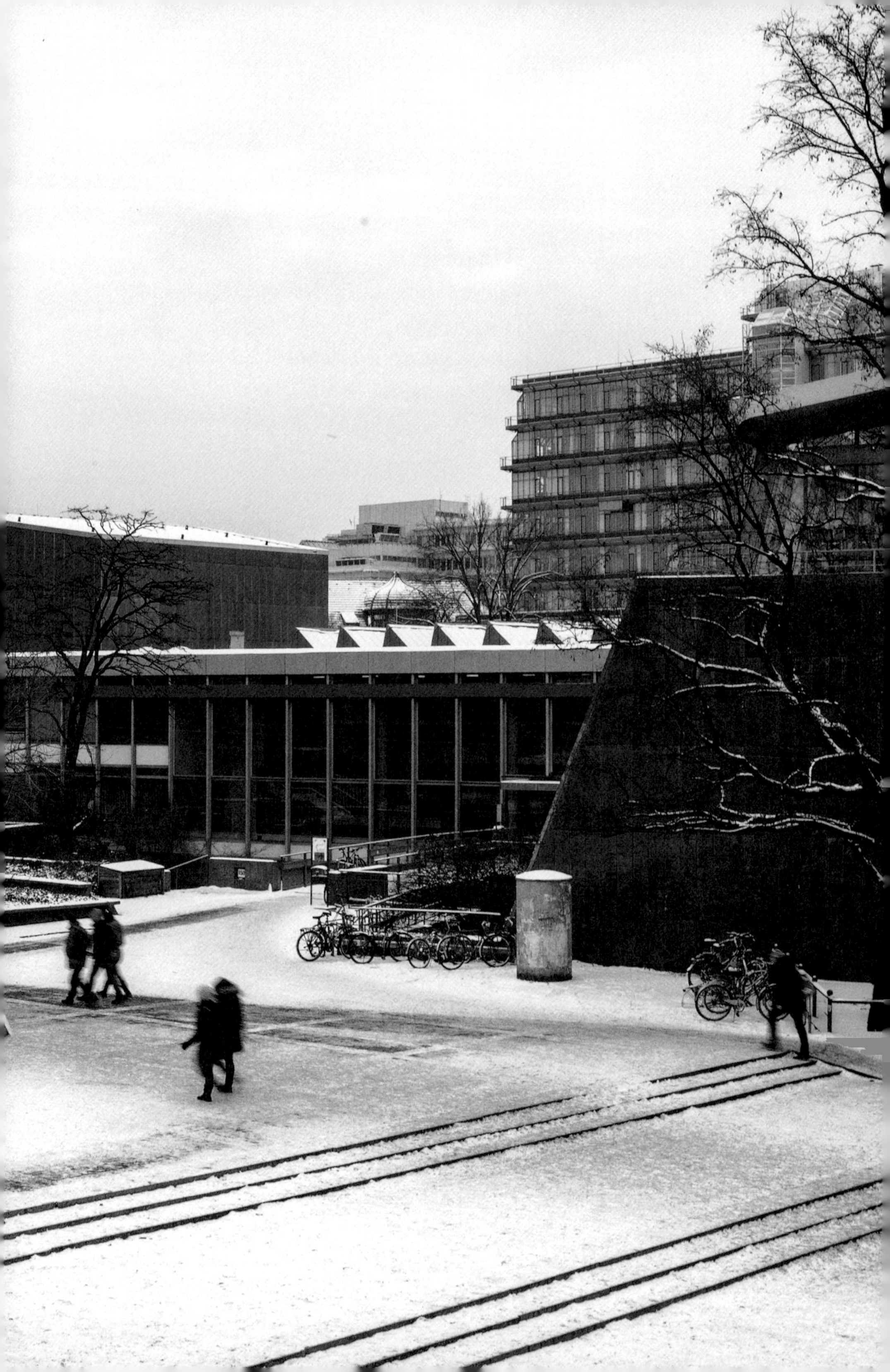

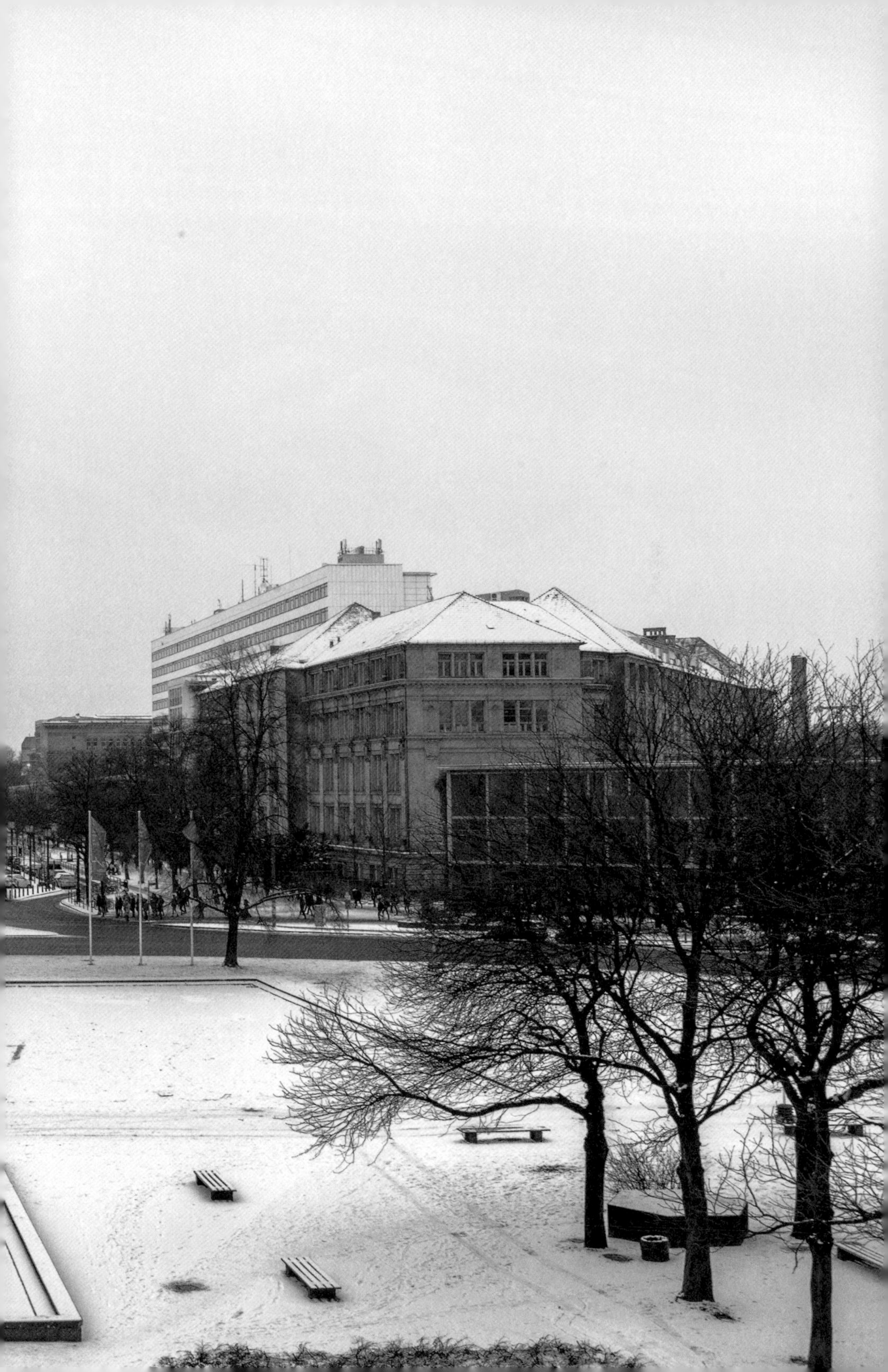

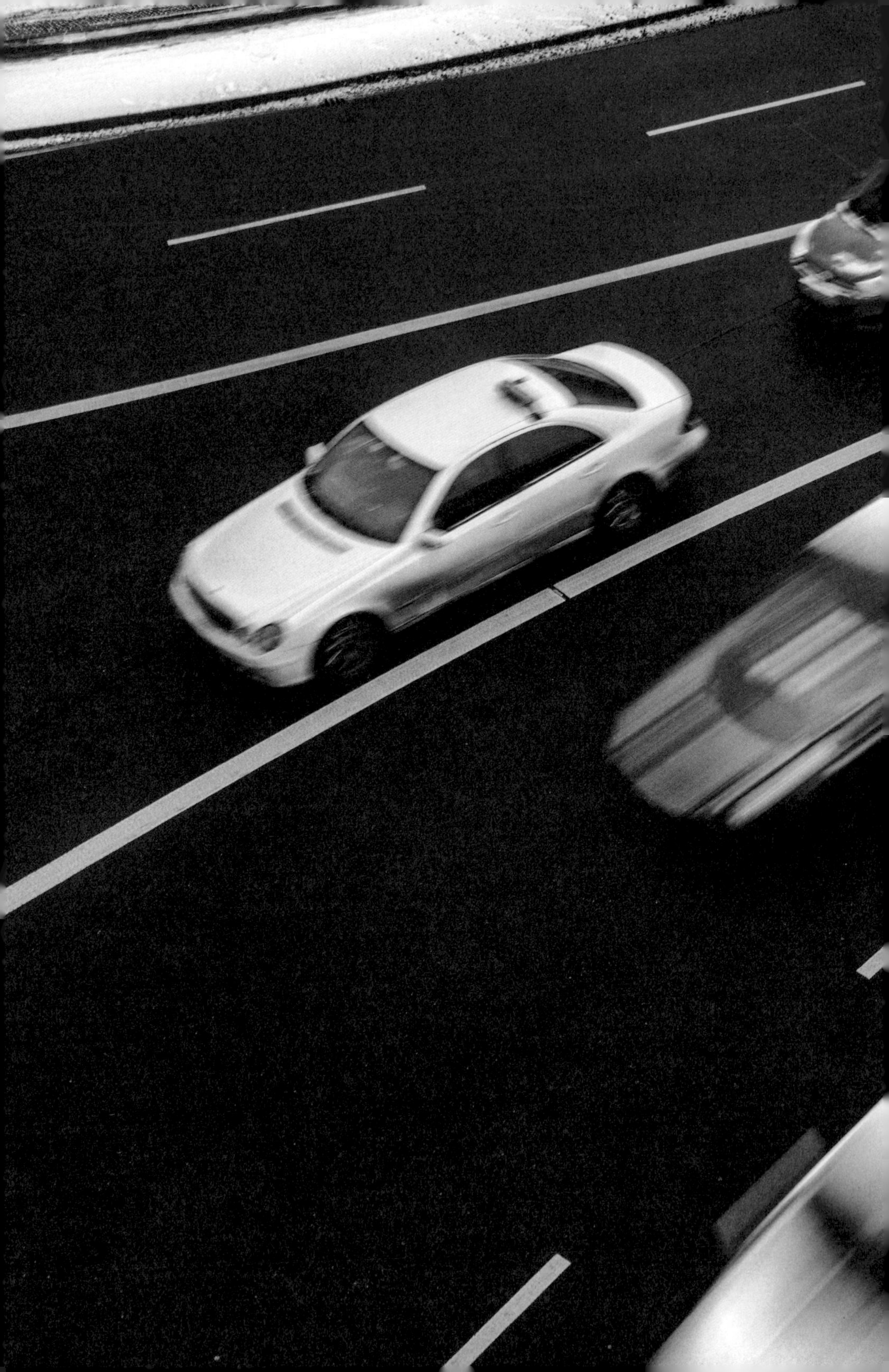

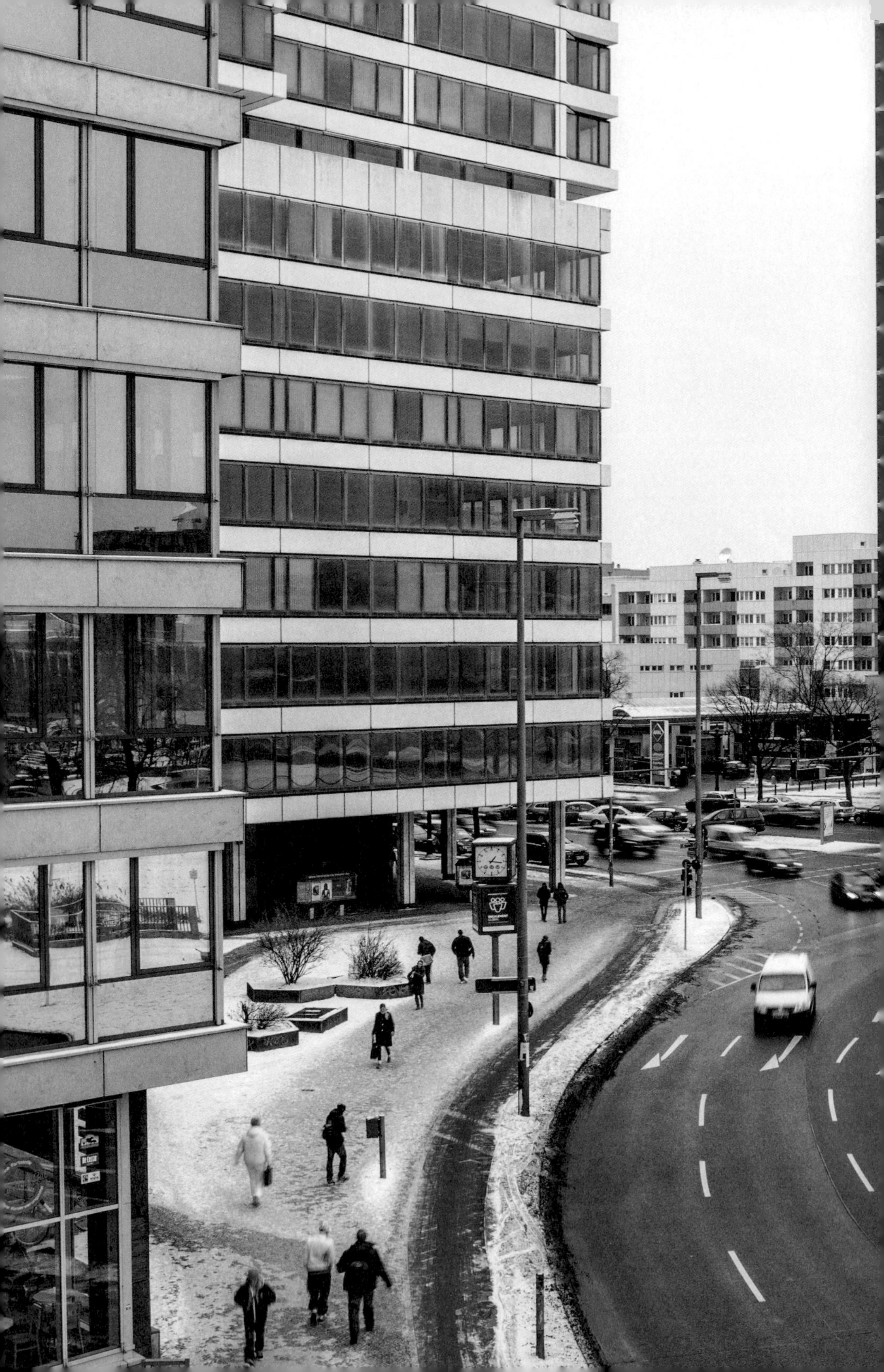

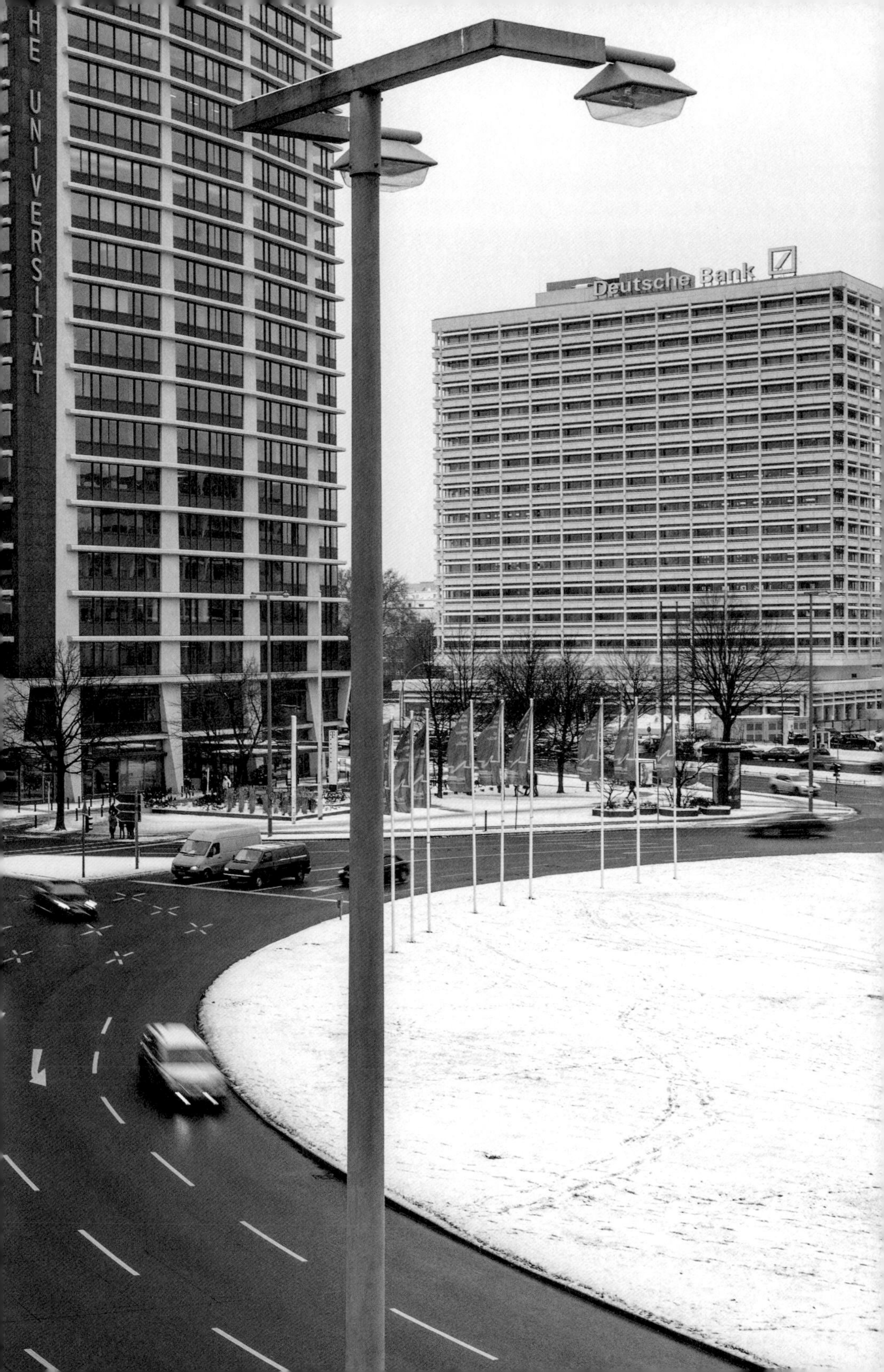

HE UNIVERSITÄT
Deutsche Bank

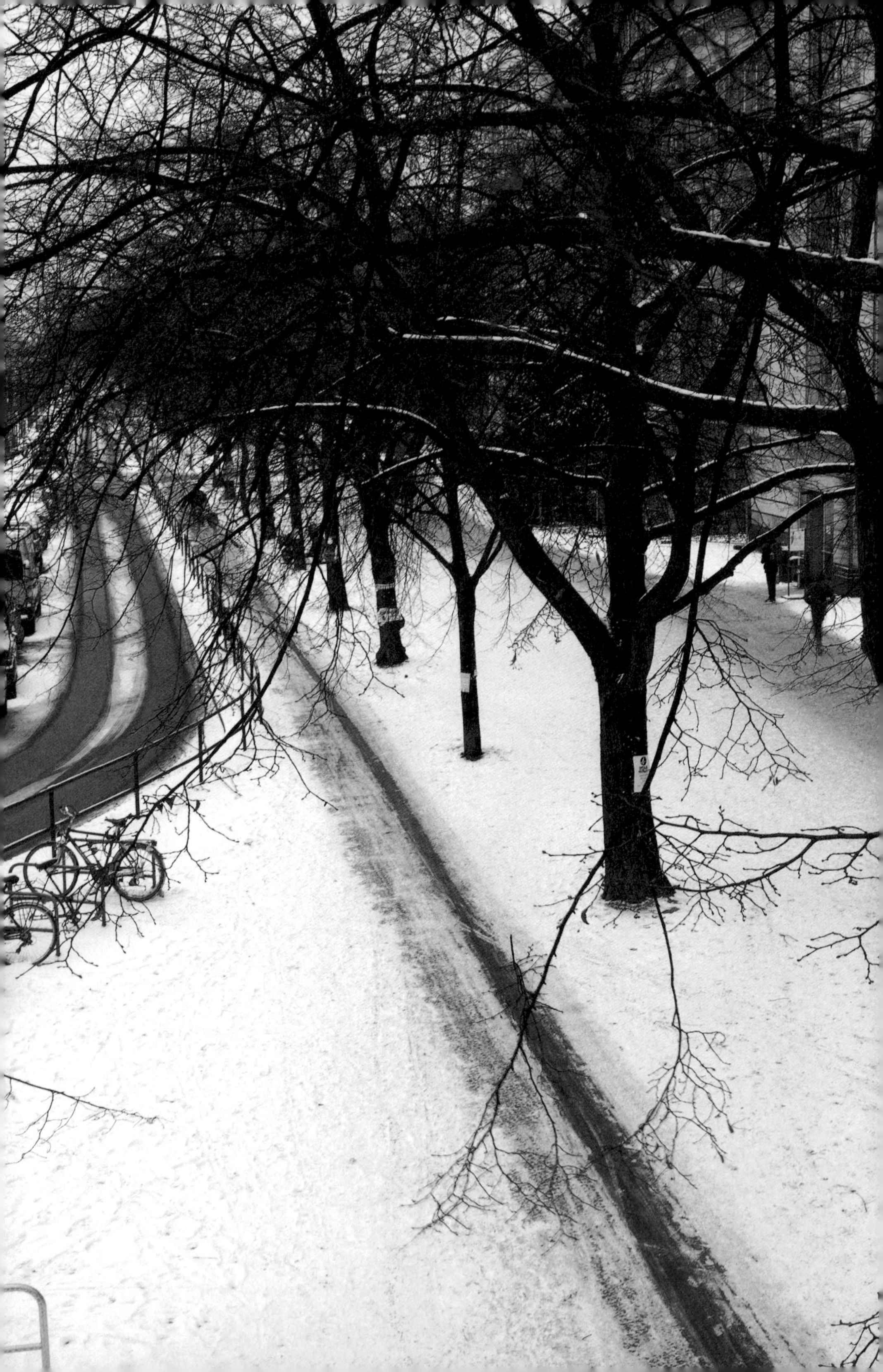

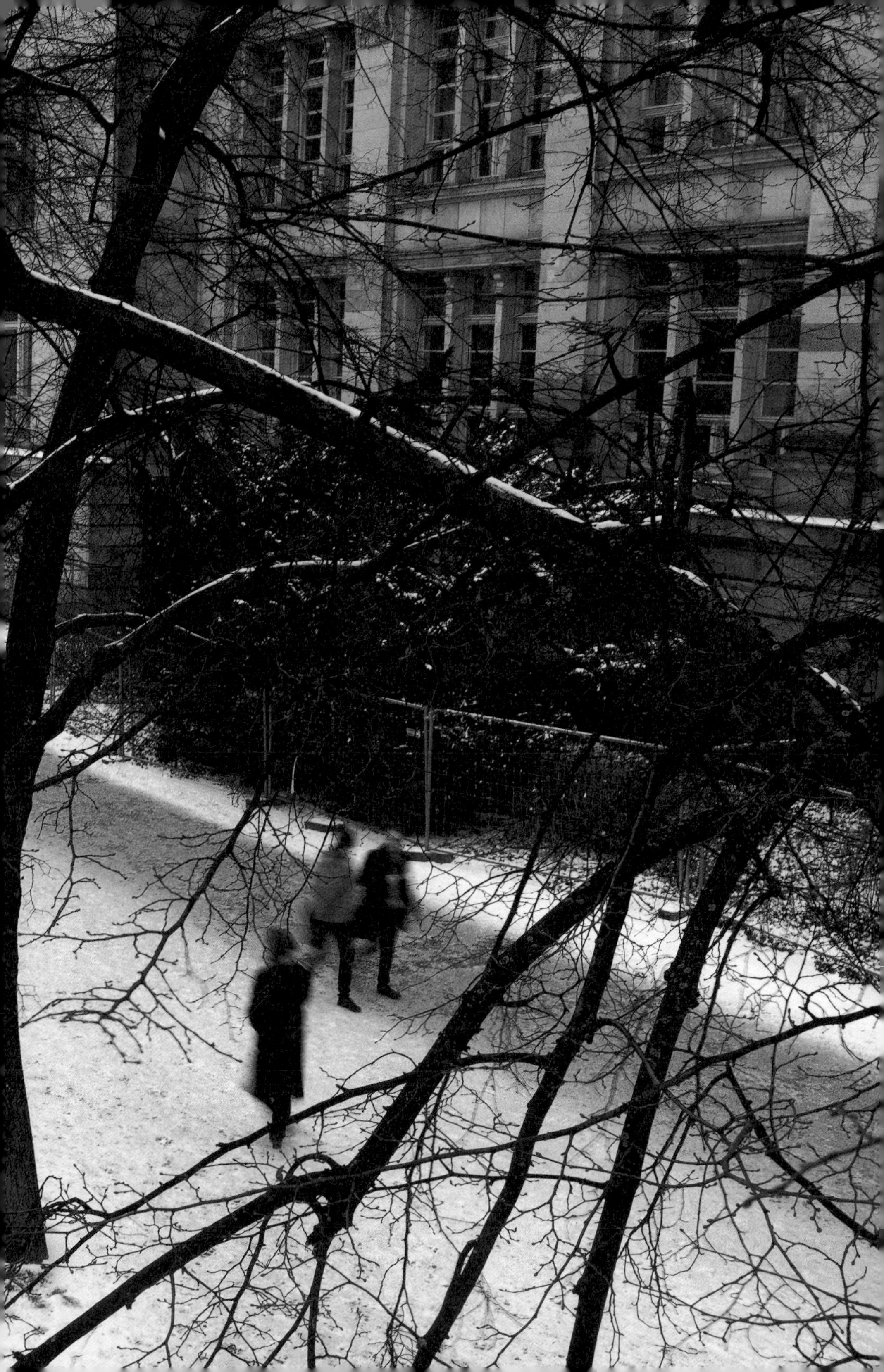

Inhaltsverzeichnis

I.1   **Auslobung Studio ERP** Als Reaktion auf die veränderten Wahrnehmungsbedingungen auf dem Ernst-Reuter-Platz wird dieser in den folgenden Jahren zu einem temporären Studio für experimentelle Gestaltung. In Anlehnung an den Namenspatron, den ehemaligen Bürgermeister Berlins Ernst Reuter, wird der Wettbewerb eine Kommunikation zwischen Berlin und Istanbul, dem Exilort Reuters, herstellen. Es ist vorgesehen, den Gewinnerentwurf des Wettbewerbs für den Ernst-Reuter-Platz nicht länger als zwei Jahre dort auszustellen um ihn anschließend auf der Biennale in Istanbul zu zeigen.

I.2   **Einleitung** Als einer der größten Verkehrsknotenpunkte Berlins prägt der Ernst-Reuter-Platz seit nunmehr 60 Jahren das Bild der Stadt. Eingebettet in das städtebauliche Ensemble Bernhard Hermkes gilt der Platz als Paradebeispiel der Architektur der Nachkriegsmoderne und der frühen autogerechten Stadt. Der Kreisverkehr wird durch die fünf anliegenden Straßen Marchstraße, Straße des 17. Juni, Hardenbergstraße, Bismarkstraße und Otto-Suhr-Allee gespeist.
Historisch gesehen befindet sich der Platz auf den Achsen zwischen Berliner Stadtschloss und dem Schloss Charlottenburg, was ihm vor dem Umbau den Spitznamen "am Knie" einbrachte.
Die spätere Umgestaltung durch Albert Speer überlagerte den Ort als Teil der Ost-West-Achse Germanias und überschrieb die vorher prägende Verbindung.
Nach Ende des Zweiten Weltkriegs konnte Bernhard Hermkes den Wettbewerb für das durch Kriegsschäden stark zerstörte Areal um den Platz für sich entscheiden. Als Reaktion auf die turbulente Geschichte des Ortes formte Hermkes einen freie, offene Platzform, die durch freistehende Solitäre gerahmt wurde. Der Entwurf sah einen großzügigen Stadtplatz mit guter Anbindung vor, die es Besuchern ermöglichen sollte, das Ensemble aus der PKW-Perspektive zu erleben.

I.3   **Aufgabe** Die heutige Wahrnehmung des Ernst-Reuter-Platzes ist bestimmt durch seine Funktion als infrastruktureller Verteilungspunkt im städtischen System. Durch das erhöhte Verkehrsaufkommen verliert der Platz seine ursprüngliche Qualität als Aufenthaltsort oder Schmuckplatz und wird zu schierem Verkehrsgrün degradiert. Auch die Erschließung durch den U-Bahnhof sowie die angewandten Gestaltungsmittel werden dem Ort in seiner heutigen Ausprägung nicht mehr gerecht.

Von hervorgehobener Bedeutung für den Wettbewerb soll jedoch die ursprüngliche Intention des Entwurfs aus den 50er Jahren des letzten Jahrhunderts stehen. Werner Düttmann kontert mit seiner Planung dem gesamtstädtischen Kontext des Ortes und dessen Lage auf der Ost-West-Achse Germanias. Als Reaktion auf den offenen, städtebaulichen Kontext erzeugt Düttmann mit Hilfe der versetzten Wasserbecken auf der Mittelinsel und dem über die gesamte Fläche gezogenen Raster einen Platz ohne klar erkennbare Mitte. Die Achse wird von der Fläche überlagert und rückt somit wahrnehmbar in den Hintergrund.

Ziel des Wettbewerbs ist die Entwicklung einer Gestaltungsidee, welche die Lesbarkeit des ursprünglichen Entwurfs Düttmanns, angepasst auf den aktuellen Kontext, erneut erfahrbar macht.

I.4	**Bedingungen**	- Das Wettbewerbsareal ist nach außen durch das von Düttmann geplante Bodenraster begrenzt. - Der unter Denkmalschutz stehende Platz ist in seiner Substanz vollständig zu erhalten. Der Entwurf darf sich lediglich als neue Ebene auf den Bestand legen.
II.1	**Art des Verfahrens & Turnus**	Die Auslobung erfolgt als offener Ideenwettbewerb. Das gesamte Verfahren wird bis zum Abschluss anonym durchgeführt. Mehrfachteilnahmen sind nicht gestattet. Eine Einteilung in Fachsparten erfolgt nicht. Es gibt keine Teilnahmebeschränkungen. Eine Ausschreibung des Wettbewerbs erfolgt im zweijährigen Turnus. Zukünftige TeilnehmerInnen dürfen nicht schon einmal den Wettbewerb gewonnen haben.
II.2	**Art & Umfang der Wettbewerbsbeiträge**	Die Präsentation der Beiträge ist den BearbeiterInnen freigestellt und entwurfsspezifisch auszuwählen. Die Jury sieht von einer normativen Vorgabe ab, um den Ausgang des Verfahrens bewusst offen zu gestalten.
II.3	**Beurteilungsverfahren & Jury**	Die Jurykommission besteht aus VertreterInnen beteiligter Interessengruppen (AnwohnerInnen, AnliegerInnen, Stadt, UdK Berlin und TU-Berlin) und wechselnden GastpreisrichterInnen. Nach Vorprüfung der eingegangenen Arbeiten entscheidet die Jurykommission über Rangfolge und Zuteilung der Preise, Anerkennungen und ggf. Sonderpreise. Der Beschluss erfolgt mehrheitlich und unter Ausschluss des Rechtsweges.

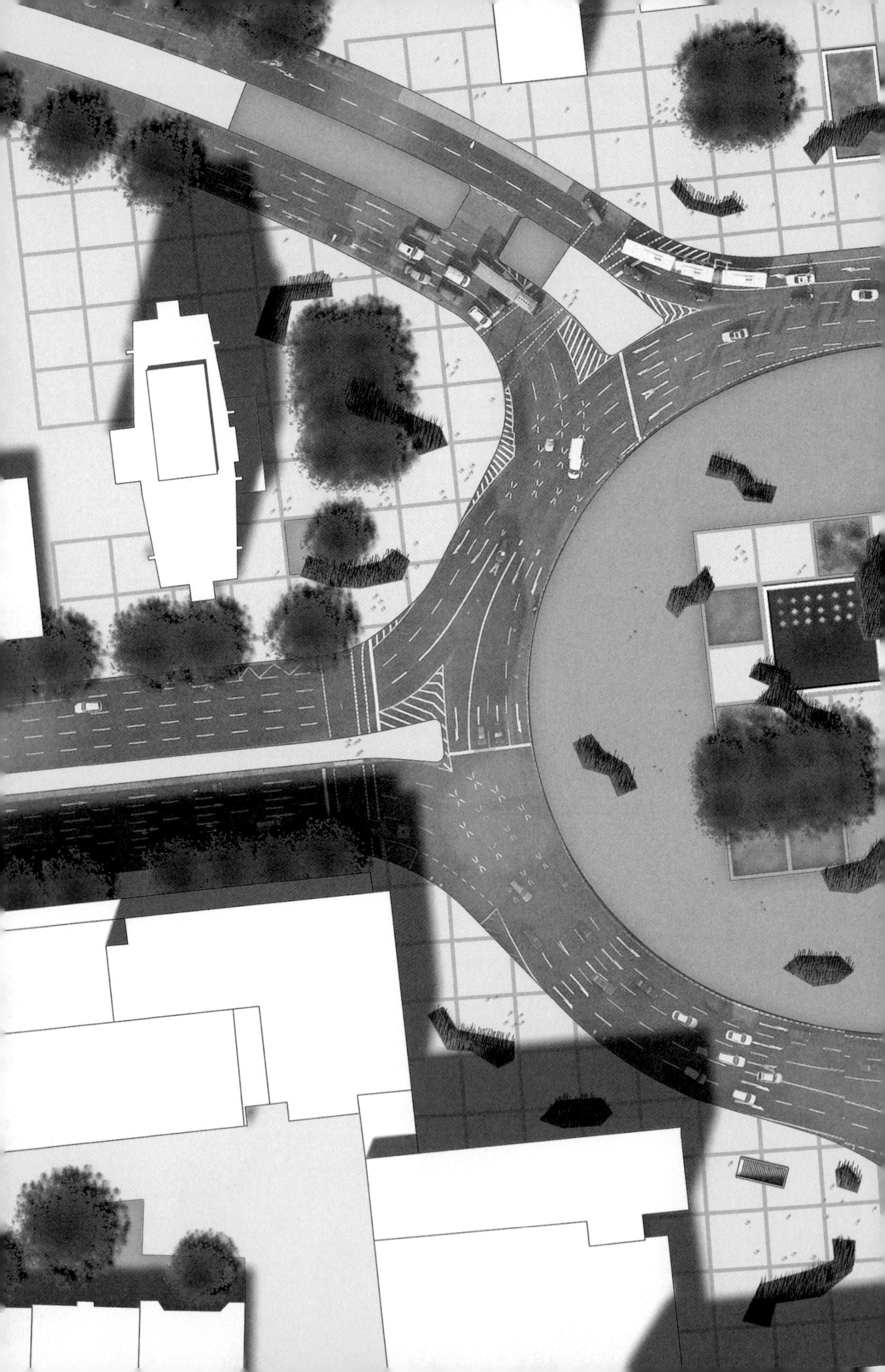

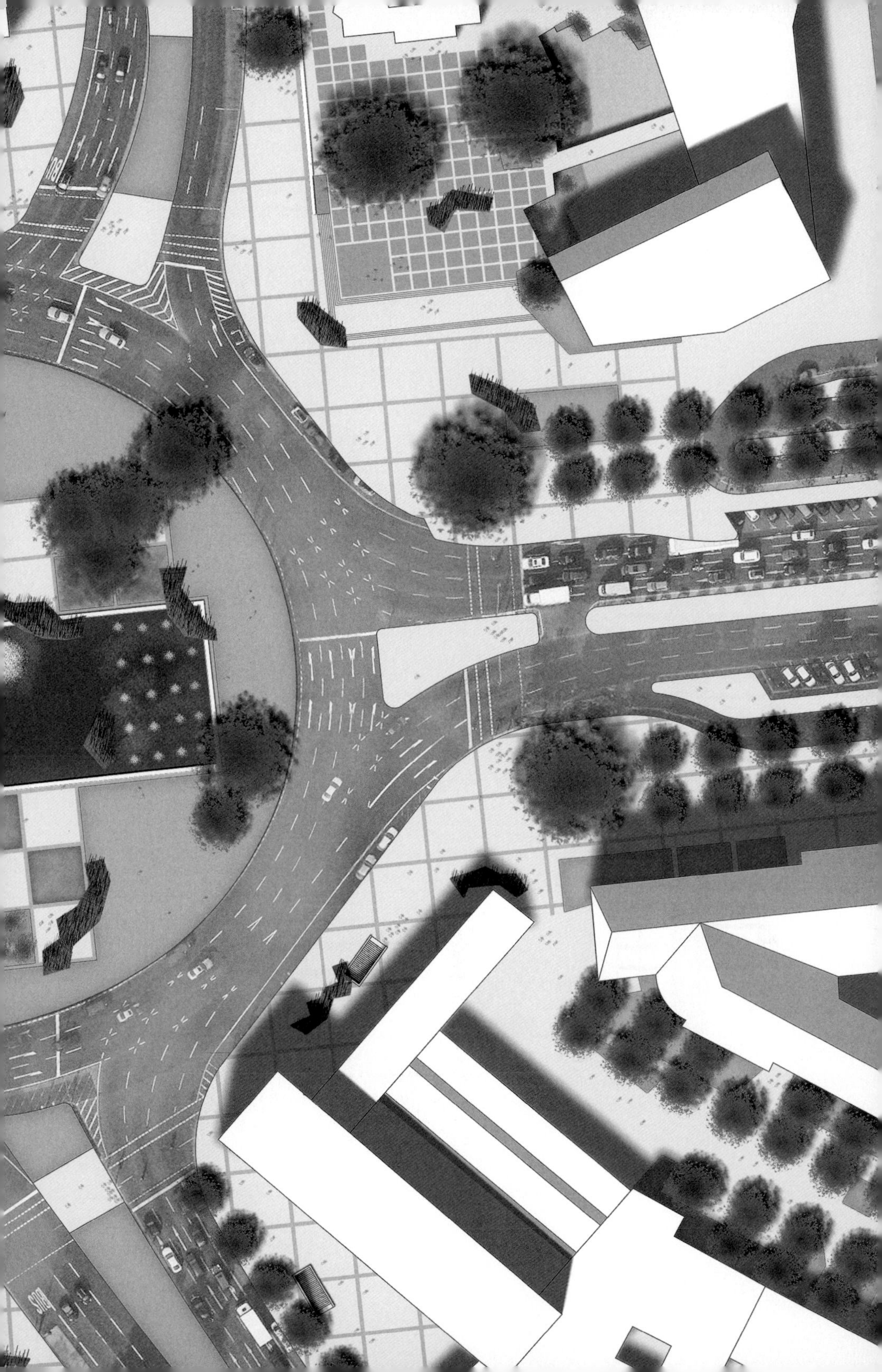

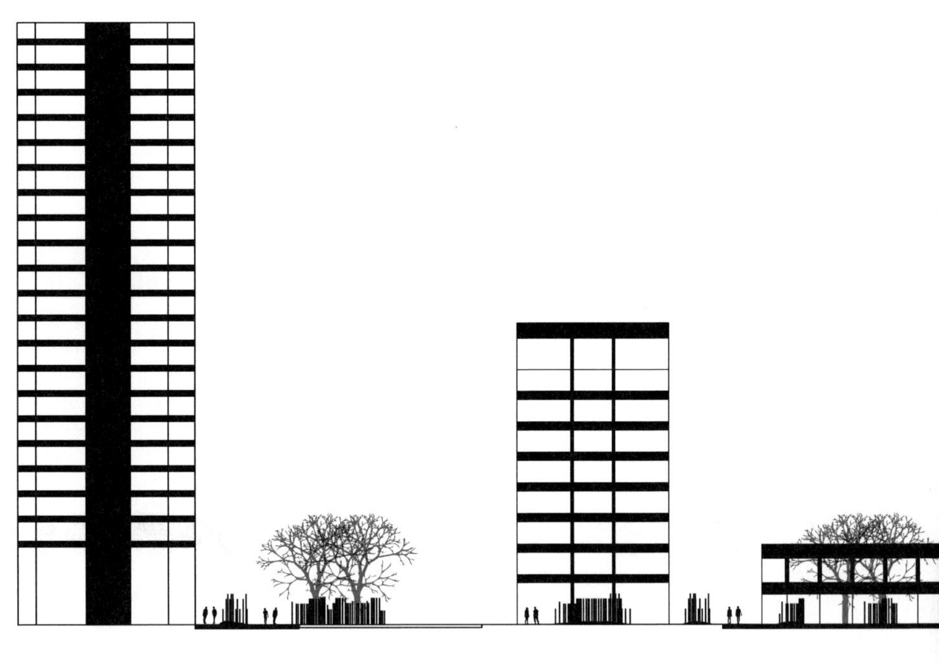

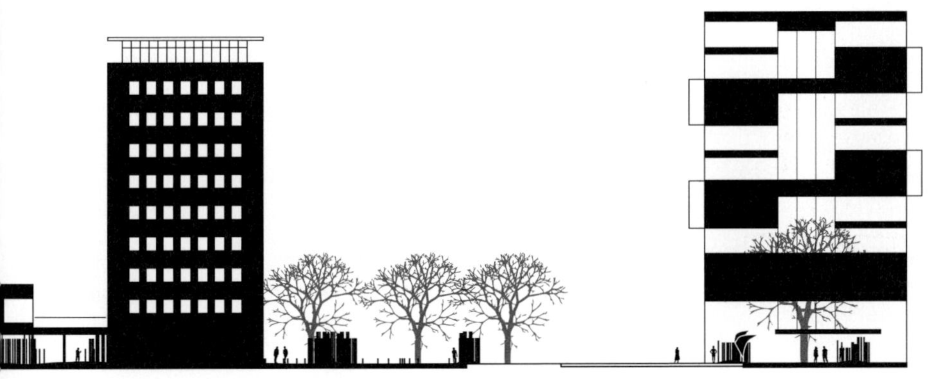

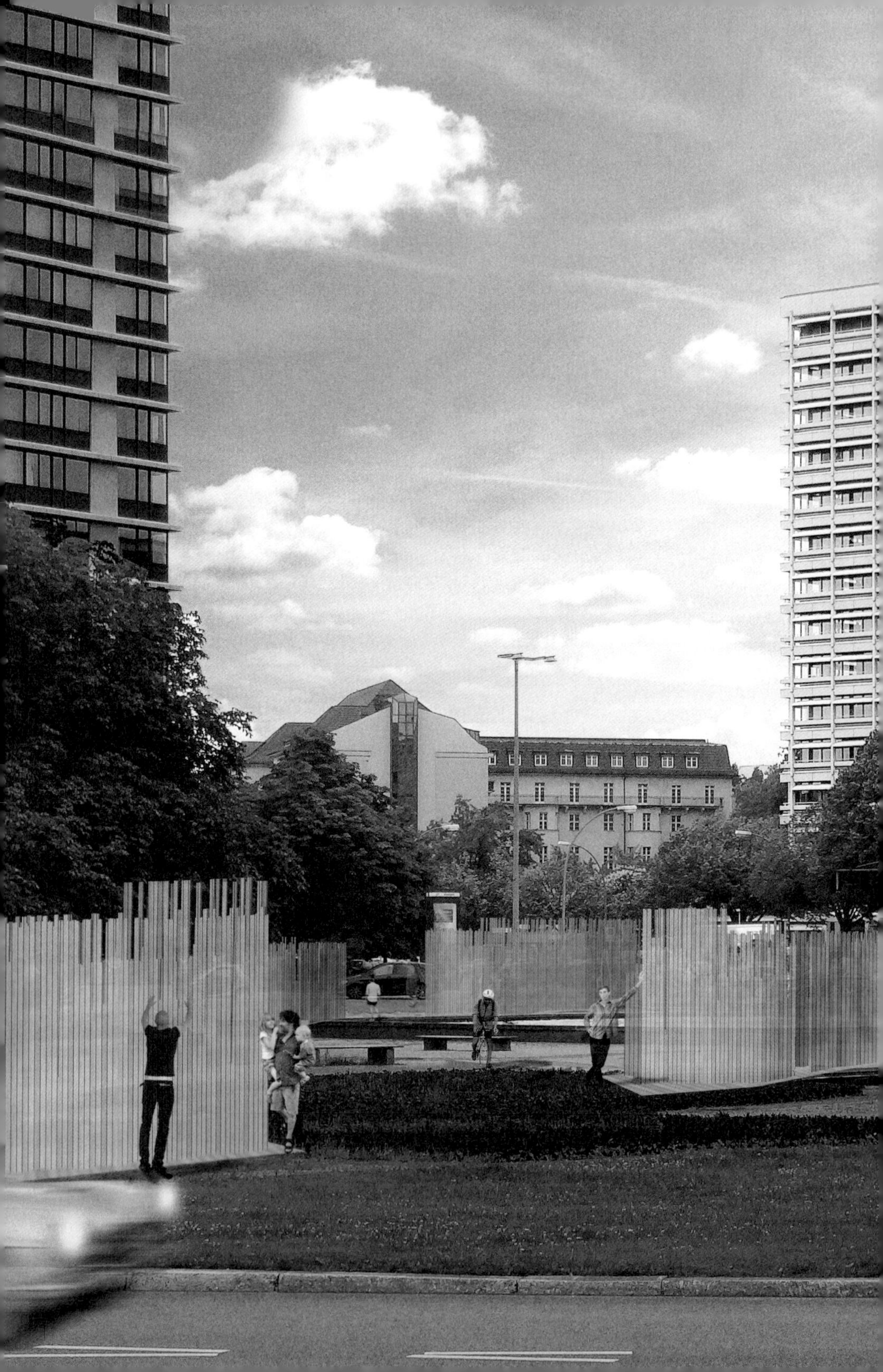

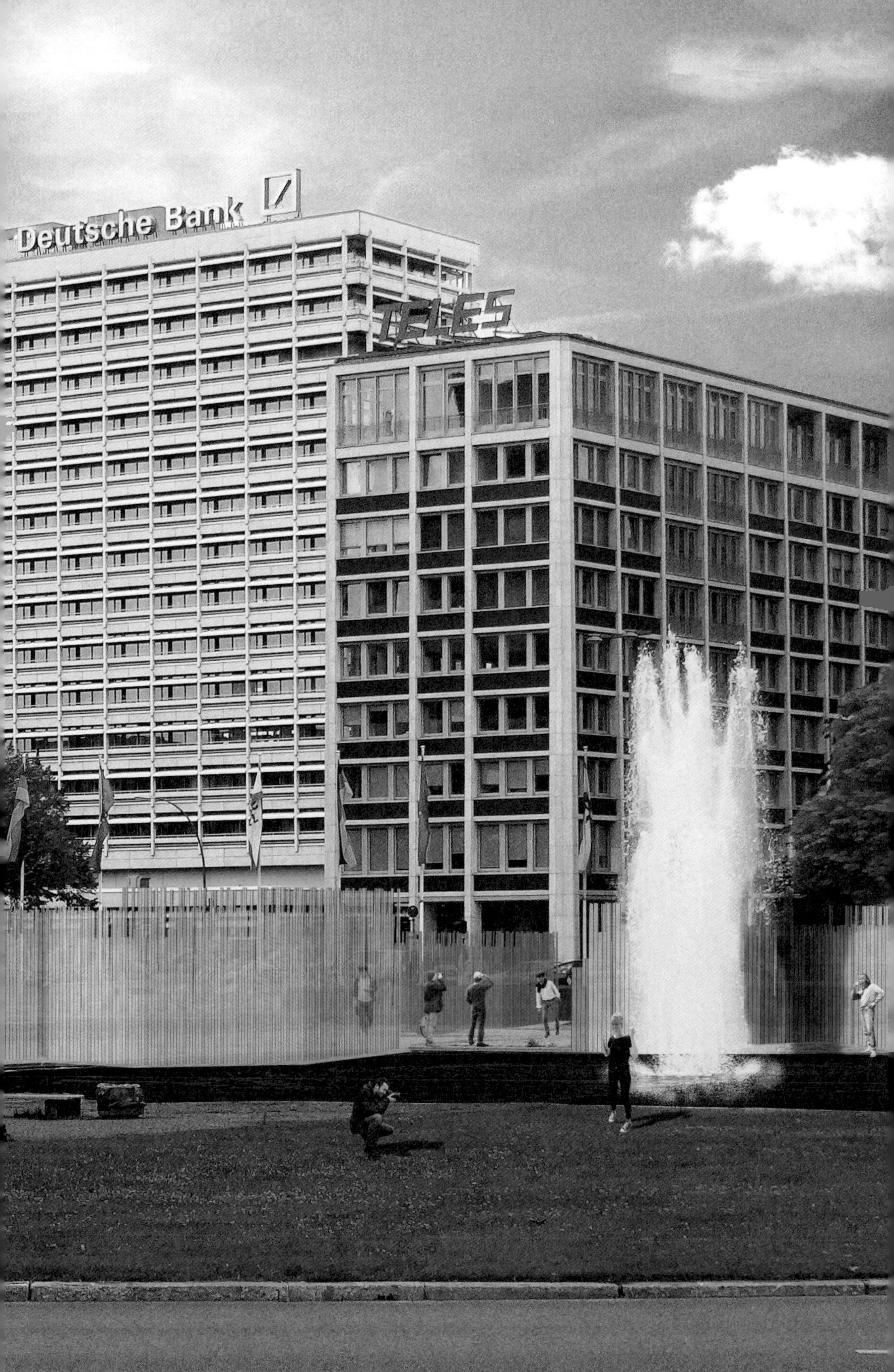
Deutsche Bank
TELES

am tag schlafen die kröten unter steinen u
hat seine zeit am wasser. die menschen leb
wurden. den wasserkreis haben sie mit wies
ein schmaler waldgürtel umringt schützen
fangen die felder an. kleine felder. auf jed
gurken neben mais und klee neben erdbe
kümmert. mittags, wenn die sonne hoch s
aus und essen, was sie sich mitgebracht hab
feigen und raukeblättern. ihre blicke schwe
bekommt, geht sie zu dem kleinen bach d
wasser in den mund. das wasser ist nicht gif
feldarbeit fertig und kehren in ihre häuser z
abendessen gemacht und jetzt tragen sie tisc
treffen sie sich und essen zusammen. es gib
von ihm angelockt, kommt eine gruppe jug
auf der suche nach ärger und mädchen setze
achtet darauf. dann steht plötzlich ein bär a
verstecken sich schnell in ihren kleinen hä
die sie laufen konnten und stehen ängstlich
und ist dabei riesengroß. mit drei hieben h
den wald. die dorfbewohner haben alles du
toten. sie beschließen die drei zu verbrennen
jemand muss noch im nachbardorf bescheid

chts schlafen die menschen in betten. jeder
dörfern, die um runde wasserstellen gebaut
geben, in die eingebettet ihre häuser liegen.
leine häuseransammlung. hinter dem wald
ächst etwas anderes. kürbis neben weizen,
eder im dorf hat sein feld, um das er sich
uhen sie sich im schatten der alten bäume
eute ist es brot mit ziegenkäse, getrockneten
die ferne, über das offene land. als sie durst
ischen den feldern fließt und schöpft sich
ist rein. zum frühen abend sind alle mit der
die, die nicht auf den feldern waren haben
d stühle auf den großen dorfplatz. am wasser
euer. weit leuchtet sein schein in der nacht.
cher über den verbindungsweg in das dorf.
ch ans feuer. es knackt im unterholz. niemand
n dorfplatz. alle rennen durcheinander und
nur die drei jungen hatten keine häuser in
uer. der bär stellt sich auf seine hinterbeine
ie drei erledigt und verzieht sich zurück in
e fenster mitangesehen. sie begutachten die
ann als dünger auf ihre felder auszubringen.
n.

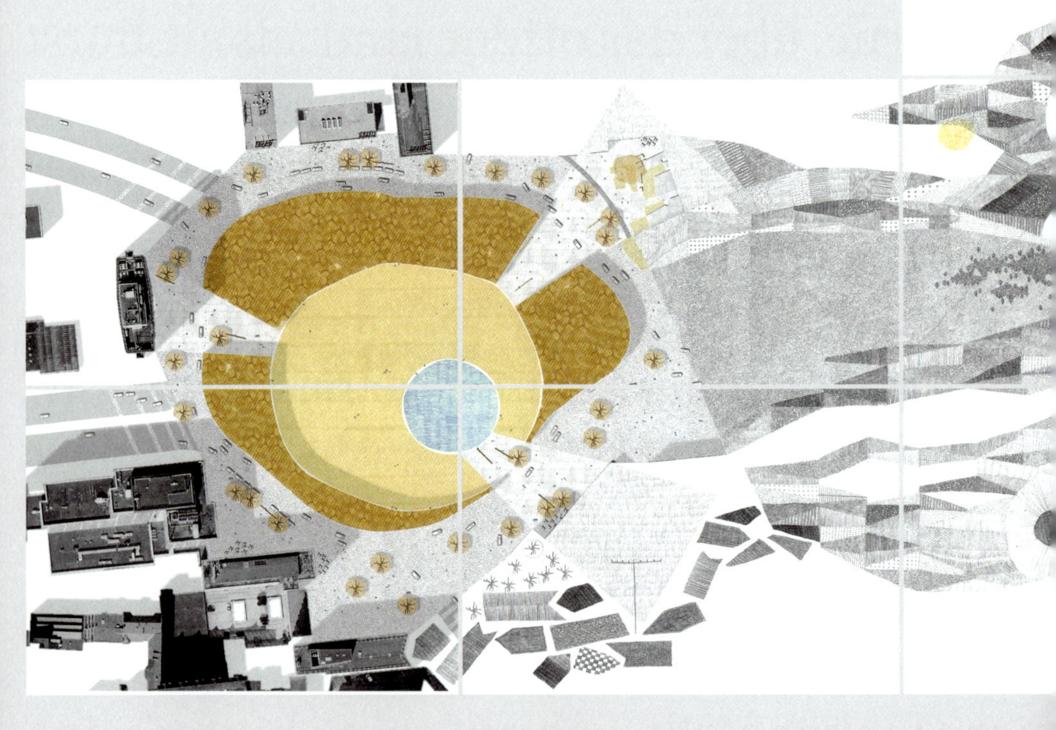

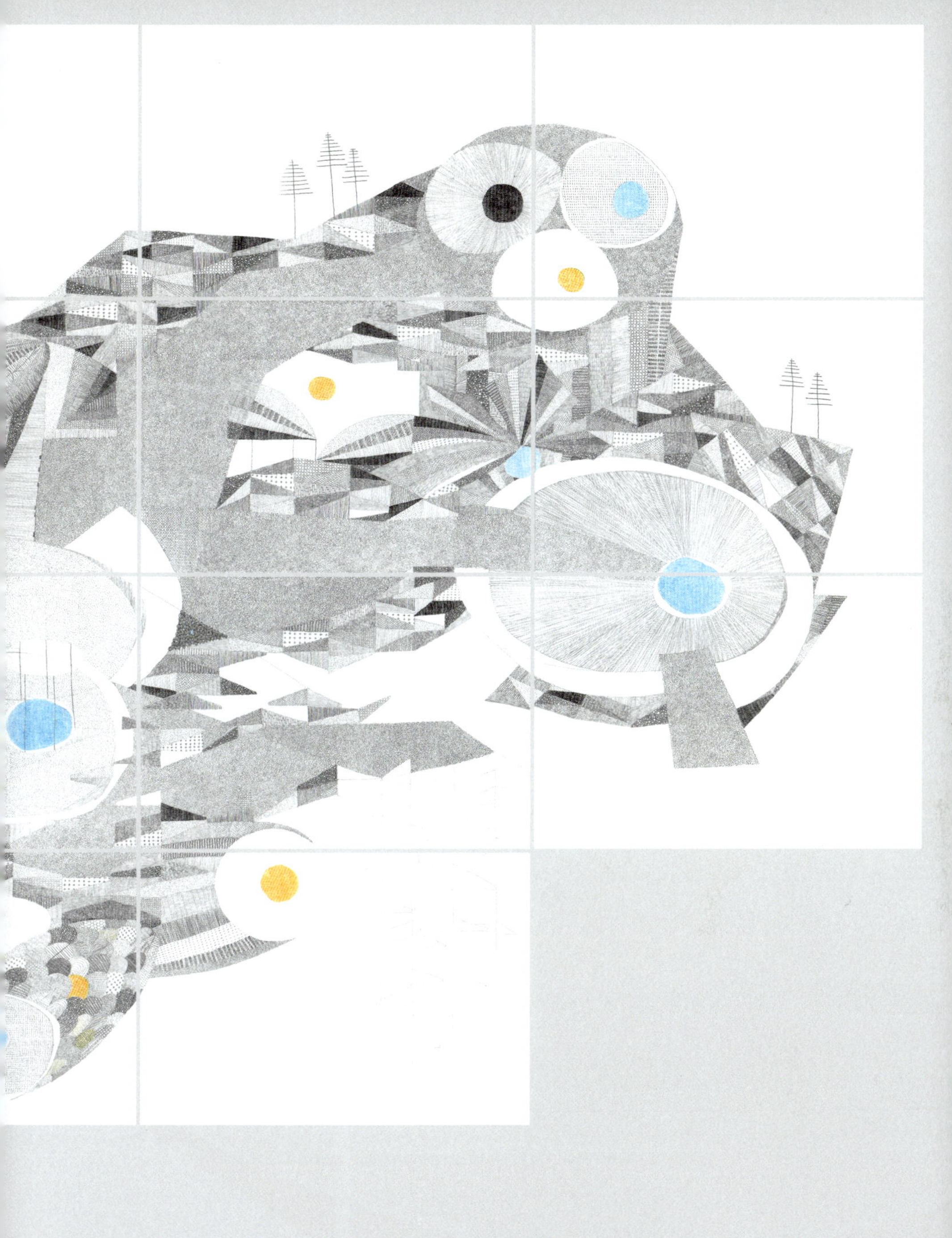

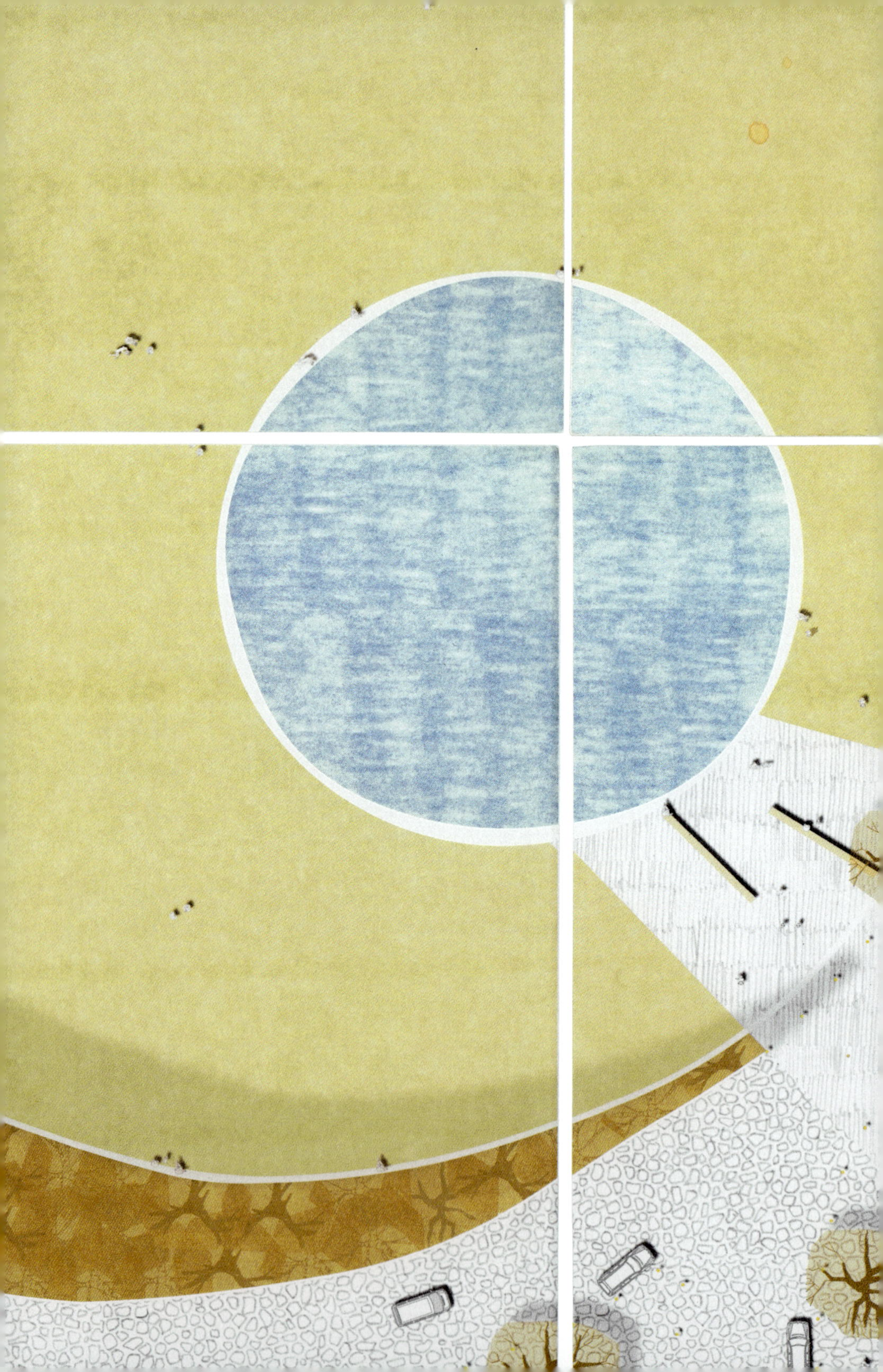

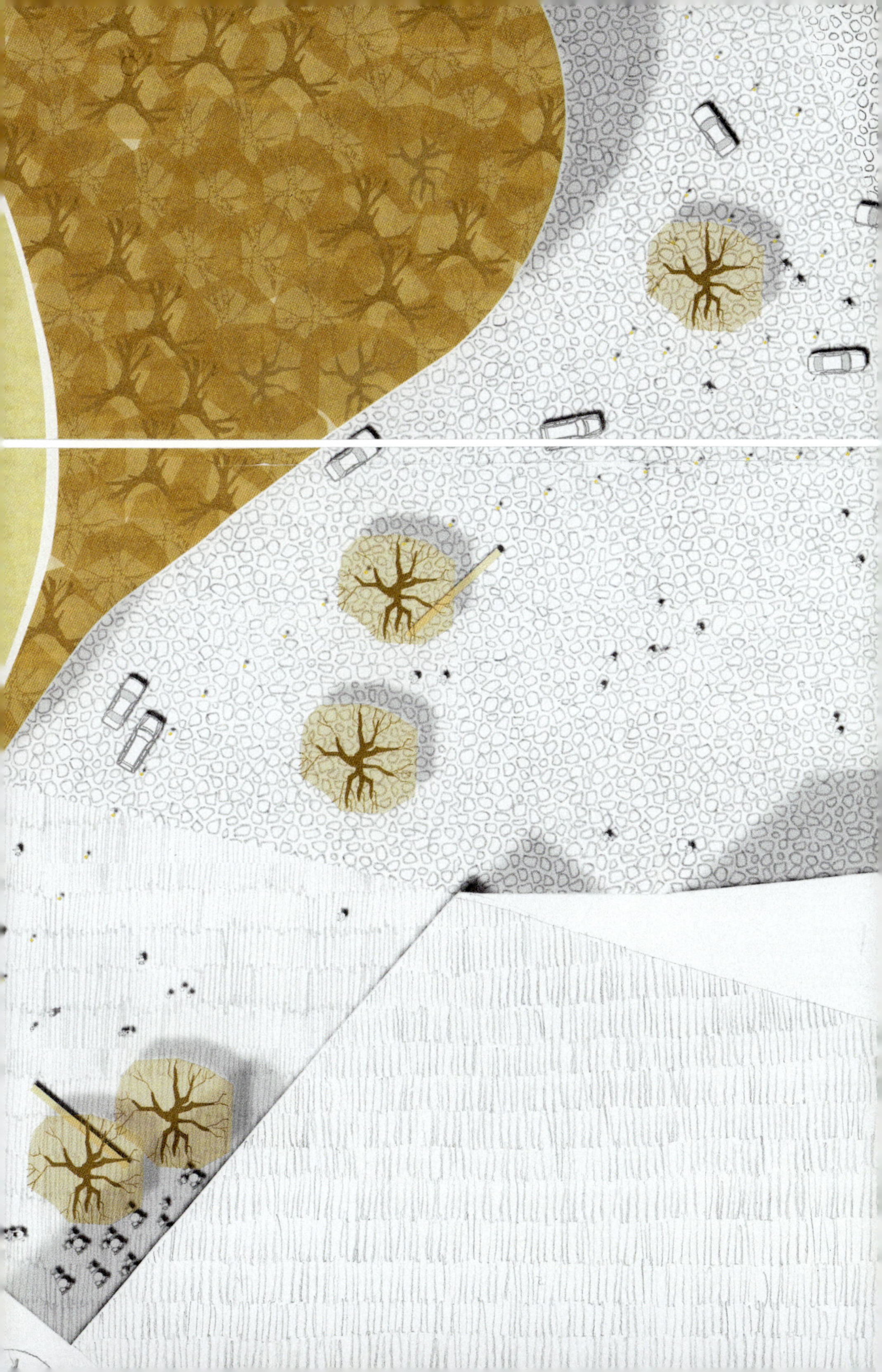

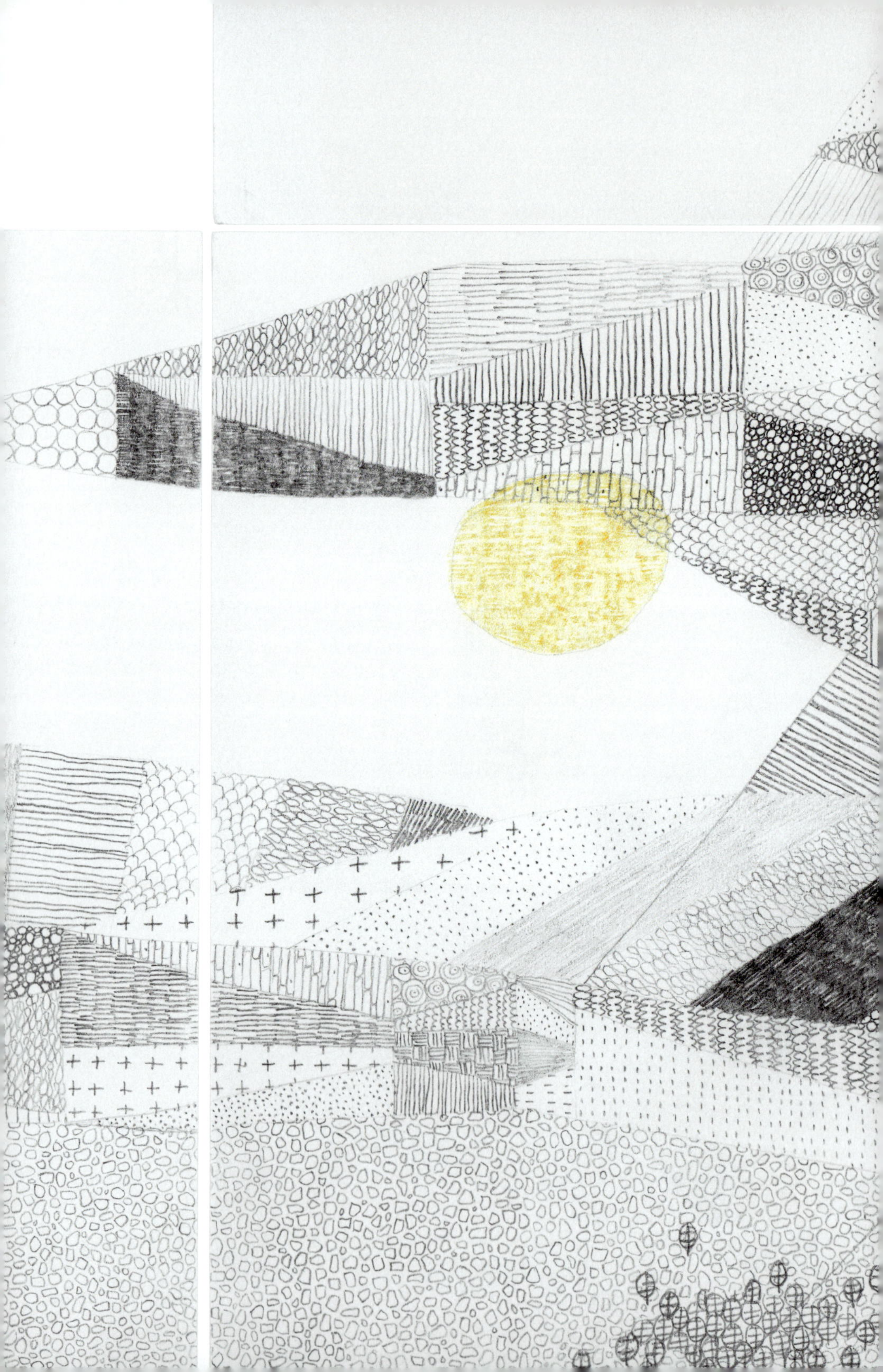

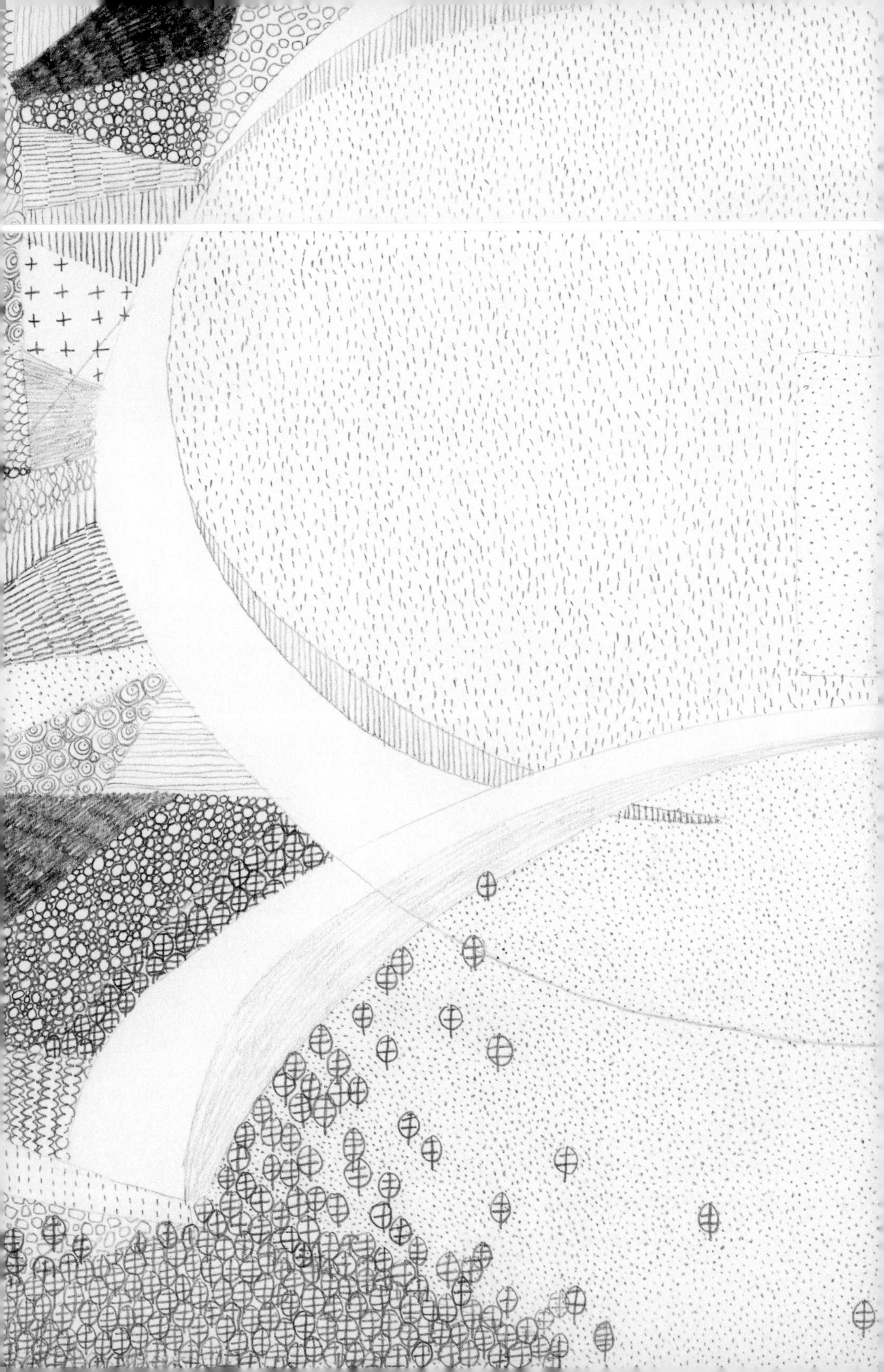

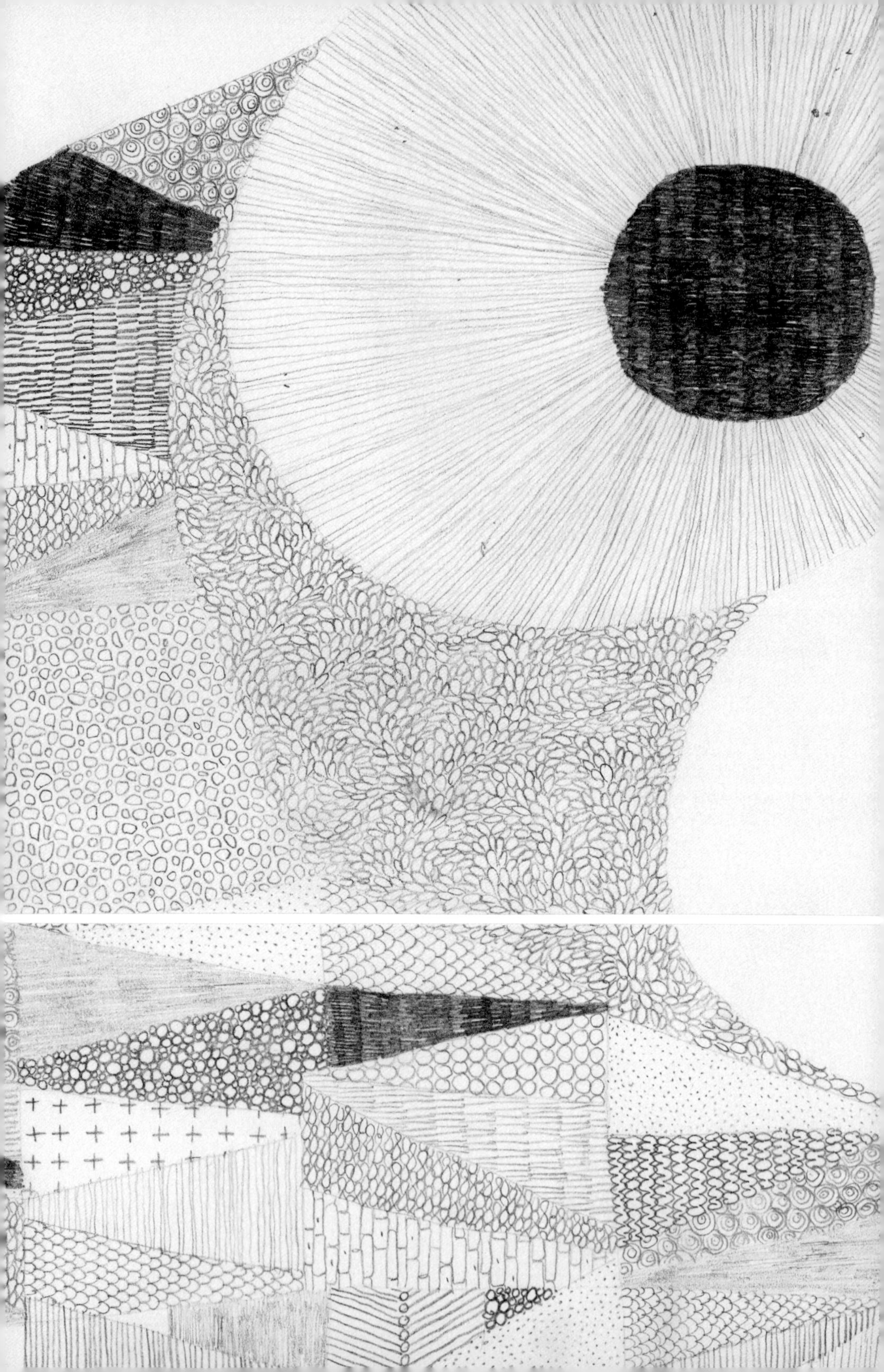

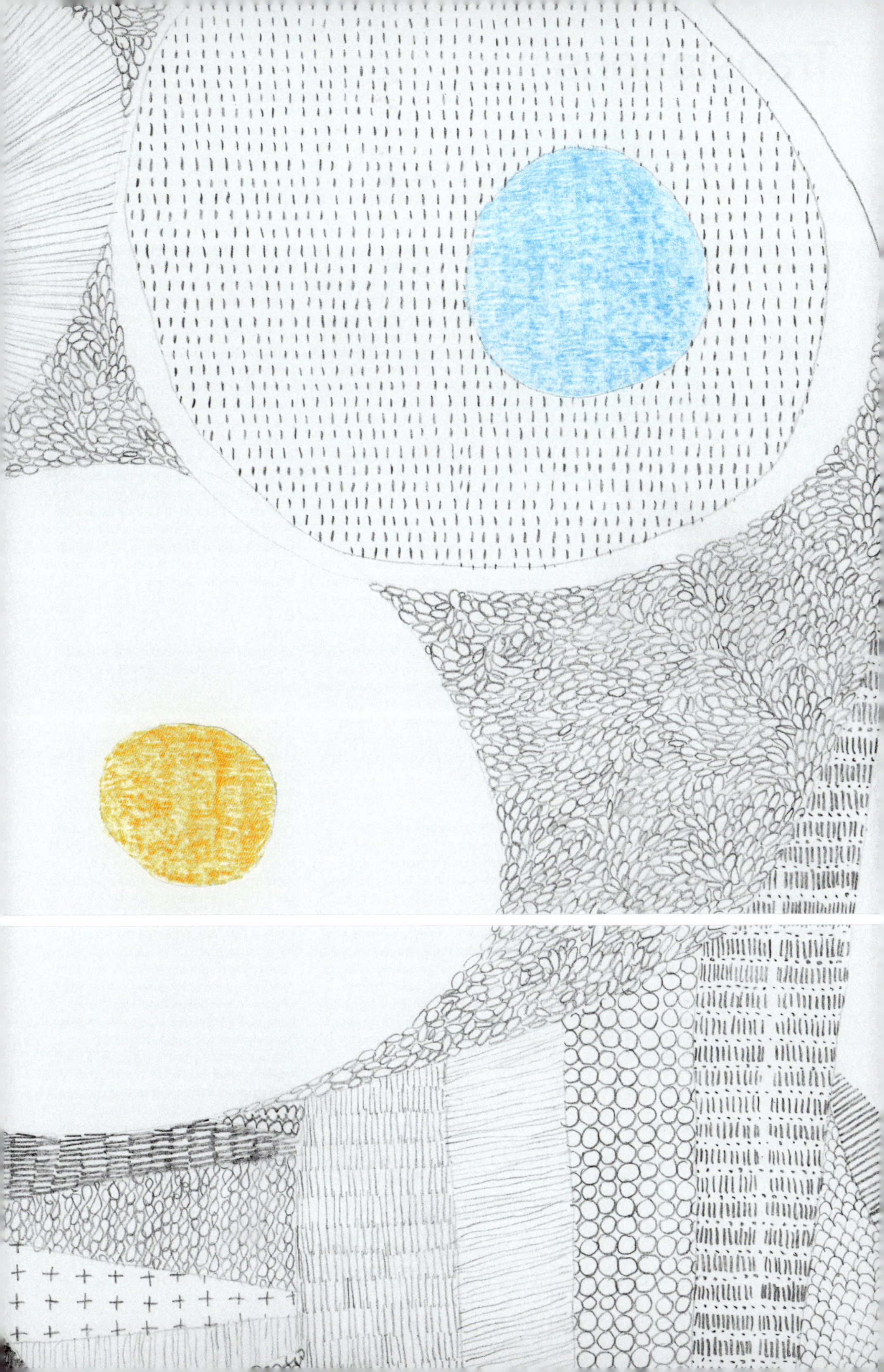

BEYOND ERP

First Issue, Friday, June 12, 2013
Beyond Ernst-Reuter-Platz

12
Other
"sometimes reality is too complex. fiction gives it form."[1]
beyond
The work beyond erp is an attempt to come closer to Ernst-Reuter-Platz, and not in the framework of a material transformation. What does beyond mean here? * Beyond is the space, both actual and symbolic, that allows for the projection of reasonable doubt, the place of uncertainty that defines the limitations of the self and goes in search of the other, the unknown, the unforeseen, the yet to come.[2] * Today there is no consensus on how to resolve the question: "What should happen with Ernst-Reuter-Platz?" It (ERP) is in the middle of controversial discourses, which are subject to two perspectival poles: The historical should be maintained (even if it is not timely). A new square should emerge in conformity with contemporary requirements, thereby not preserving the historical substance. * Yet these two hardened perspectives do not allow for productive discussion. In this indecision, by default, Ernst-Reuter-Platz today remains almost an open-air museum. * With the work beyond erp, the framework should be put in place to imagine a hybrid, * manifold Ernst-Reuter-Platz. Through conversion, the work is meant to create new stories out of existing history, yet to come, or maybe not. beyond erp constitutes a contribution against a homogenized cityscape that establishes the city as a brand. The imaginative narrative is meant to serve as a means of doing justice to a complexity that is worth thinking about. * The berp is a call to courage and audacity, to fantasy and lightness, to a non-functional life form, to joys and experiments, to being non-trivial. It wants to be unconventional, but not as a priority. In this first issue, dear reader, we would like to invite you to laugh, to cry, to revel. Laugh, and laugh out loud!

6
I dreamt about you and your traffic lights last night.
It was dark, time to flee, we were all running. Finally crossing and hiding in the warmth of your center.
Kreuzberg, Berlin, Germany.

1
I have no image of Ernst-Reuter-Platz whatsoever. It is one of the many non-places of this world. * Some places exist in my head because I have traveled them, others, because I have read them. Los Angeles is a place that I only know from Bukowski and Chandler, just like Paris from Henry Miller. * Ernst-Reuter-Platz is not among them. I have never been there, nor have I ever read about it. Hans Fallada never went through Ernst-Reuter-Platz, as far as I recollect. Franz Biberkopf was at Alexanderplatz. * I've been told it's a square in Berlin. Berlin was always too cold and much too fast for me, as a city. The nicest thing I know of Berlin is a film, "City of Angels" by Wim Wenders. When I was there physically, I always felt it to be blue on an emotional color spectrum. Not a dreamy blue, a colder, technoid blue. * That is also how I imagine this square in the middle of Berlin, too cold to stay there for long. It is not a square where a revolution would start. A lot of traffic and hurried people who scurry by a statue or commemorative plaque. The name Ernst-Reuter sounds like a great person, it sounds like Willy Brandt, presumably he was the mayor or he was killed by the Nazis, which always makes one predestined for a place name in larger cites.
Dunmanway, Ireland

3
Three-legged cat rescued A cat was found in the middle of Ernst-Reuter-Platz, Wednesday shortly after lunch hours. Overtaken by bravery it had stumbled onto the island in the middle of the roundabout, but was unable to gather courage to embark on the journey back. While approached by local onlookers, the three-legged cat started to sing russian folk songs, paying little or no attention to the growing crowd. The fire brigade was brought to the place, and after 3 hours successfully managed to return the cat to its owners on the mainland.
Friedrichshain, Berlin, Germany

4
"I know this place," said the old lady in her green skirt with white dots, that made her somehow something. She wore big glasses and owned one of those golden necklaces that many old ladies wear these days. We were just standing next to the gravis building, when she started to tell her story. * "driving through at night, they pointed out to me the tall buildings left and right. But I was not amazed at the colossi that grouped around me in a circle, these monsters of concrete.

As I drove through the streets, I saw the lights blinking from hundreds of windows. Light playing on the trees in their negligible position in the middle of the island. * The twinkling of the movie theaters and warehouses. A pleasant, homey image. No one of these buildings could impress me on its own, I thought. I immediately had a harmonious relationship to all of them. They were not too big. The square was not too big. It was complete (vollkommen). It was a new kind of city, corresponding to the state of modernity and at the same time bringing with it everything required for aesthetics. We circulated over the square for at least fifteen minutes." * The lady left as soon as she had finished her story. It was 5 p.m. I then started to walk the place in circles for 7 * 15 minutes and wondered about the word "vollkommen."
Neukölln, Berlin, Germany

8
Fields.
and suddenly there was nothing. At least one island of Berlin had already returned to its origin.

9
When the Counsel of Circology met for the first time in the 650th year after Manimani, at first no one paid attention to the young, earnest (ernsten) Reuter who sat at the bottom right end of the table, sipping cautiously from an oily drink. * The counsel had been called because strange incidents had been reported. * All over the land there was unrest. Farmers from every part of the realm complained of huge, empty circles on their fields that minimized the harvest. Only the corners of the fields remained unscathed. The demand for those responsible swelled to bestial dimensions. And so no one was surprised that herbalist organic-inhaling Birkenstock wearers, as cause for the deficit in growth and thus harvest, were soon made responsible. * Consequently, the counsel decided to put together a commission of experts to shed light on the incidents. * When the young, earnest Reuter was put in charge of this task, he was still entirely occupied with the degustation of his oily drink. Until this time, the earnest young man had devoted himself exclusively to studies of squaring, and so he was quite surprised to be entrusted with the case of the grain circles. * After investigating the phenomenon in every

direction of the realm, he determined that the frequency of the circles always increased when the fields in question were framed by exactly seven equallings. * He probably only noticed this because his favorite drink was made from the extract of the spongy interior of the equalling. Soon they started to drill deep holes at the significant sites. More and more frequently, the rig workers struck on sources of deep black liquid that gushed up to the surface in viscous fountains from the loamy innards of the earth. * After only a few weeks, they realized that some of the workers were plagued by helplessness and enormous thirst for activity after excessive consumption of the black gold. * The earnest Reuter as well, who had always been extremely partial to the enjoyment of the oily drink, refreshed himself more and more with the sticky spirit. One evening he even drank a whole barrel, and at sunrise on the second day of the third month he passed through a gate. The fog lifted, and he caught sight of a gleaming, strange world with carriages and horses of pure steel, fast and unfathomably elegant. In the air, dervishes whirled around their own axes and glorified progress in deafening clamor. Faster and faster and more fiercely, the world churns into infarction with hedonistic arrogance. Dark clouds draw together, angels shit, soot and metal crash in on each other. In the middle of the thundering din, the earnest Reuter found shocking fascination for the apocalyptic turmoil. As the boom and roar grew silent, he looked into the faces of seven wondrously beautiful sisters who exhaled to him the eternal cycle. And for the first time in his life, a smile formed on his face.
Berlin, Germany

2
Berlin doesn't work anymore. One day I ran from the Straße des 17. Juni, along the straight, clear, and perhaps long balustrade towards the Deutsche Oper on … street. For I wanted to finally be staged in the big bunker with the stone façade, in which one director already lost his life because presumably his heart could no longer sustain fantasy's effort to bring his own conception closer to the public [naturally they say he died of a heart attack]. * So I went along the balustrade and read on the ground, "Berlin doesn't work anymore." – a bit of stencil art. And as I get closer to the big traffic circle, my perception starts to throw a wrench in my works. [Was it my perception?] Because the otherwise inconspicuous circle had suddenly become completely gray. A sea of gray fog had seized it. Although it was not entirely possible to say whether this sea had really emerged as an external fog from my perception, or whether the color of my surroundings had manifested itself to such

an extent that logically I only saw gray. * I let myself get defiled in the gray, very gray current. * As I reemerged, I stood in the middle and nothing worked anymore.
Berlin, Germany

5
A SQUARE
a place, what can it be?
come from afar
imagining oneself at the destination
do you see the deception?
do you never see?
the knee!
that once formed this square,
the knee turned into a circle,
the circle whether it stays who knows exactly
will still be tomorrow –
what today seems to you stable?
driving away from the circle
centrifugal force pulls you today, tomorrow
desire drives you,
which river will you follow,
which path will you take
which wind follow after
which temptations will you not withstand?
one square follows the other whichever path
you chose centrifugal force pulls you today
day after tomorrow desire,
whichever path you take
which current pulls you along,
here too and on other squares
that stand before you,
some temptations you cannot resist
only when you have seen the deception, had
taken so long to see this,
it should never happen
i saw your knee.
Bamberg, Germany

10
bells and ice cream were ready. the carousel had already started to turn the carousel had already started to turn. children and beep-beep of passing cars driving do not disrupt rumm-rumm existence. mother, mother, mother, and children, 1, 2, 3, gather at food stands and ticket booths to shoot where are the fathers when there is shooting? they are at war. but isn't the war long past? it is, it is, but where are the fathers when the children splash in the pool under the fountain? under the fountain when the splashing children in the pool where are the fathers? on the side a lady in blue (*blao*) sings and blao is old German like her face when she suddenly opens her mouth and cries: … in this city I am at home in this city I know my way around… and when she then takes a turn on the car-carousel on the square the text sounds from the crumpled sandwich paper to

the empty cigarette packs and on the bench sat fritz who cannot kiss the old German goes around again on the carousel but she wants to go away away from home is fritz and licks his ice cream. and next to him clamor continues. the brass band is about to arrive says the boy in the yellow frock. there they come already. and everything is still the brass band strides with horns and trumpets in a circle around the square.
Berlin, Germany

7
On Tuesday, the company cancelled its general affiliation agreement for new construction of the academy on Ernst-Reuter-Platz. Ernst-Reuter-Platz will unfortunately become an element of uniformity. * There may be squares where this is thinkable, not Ernst-Reuter-Platz. * A 25-meter wide safety strip, traffic posts, guardhouses with bullet-proof glass, retractable barriers, and a insurmountable fence – this is how the USA want to protect their new server on Ernst-Reute-Platz. * Their administration is above all identified with reconstructions that restore a seemingly vanished state of affairs: for example on Ernst-Reuter-Platz or in Klein-Glienicke. * For the office of XXXXX from Boston, worldwide there were "few empty construction sites of such great significance" as Ernst-Reuter-Platz. * During the final meeting, starting at 6 p.m., fire will blaze in a bowl on Ernst-Reuter-Platz. * In the dispute over the US server on Ernst-Reuter-Platz, indications of a possible solution are intensifying.
Nuremberg, Germany

11
1. it was midnight when time arrived at Ernst-Reuter-Platz in order to present itself in its megalomania. velocity always tied to its apron strings. both discovered slowness only later, not on this square at this time.
2. time had sunken into change and the logic of the duplicate emerging in its appearance.
3. the present takes on the character of the supposed past of a future that is still to come.
4. it was midnight when the three stole away.

1 Alpha 60, the fictional controlling computer of alphaville in Jean-Luc Godard's Alphaville.
2 Sophie Warren & Jonathan Mosley: beyond utopia
* hybrid: two elements that are transformed based on their particularity/disparity into a new element, in which the originality of both remains recognizable, yet something new emerges. Conflict is a central component of this process [driving force].

STUDIO ERP

Ideas Contest for the Redesign of Ernst-Reuter-Platz

I.1 Studio ERP: Call for Entries

In response to the altered conditions of perception on Ernst-Reuter-Platz, during the next few years the site will become a temporary studio for experimental design. Inspired by the site's namesake—former mayor of Berlin, Ernst Reuter—the contest will establish communication between Berlin and Istanbul, where Reuter lived in exile. The plan is to exhibit the winning design at Ernst-Reuter-Platz for no longer than two years, following which it will be on display at the Biennale in Istanbul.

I.2 Introduction

As one of the largest traffic junctions in Berlin, Ernst-Reuter-Platz has influenced the urban landscape for over 60 years. Embedded in the urban ensemble created by Bernhard Hermkes, the site is considered a prime example of post-war modern architecture and early car-friendly city planning. Five surrounding roads feed into the traffic circle: Marchstraße, Straße des 17. Juni, Hardenbergstraße, Bismarckstraße, and Otto-Suhr-Allee.

Viewed historically, the square is on the axis between the Berlin City Palace and Charlottenburg Palace, a location that earned it the pre-renovation nickname "on the knee." Later redesign, conducted by Albert Speer, superimposed the square onto the planned East-West axis of Germania, thereby overwriting previous associations. After the Second World War, Bernhard Hermkes won the competition to redesign the site around the square, which had been badly damaged during the war. As a reaction against the turbulent history of the location, Hermkes proposed a free and open space that would be framed by freestanding solitary constructions. The design proposed a generous city square with good connections, which would enable visitors to experience the ensemble from their cars.

I.3 Task

The perception of Ernst-Reuter-Platz today is determined by its function as an infrastructural hub within the city system. Due to the increase in traffic volume, the square has lost its original quality as a place to spend time or as an ornament in the urban landscape; it has been degraded to a bit of greenery amidst traffic. U-Bahn station development and applied design elements also fail to do justice to the location in its current form.

More significant for the contest, however, should be the original intention of designs from the 1950s. In his plans, Werner Düttmann reacted to the citywide context of the location, and its situation on the East-West axis as planned by Albert Speer. In reaction to the open city-planning context, Düttmann used the staggered water basins on the central island and the grid pattern covering the entire surface area to create a square without a clearly identifiable center. Overlaid by this pattern, the axis moves into the background of perception.

The goal of the competition is the development of a design concept that will make it possible to newly experience Düttmann's original design, adapted to the current context.

I.4 Conditions:

The area in question for the competition has as its external borders Düttmann's original surface pattern. As a recognized, protected monument, the square is to be fully preserved in its substance. The design must limit itself to a new level to be applied to existing structures.

II.1 Process and Cycle

The call for entries will be conducted as an open ideas competition. The entire process will be conducted anonymously up until its conclusion. Multiple entries are not allowed. There will be no division according to specific categories. There are no constraints on participation. A call for proposals will occur in two-year cycles. Future applicants may not have previously won the contest.

II.2 Type and Extent of Contest Entries

Presentation of the entries is at the discretion of applicants, and is to be selected according to specific design. To allow the outcome of the process to be as open as possible, the jury will not implement normative guidelines for entries.

II.3 Assessment Process and Jury

The jury commission consists of representatives from participating interest groups (residents, neighbors, the city of Berlin, Berlin University of the Arts, and the Technische Universität Berlin), as well as alternating guest jurors.

After preliminary examination of received entries, the jury commission will decide on ranking and assignment of the prizes, special mentions, and, where applicable, special awards. The decision is by majority and without recourse to legal action.

AT NIGHT THE TOADS

during the day the toads sleep under stones and at night the people sleep in beds. everyone gets their turn at the water. the people live in villages built around watering holes. they have surrounded the circle of water with meadows in which their homes lie embedded. a narrow belt of forest protectively encircles the little clutch of houses. beyond the forest the fields begin. little fields. something different grows in each one. pumpkins next to wheat, cucumbers next to corn, clover next to strawberries. everyone in the village has their own field to tend. at midday, when the sun is high, they rest in the shade of the old trees and eat the food they have brought with them. today there is bread with goat's cheese, dried figs, and arugula. their gazes drift to the distance, across the open country. when she is thirsty she goes to the little stream flowing between the fields and scoops water into her mouth. the water is not toxic. it is pure. by early evening they have all finished their work in the fields and they return to their homes. those who were not in the fields have prepared the evening meal, and now they carry tables and chairs out onto the village square. they meet at the water and eat together. there is a fire. its light radiates deep into the night. lured by the flames, a group of youths enter the village through the connecting path. in search of trouble and girls they take a seat at the fire. there is a crack in the underwood. no one pays attention. then suddenly a bear is standing in the village square. everyone runs in different directions and they hide in their small houses. only the three young men didn't have homes into which they could run and hide, and they stand afraid by the fire. the bear gets up on its hind legs and it is huge. with three blows it kills the three young men and then returns to the forest. the villagers have seen everything from their windows. they examine the dead. they decide to cremate the three bodies and scatter the ashes as fertilizer on their fields. someone should tell the people in the next village.

The Auditory Architecture Research Unit's design for Ernst-Reuter-Platz

Alex Arteaga

Boris Hassenstein

Maria Horn (drawings)

The design for the transformation of Ernst-Reuter-Platz described in this text was realized by Boris Hassenstein and Alex Arteag, with assistance in the graphic realization from Maria Horn. It has been presented as the design of the Auditory Architecture Research Unit because it culminates a collective process initiated four years earlier on this platform.[1] The conceptual and operational core of this research/design process is exhaustively exposed in the chapter, "Steps towards an Architecture of Embodiment: thinking the environment aurally." This text contains an explanation of the main concepts used here and the practices that enable this design.

In the following lines, we are not going to describe the process of design but only its results: the constellation of interventions defined as a means of reinstating the potentiality of this place as an agent of urban significance. The square's progressive loss of signification since it was built according to the design of Bernhard Hermkes, that is, the increasing difficulty of collectively understanding and inhabiting this place in ways that cohere with its daily and occasional uses, is precisely what presents Ernst-Reuter-Platz as a "problem" in the context of current deliberations to redefine Berlin's City West,[2] and, more specifically, Campus West.[3] This "problem" has been articulated as a "dilemma." On the one hand, the square is not experienced as pleasant, enjoyable, agreeable, gratifying, interesting, or enriching by those who work or study there—or even by those who visit occasionally or simply cross through to get somewhere else. Neither it is still attractive for investors or entrepreneurs searching for a suitable location in Berlin. On the other hand, the architectural and historic value of this urban ensemble as a paradigmatic example of post-war modernity is not unanimously but broadly accepted, justifying its classification as protected urban landmark. This conflict has been addressed mostly by stressing one of the operative terms derived from these divergent perceptions—the necessity of change or the imperative of conservation—and understanding the other one as its antagonist. Our design takes this situation as a point of departure, proposing a network of transformative interventions able to deactivate the conflict between renewal and preservation while further establishing sustainable synergy between these poles. The integrative quality of our design stems from our approach to architectural design as a process of *immanent transformation*: a modification of the enabling conditions of the emergent environment to be designed, and/or the introduction of new constraints into this process of environmental emergence, the structure of which is revealed by our research practices. This approach brings novelty in continuity to what is already constituted, based on an understanding of both states—the present and the one to come—as temporary stabilizations of a continuous and collective process rather than static formalizations to be substituted for one another.

I will begin the description of our design by outlining the presence that our object of design acquired through the performance of practices of aural-architectural research.[4] Ernst-Reuter-Platz appeared as a *space of radical circulation,*

1 The first and most exhaustive public presentation of this design took place in the glass gallery of the former IBM-Building in Ernst-Reuter-Platz. For a general description of the whole project and an exhaustive list of people involved, see the foreword of this book. 2 For an overview, see the websites of the Regionalmanagement CITY WEST: www.berlin-city-west.de/ and of the Bezirksamt Charlottenburg-Wilmesdorf: http://www.berlin.de/ba-charlottenburg-wilmersdorf/ueber-den-bezirk/ (both websites in German). 3 For an overview, see the website of the Senatsverwaltung für Wirtschaft, Technologie und Forschung: https://www.berlin.de/sen/wirtschaft/wirtschaft-und-technologie/technologiezentren-zukunftsorte-smart-city/zukunftsorte/campus-charlottenburg-city-west/artikel.95837.php and of the Senatsverwaltung für Stadtentwicklung und Umwelt: http://www.stadtentwicklung.berlin.de/planen/stadtplanerische_konzepte/leitbild_city_west/de/teilprojekt_leitbild/leitbild/vertiefungsbereich_masterplan_tub/index.shtml (both in German). 4 In realistic terms—which do not recognize the constitutive function of the practices of observation—this would be expressed as a description of the "actual state" of the object of design.

dominated by motorized traffic but also including pedestrians and cyclists. Furthermore, circulation here appears to be absolutely functional: all moves are performed in order to reach a predetermined target, a target not originating in, by, or with this square but rather set before encountering it. More concretely, the square manifests as a surface on which movements are mostly performed to reach places within or beyond its margins in the most efficient way, that is, as fast and undisturbed as possible. Movements in this place, therefore, implicitly aim to abandon the square after having crossed it by necessity. Ernst-Reuter-Platz appears as a *functional place*: an environment in which the performance of sensorimotor skills almost exclusively obey the achievement of utilitarian goals not related to any other potential presences in the square, but rather related to the function of architectonical units situated on its periphery or beyond (university buildings, offices, shops, and, marginally, cafés or restaurants). The square appears as a constellation of departure and arrival points linked by lines describing the best possible connection between them: a field of *functional conduct*.

This kind of behavior, characterized by tense, focused motor activity and analytical awareness, hinders the implementation of *aesthetic* behavior, which is characterized by a more passive attitude, endowed with a wide focus of awareness, receptive to the qualitative and emotional components of the environment and, simultaneously, those of the observer. Nevertheless, when we voluntarily adopt aesthetic conduct to methodically reflect this square as an emerging environment, Ernst-Reuter-Platz appears as a unique urban space. Aside from the singularity of some of the delimiting buildings, three main traits constitute its uniqueness. The first is its *wideness*. This square appears as a broad, open space whose presence transcends its topological limits. Factors contributing to the emergence of this quality are: the physical broadness of the circular surface in the center, e.g., the so-called *Mittelinsel* (middle island); the openness and extension of the five segments of sidewalks around it; the largeness of the three avenues (Straße des 17. Juni, Otto-Suhr-Alle, Bismarkstraße), which together with two other spacious streets (Hardenbergstraße, Marchstraße) articulate this square; and the volume and very particular disposition of surrounding buildings. The second most outstanding trait, *processuality*, further reinforces its panoramic character. The predominance of moving objects with a centripetal flow hinders the fixation of attention on any concrete spot or element, so that perception sweeps out to follow objects on the move. Observed with an aesthetic variety of awareness, circulation appears as *organized dynamics* leading the focus of attention through this square and beyond its limits. Thus perceived, the square does not eliminate its own presence as is the case when it is perceived as conditioned by functional conduct; it rather presents itself as the condition of possibility for a fascinating *panoramic observation*. The third coalescent quality arising out of aesthetic reflection is *transparency*. The square's totality can be perceived from almost every spot with few obstacles, the urban context can be perceived through the boundaries of the square, and this contributes to a sense of clearness that in turn reinforces the presence of its wideness.

These three qualities can be identified through practices of aesthetic reflection of Ernst-Reuter-Platz,[5] but their presence does not appear in an absolutely distinct, clear, and unambiguous way. They appear rather as *potentialities* that, if developed, could achieve a more comprehensive and immediate level of evidence. These qualities can be present but latent to a large extent, occluded by three other mutually reinforcing qualities that also appear: *homogeneity*, *non-differentiability*, and *stress*. Especially aural-aesthetic research into this place reveals these other qualities and their complex relationship with those described above (*wideness*, *processuality*, and *transparency*).

The predominant sound in this square is the sound of traffic. With variations depending on date and time of the day, this place is flooded by the sounds produced by cars, mainly, but also, to a lesser extent, trucks and, marginally, motorcycles. Although this flow is regulated by traffic lights, its aural presence takes the form of a continuum, almost independently of the spot where one hears. Only an attentive form of listening presents this sound mass as rhythmically structured, thus breaking the homogeneity with which it commonly appears. The square emerges as an allover volume of traffic sound, surrounding the observer wherever she goes. Single and singular sounds—bikes passing by, steps, voices, birds, the fountain and spouts in the central circle (only functioning in the summer), or even particular traffic sounds—disappear or at least lose their significance under the massive and penetrating presence of the bulk of traffic sound. The sounds produced in the distance tend to vanish as well, limiting the aural wideness of this environment. The differentiability of single sounds and, consequently, of their source is extremely limited. Their blurry and hidden presence hinders the manifestation of this square as clear and transparent; it rather tends to manifest as covered and opaque.

In addition to the pressure produced by the constant presence of this perceptual blurriness, a sense of stress is generated by the aggressive presence of individual vehicles, conditioned by the amount of traffic and, even more, by the way its flow is organized, which is clearly manifest the closer the observer comes to the circulating cars, especially when they abruptly accelerate. Additionally, the difficulty of discerning singular objects induces a lack of orientation. The uneasiness and incipient anxiety coloring this environment reinforce its functional use and limit the potential wideness of its presence. Stress leads to a reduction of the scope of awareness and concentration on the immediate surroundings, bringing the totality of the square and its context out of focus. It also contributes to the negative connotation of the present sounds; they turn into undesirable noises associated with a latent sense of danger.

Taking this meshwork of qualities as our object of design, we determined two fundamentally interlaced goals for its transformation: to potentiate the factors that contribute to increasing the presence of those qualities that present this place as a singular urban space, and to create conditions that make it possible to experience this place aesthetically, that is, to behave in an aesthetic mode in the square. Both goals operate in a relation of circular causality: adopting aesthetic conduct contributes to the emergence of a comprehensive presence of Ernst-Reuter-Platz, a presence that is not reduced to its functionality and therefore includes finely differentiated qualities of the square as an autonomous whole in a specific context. In turn, the reinforced presence of wideness, circulation as organized dynamics, and transparency contributes to spontaneous inducement of aesthetic conduct. The two goals thus reinforce each other.

Our concrete proposals to achieve these goals can be categorized under three operations: *to clear, to differentiate,* and to *attract.* To clear means here to remove all material elements that are not constitutive part part of Hermkes's design, hindering the perception of and, mainly, through the square. In other words, we seek to eliminate those objects that act as obstacles to the presence of Ernst-Reuter-Platz as a wide, transparent, dynamic environment that provides access to its urban surroundings. Concrete proposals to unblock the square are as follows: all parking lots should be eliminated. Parking and stopping at any time should be prohibited on the whole surface of the square, which in our design includes the whole area delimited by the grid designed by Werner Düttmann. This measure would reinforce the square as a radical space of circulation. Accordingly, all bicycle stands and bus stops should be displaced outside of the square. Further elements to be removed are: plant tubs, some trees, telephone and flagpoles, and advertisement panels. The two subway entrances on the southern part of the square can be considered elements of pedestrian circulation and therefore should not be displaced. Nevertheless, the metal constructions signaling and structuring these entrances should be replaced by transparent elements. These interventions would reinforce the presence of this square as wide and transparent—as a place of panoramic observation—exclusively on a visual level. This might seem contradictory as part of an *auditory*-architectural design, but it is not; the auditory-architectural design process approaches, researches, and thus constitutes the object of design and identifies the interventions for its transformation through different varieties of aural activity—different forms of hearing and listening—but our design proposals cannot be reduced to interventions that condition exclusively what can be listened to or heard, nor to interventions by means of sound. Aural interaction allows us to identify not only acoustical characteristics but also, mainly, general and transmodal qualities of the environment. Auditory architecture is neither acoustic design nor sound art but rather architectural research/design based on aural reflection.

Nevertheless, the main intervention proposed in order to increase *differentiability* in Ernst-Reuter-Platz would also help to increase its aural wideness and transparency. Before describing this, we would like to introduce some other small-scale proposals intended to increase the possibilities of perceptually discernment, or, in other words, to reduce the oppressive homogeneity of this environment. In this square, three varieties of circulation coexist: power-driven vehicles, bicycles, and pedestrians. In order to facilitate the presence of the complexity of this flow, the latter two types should be reinforced. Bicycling should be enhanced by widening the bicycle lane in order to allow for circulation in both directions. This measure has been recently implemented in another important square in Berlin, namely the Grosser Stern. Pedestrian circulation would be improved by the elimination of obstacles as already mentioned. Widening the bicycle line would also indirectly create better conditions for pedestrians by increasing the distance between them and the automobiles. However, the intervention that would generate the most relevant increase of differentiability is a fundamental *reorganization of the circulation flow*, which would entail a change in the way these three modes of circulation relate to each other timewise. What we propose is to implement a new structure, hybridizing two types of organization: traffic circle and traffic light circuit. Although these two models are commonly understood as opposites—circulation is either regulated by traffic lights, or it is self-regulated based on the single principle that the car in the traffic circle has right of way—it is possible to combine both logics in one hybrid model. This is the specific type of combination we propose. Distribution and models of traffic lights should be modified as follows: first, eliminate traffic lights in the central circle; second, replace current traffic lights in the streets providing access to the circle with new ones that only have two states for automobiles (steady red and blinking yellow), and two for pedestrians and cyclists (steady red and steady green); and third, replace the lights currently situated in the streets leading traffic out of the square with new lights that have two states for automobiles (steady red and no light), and two for pedestrians and cyclists (steady red and steady green). All these traffic lights will change colors simultaneously, generating two states of circulation in the whole square. In the first state, all traffic lights would be red for automobiles, and green for pedestrians and cyclists, who could thus circulate in the whole square while automobiles would be stopped everywhere. In the second state, all traffic lights for pedestrians and cyclists would be red, and those for automobiles would blink yellow in the access streets and show no light in the streets leading out of the square. In this second state, automobiles could circulate within the center and through all surrounding streets, self-regulating their relationships according to the rule of a traffic circle. This model would generate a clear and steady two-phase rhythm in Ernst-Reuter-Platz as a whole, according to which either cars or pedestrians and bikers would be the main agents of movement and sound. Especially in the timeframes when there would be no automobile traffic, all other sounds—also the quiet ones—would be much more present, reducing the pressure of traffic noise, expanding the aural field, and thus reinforcing the visual wideness and transparency that is already present. In addition, the new basic rhythm of the square would break current monotony and provide new intervals for aesthetic observation, that is, for the qualitative emergence of this environment beyond its functional appearance.

The third kind of intervention we propose in order to endow Ernst-Reuter-Platz with a renewed significance, to *attract*, is based on the former two—they constitute the conditions of possibility for its realization —and, in turn, constitutes their necessary complement. To clear, to differentiate, and to attract are not to be understood as forms of intervention related to each other by addition but rather by mutual determination. They configure an organic meshwork in which each component is necessary in order to achieve the intended transformative power.

What does the operation of attracting mean in this context? Once the square has increased its perceptual wideness and transparency, and reduced its homogeneity and monotony—thus increasing the possibility of differentiating single events and objects in a framework of panoramic observation—it is necessary to introduce new elements that actualize these potentialities by concentrating attention. The open and unstressed field should be activated through the introduction of new elements of interest that constitute foci of awareness throughout the place, breaking the functional blindness that currently occludes the square. We propose to achieve this goal through two kinds of operations: activating the ground-floor spaces of buildings demarcating the square, and instituting an international competition for temporary architecture.

In the current state, only a few adjacent ground floors contain activities that can be perceived from the outside as appealing poles. The responsible city departments could encourage and facilitate private and public investments to bring attractive activities to these spaces, and, in turn, set up quality criteria and curate new urban presences in dialogue with those in abutting buildings.

The second intervention we propose in order to reinforce the presence of the square through attraction is the conception and organization of an international competition of site-specific, temporary architecture. The particularity of this competition lies in the function of the targeted architectural artifacts. They should be designed specifically for Ernst-Reuter-Platz in order to accomplish a very specific function: to contribute to increasing the presence of this place while respecting the limitations derived from its condition as urban landmark, that is, without altering its original materiality. More specifically, provisory architectural interventions should function as *catalyzers of awareness*, attracting attention to themselves only in order to conduct concentrated awareness to the square, that is, without keeping hold of attention. This very particular function constitutes the unique feature of this competition, and differentiates it from other contests also devoted to the realization of site-specific architectural pieces.

Attending to this singularity, and in order to provide a preliminary material concretization of the competition's concept, we have designed a first temporary architectural object. More precisely, this is a first intervention through a provisory architectural artifact. This object—an *observatory* to be located on the central circle—should exemplify the kind of intervention intended. The observatory is a rectangular building, 40 meters long, 10 meters wide, and 5.65 meters high. It is elevated 1.35 meters over the square's surface—thus achieving a total height of 7 meters—and situated between the two water basins. These dimensions refer to elements already present in the square: the 10 x 10 meters grid on the surface, and the elevations and heights of the ground floors of the surrounding buildings. The observatory's location and orientation respond on the one hand to the possibility of having a panoramic perception of the whole square from a single spot, and on the other hand to the aim of reinforcing the function of Düttmann's landscape design as an element of resistance—*Gegenbau*[6]—against the East-West axis defined by the urbanists of National Socialism.

The six surfaces of this observatory are completely transparent. Its external surfaces configure a rectangular cuboid of glass. This allows people to see the whole square from inside the observatory but also through it. In contrast to its visual

6 Martin Warnke, "Bau und Gegenbau," in *Architektur als politische Kultur*, Hermann Hipp and Ernst Seidl (eds.) (Berlin: Reimer, 1996), pp.11–18. Thanks to Gabrielle Dolff-Bonekämper for this reference.

transparency, the observatory is aurally completely opaque. It is isolated from the surrounding sounds. This acoustic insulation is made possible by a second, slightly irregular glass construction in the interior of the rectangular cuboid, sound insulating supports to avoid the transmission of vibration through contact with the ground, and an entrance and exit organized as a triple sluice gate. Visitors—the observers—access the building from a ramp aligned with the exit of the metro tunnel. According to our design, this tunnel should remain the only access point to the central circle. Providing easier access on the surface, for example through one or more crosswalks, would completely disturb the insular character of the central circle, along with one of the most unique traits of Ernst-Reuter-Platz: its *Mittelinsel* (central *island*). Instead of simplifying access, we suggest making it a bit more singular. The existing stairs should be eliminated and replaced by an elevator, whose box— half on the surface, half underground—should be constructed as a vertical glass rectangular cuboid, a counterpart to the observatory. Unlike the observatory, however, this cuboid should not be aurally isolated but should rather allow the sounds of the square to be present already while users are waiting for the elevator underground and, increasingly, as they access the surface. This progression will be reversed while accessing the observatory through the ramp and the triple sluice gate.

The observatory, reinforced by the redefinition of access to the central circle, will fulfil two complementary functions. From the periphery of the square, it will attract attention to itself without diminishing the perceptibility of the square as a whole, establishing a new and singular focus of attention detached from any pragmatic use. From inside the observatory, through the interplay between increased visibility and limited audibility—which produces an intensification of aural perception after leaving the observatory— it will provide conditions that induce and reinforce a multimodal, aesthetic observation of this singular urban environment.

In order to facilitate the international competition, which allows for the temporary construction of architectural "perceptual apparatus,"[7] we suggest that a consortium of private and public actors involved in Ernst-Reuter-Platz should be created, and eventually constituted as a foundation. This new institution should, among other functions, define the conditions of the competition, disseminate the call for proposals, select the jury, and raise funds for the realization of projects. In itself, an Ernst-Reuter-Platz Foundation would hold a twofold element attraction. From the inside, it would offer a new instrument to connect individuals, companies, and institutions relevant for the development of this square. From the outside, it would draw international attention to Ernst-Reuter-Platz as a place to think architecture and urbanism. Through this competition, the square would again find a place in the international discourses of these disciplines.

Through a combination of constructive and non-constructive interventions, the Auditory Architecture Research Unit's design allows for a reactivation of Ernst-Reuter-Platz as an agent of actual urban life. Mobilizing the potentialities of the place without negating its history, our design makes it

7 For a general reflection of this concept, see *Ästhetik x Dispositiv. Die Erprobung von Erfahrungsfelder*, E. Bippus, J. Huber, and R. Nigro (eds.) (Zurich: Springer, 2012). For a more specific account in the field of architecture and urbanism, see the website for the project, "Visuelle und auditive Wahrnehmungsdispositive. Zur Erweiterung der Evaluationsmethodik von Stadtentwicklung in der Agglomeration am Beispiel von Schlieren" (Visual and auditory perceptual apparatus to extend the evaluation's methodology of urban development in the Swiss suburban areas using the example of Schlieren): www.wahrnehmung-agglomeration.ch (in German).

possible to close the gap between a constructive structure designed according to a different urban paradigm, and the needs and aspirations of its present inhabitants. Our design, as well as the process leading to its configuration, exemplifies a concept of architecture understood not as the formalization of big-scale material artifacts, but rather as transformative intervention in an ongoing process of environmental constitution. Our design aims not only to regenerate Ernst-Reuter-Platz, but also to provide an example of architecture as a process of introduction and modification of conditions of collective sense-making in the framework of the built environment.

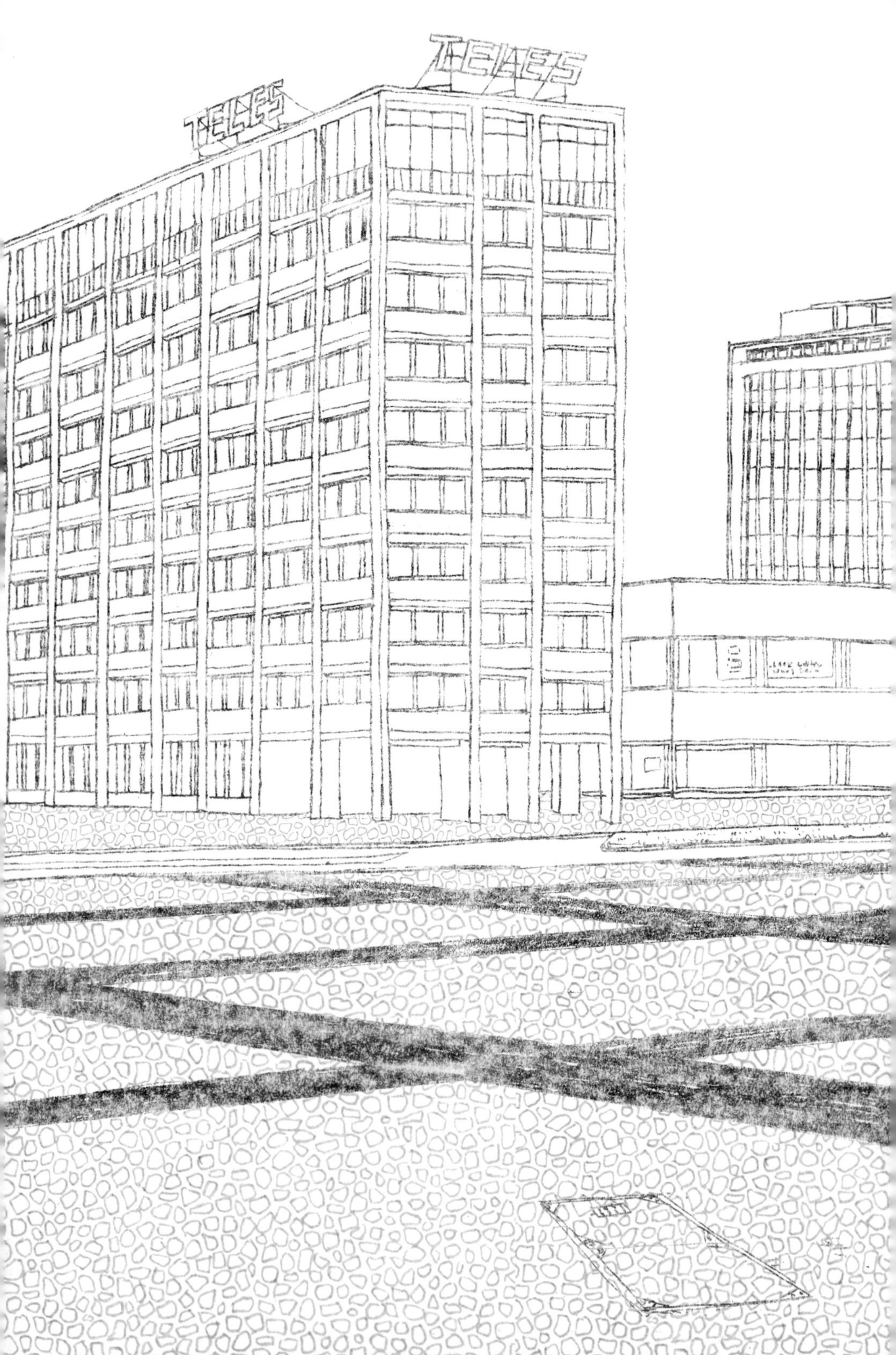

TELES
TELES

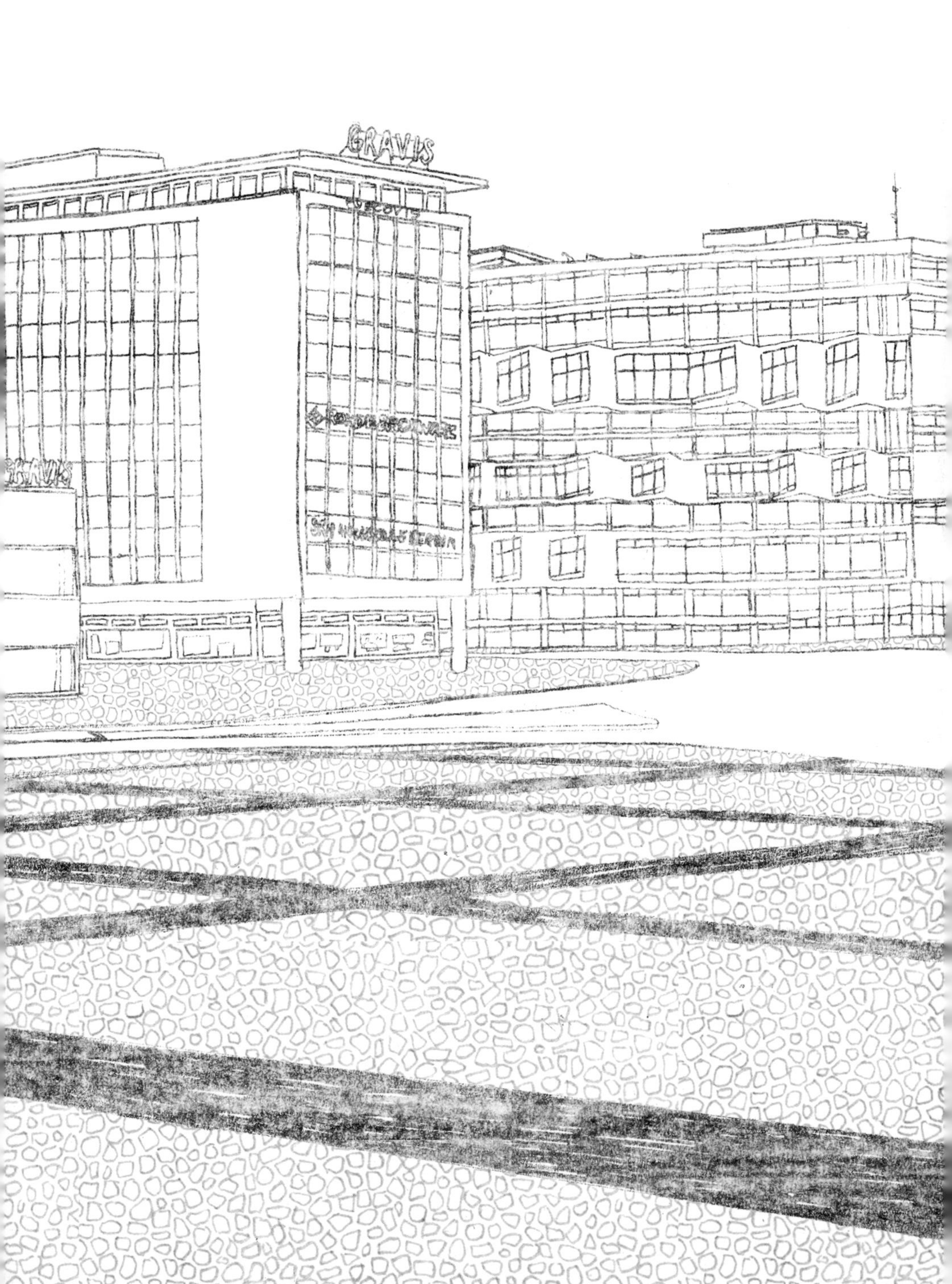

GRAVIS

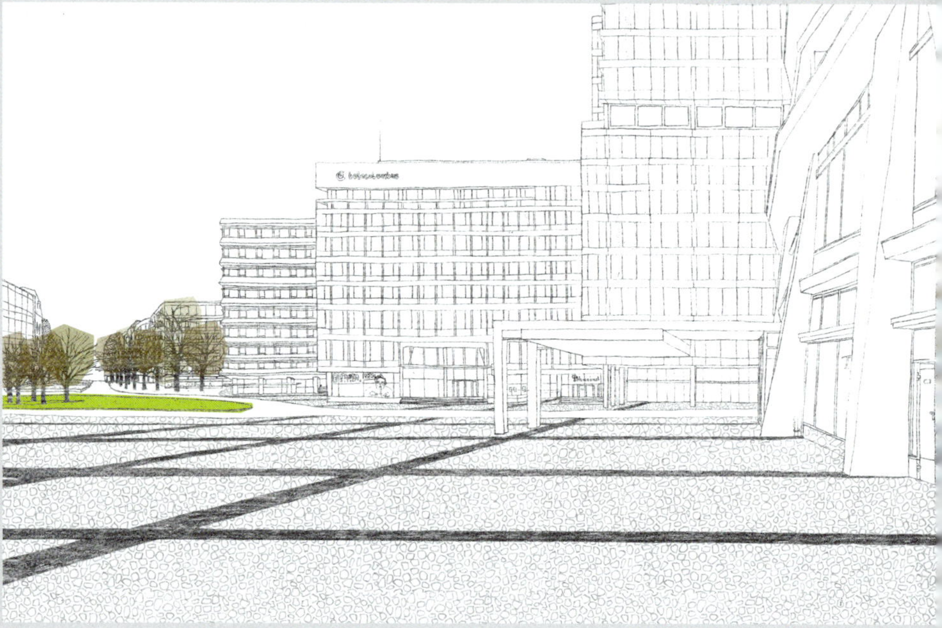

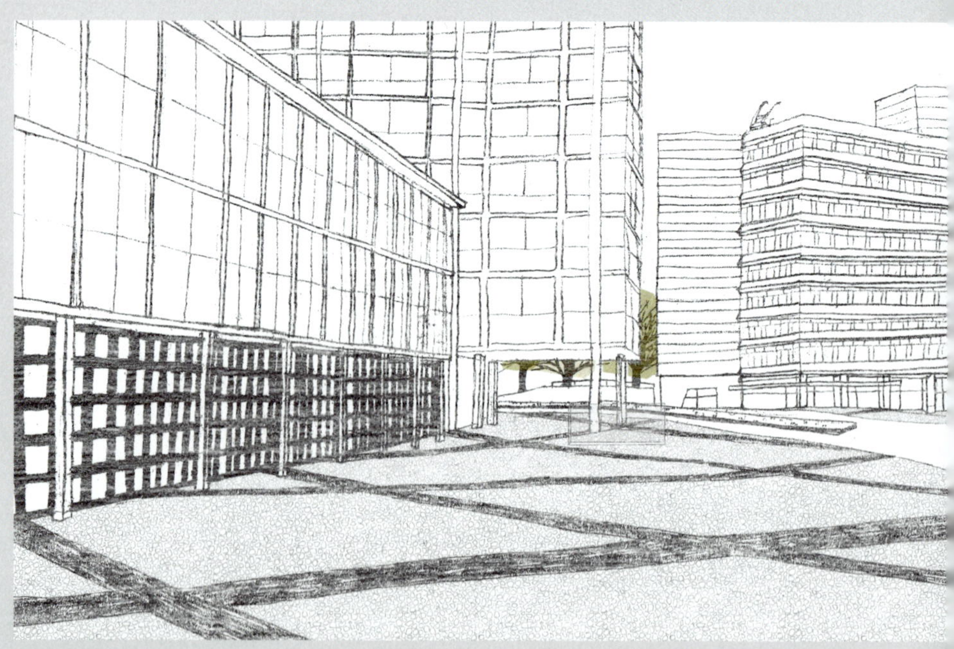

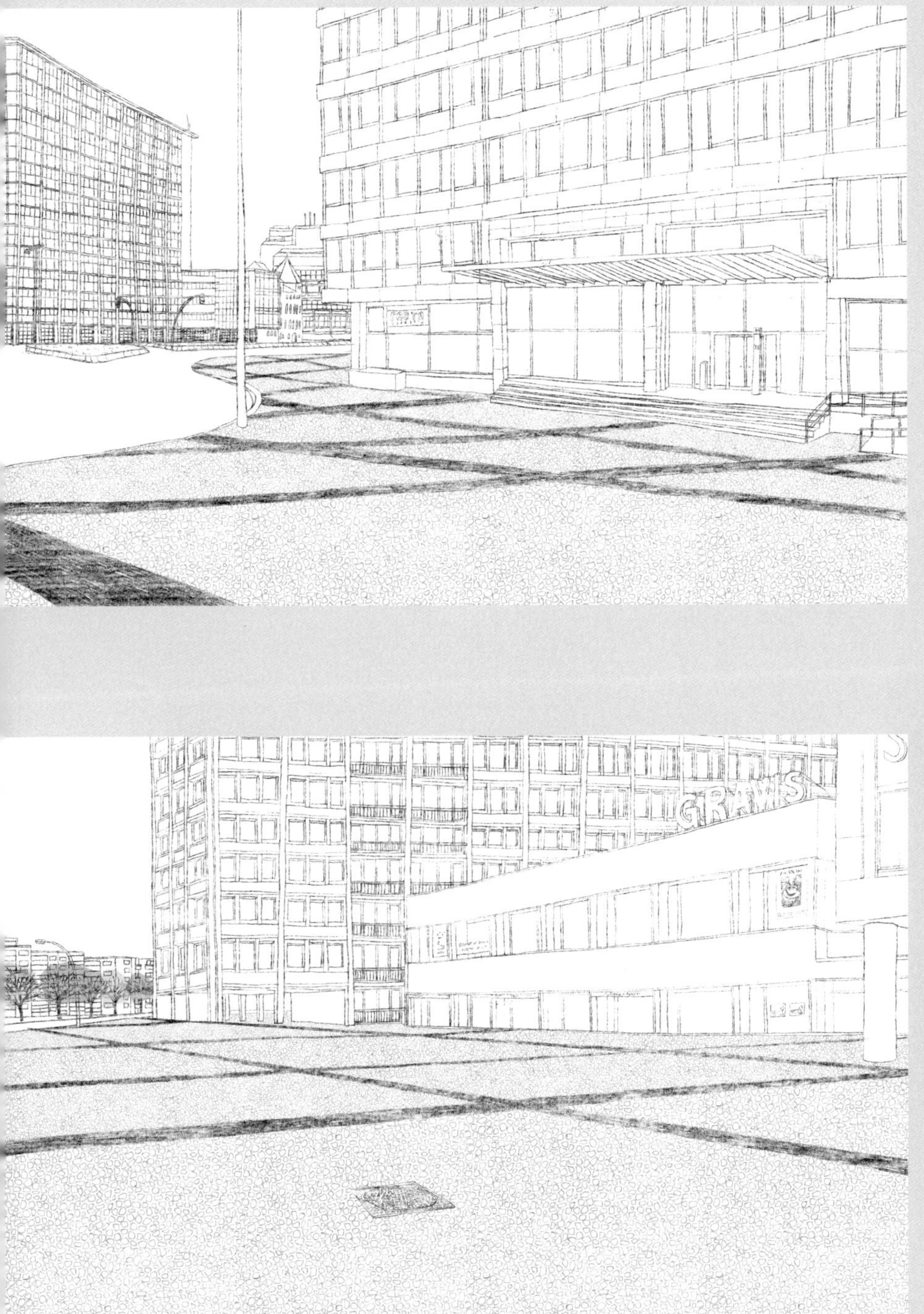
GRAMS

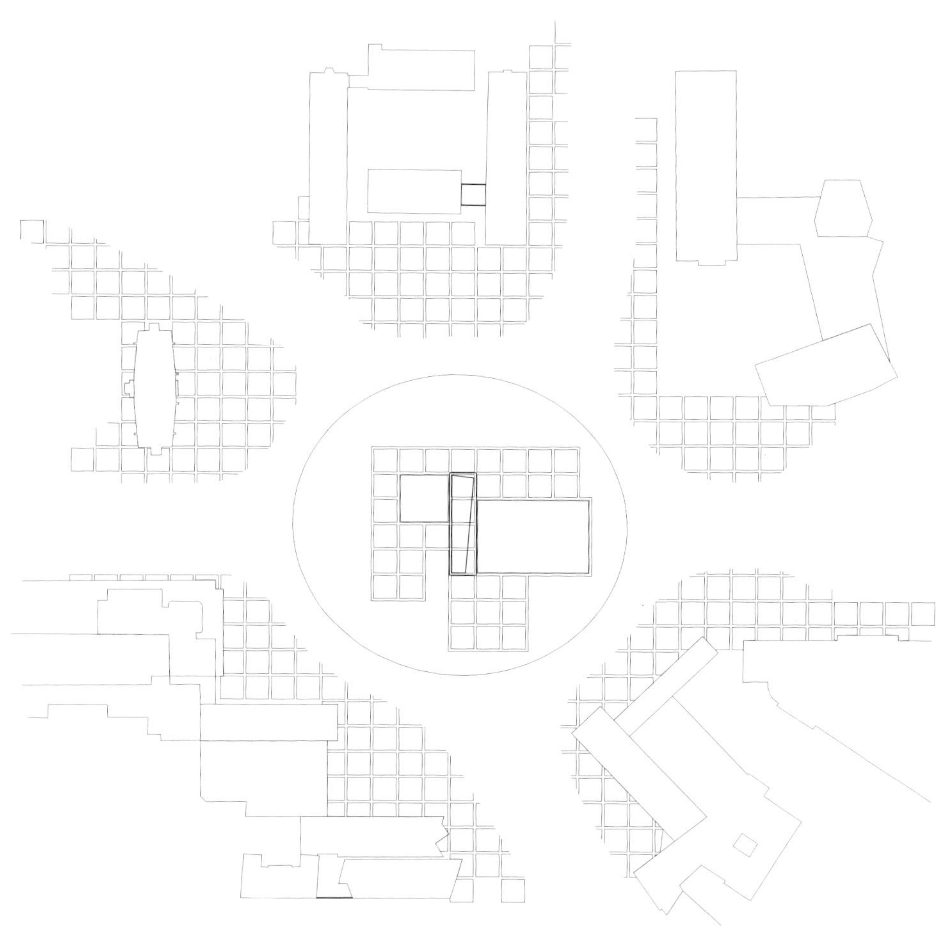

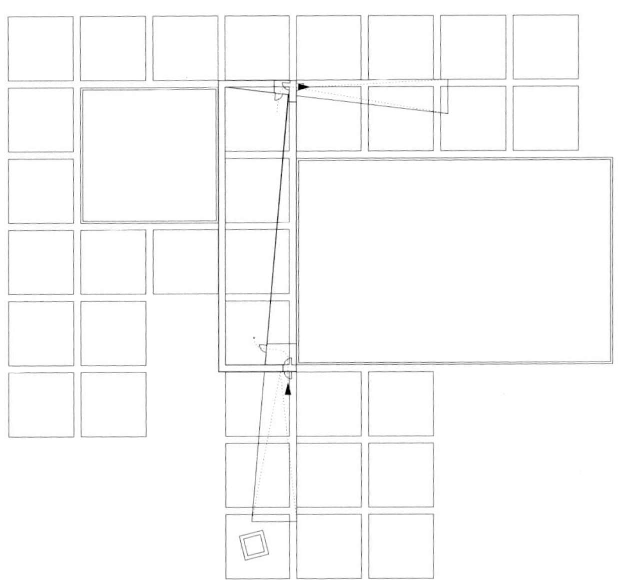

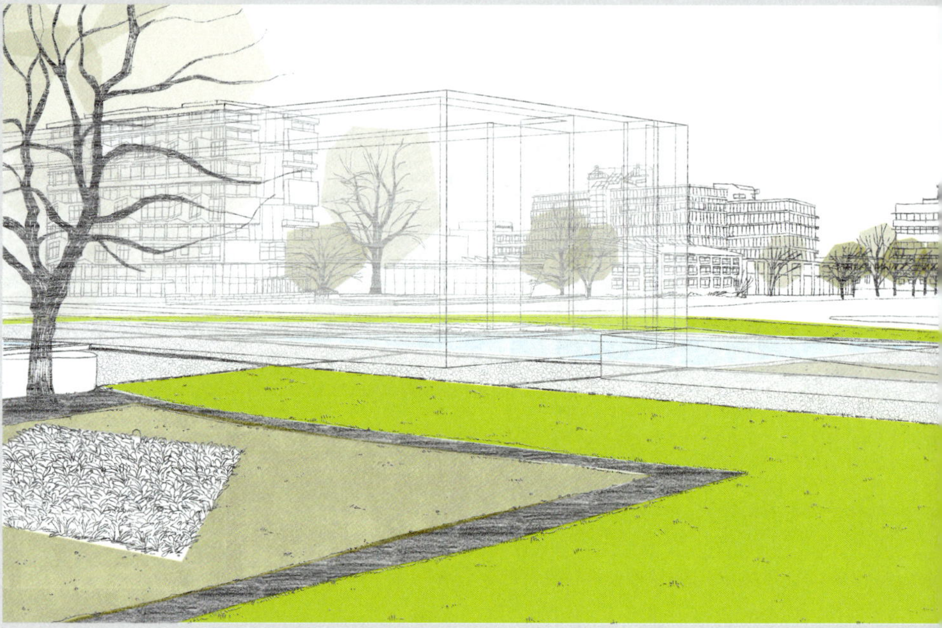

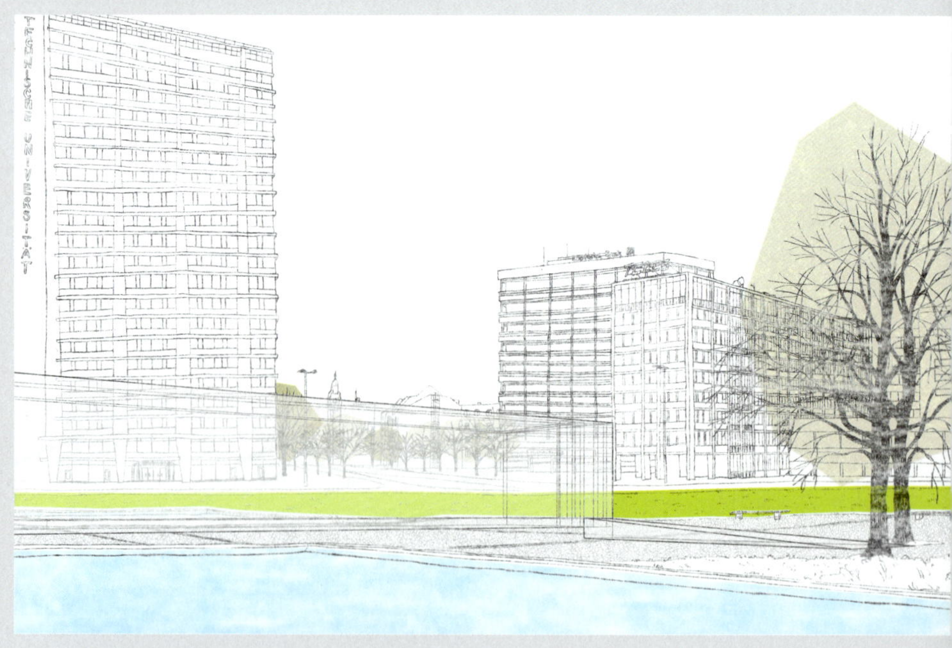

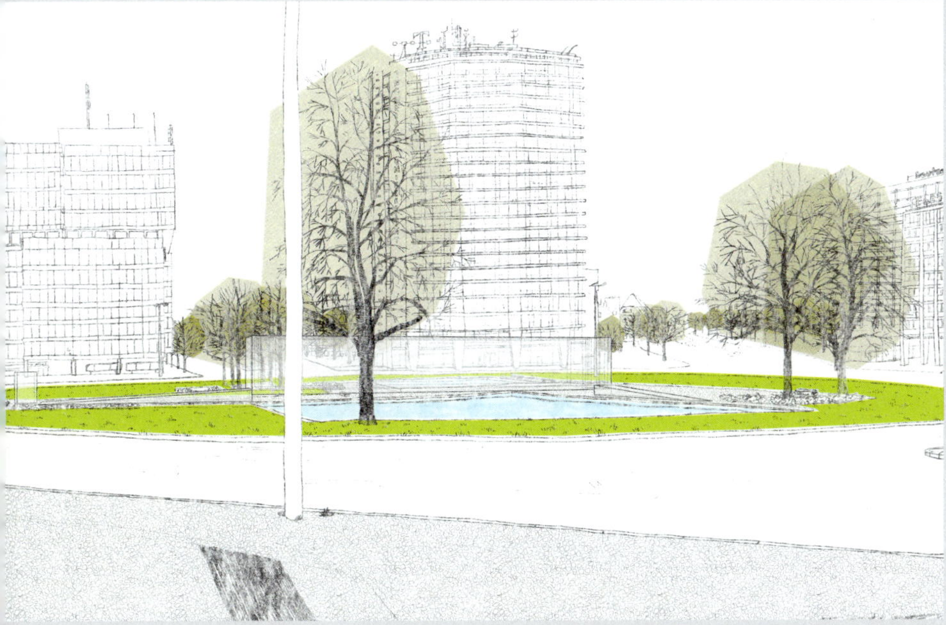

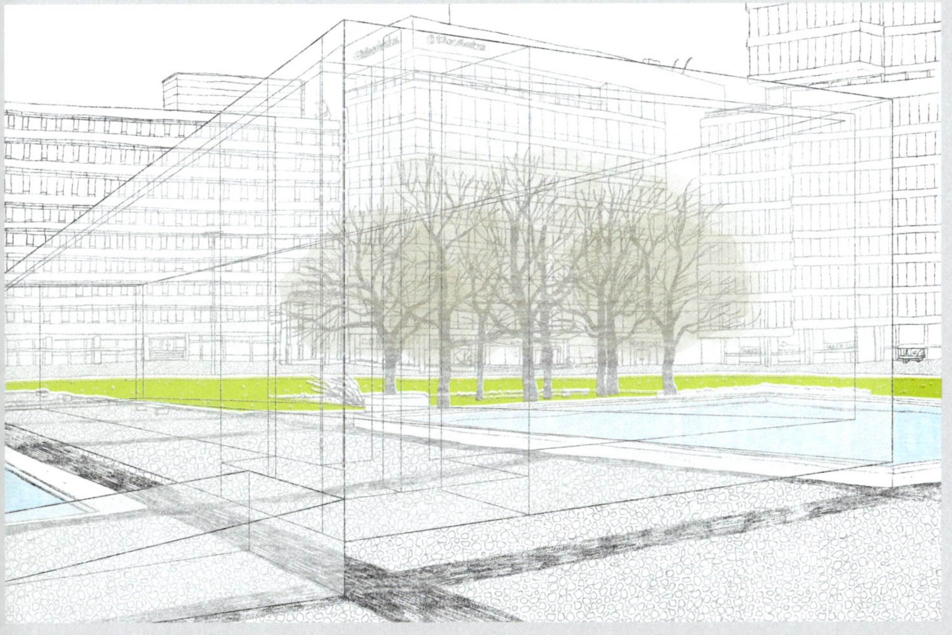

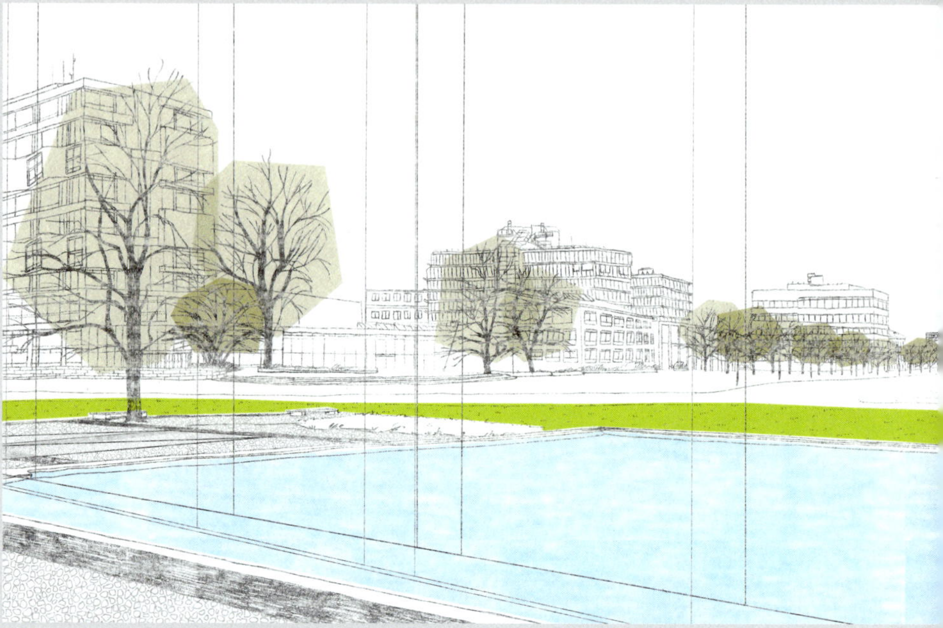

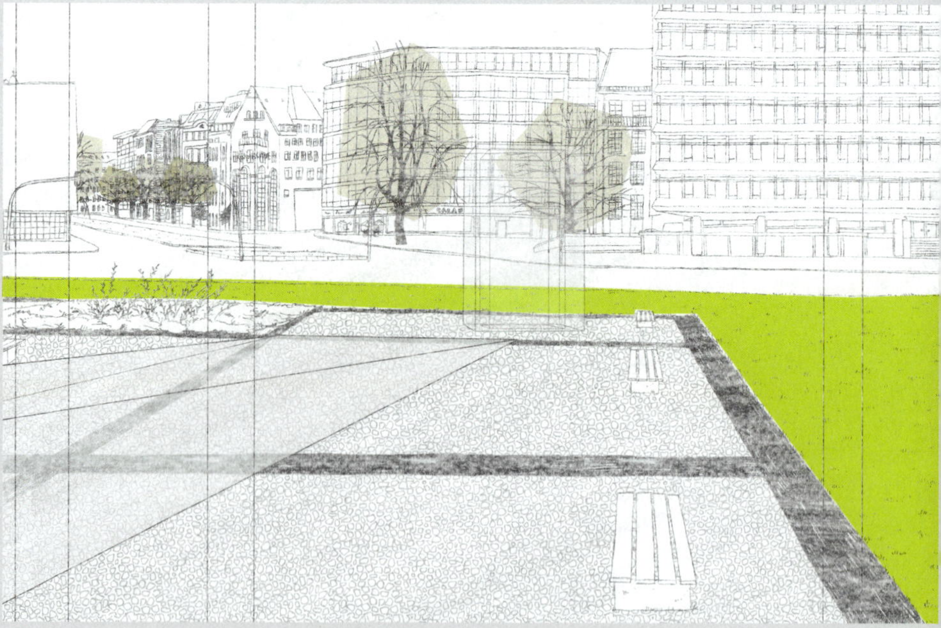

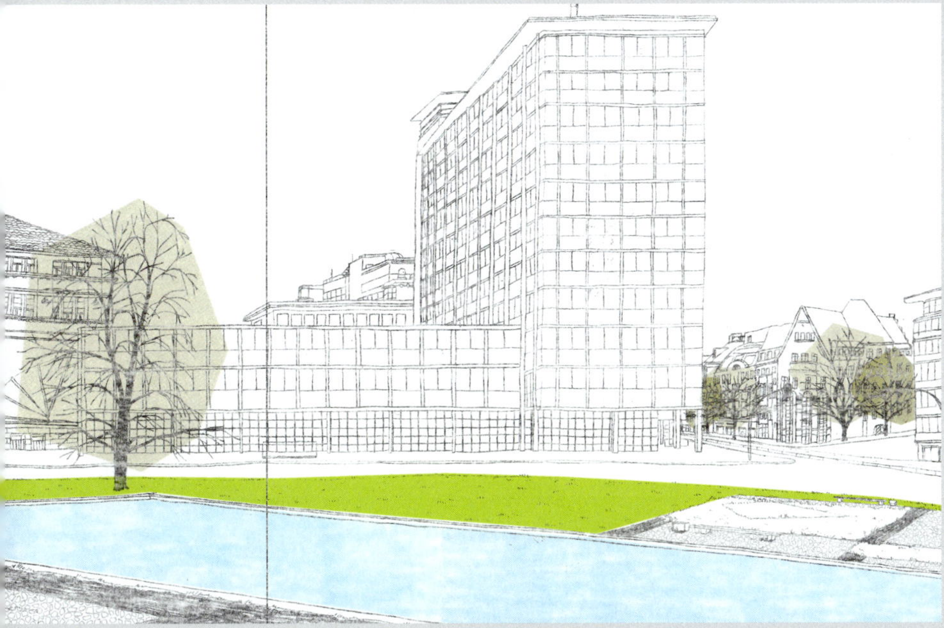

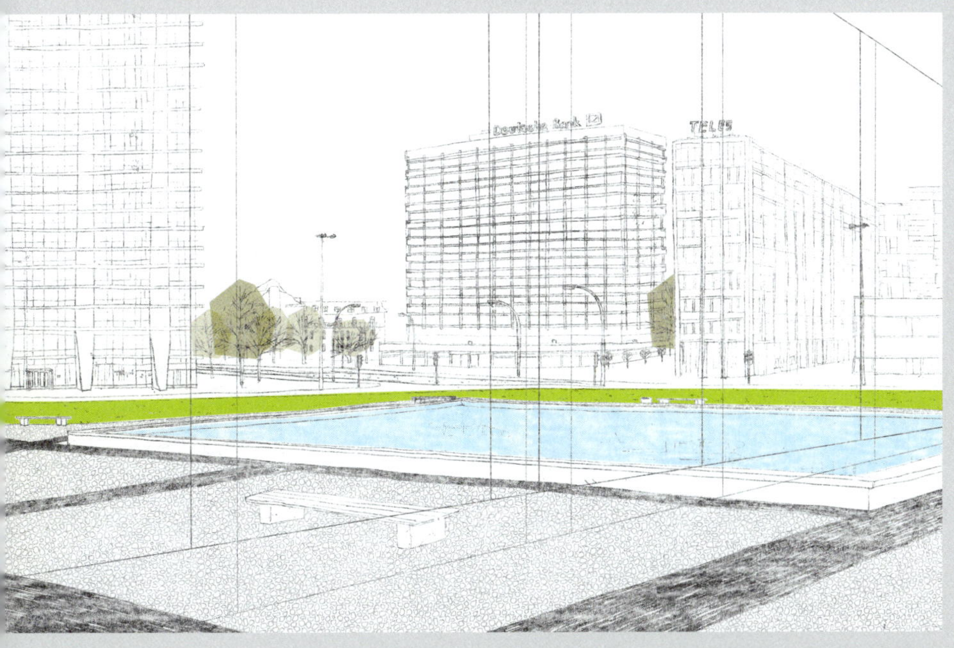

Deutsche Bank
TELES

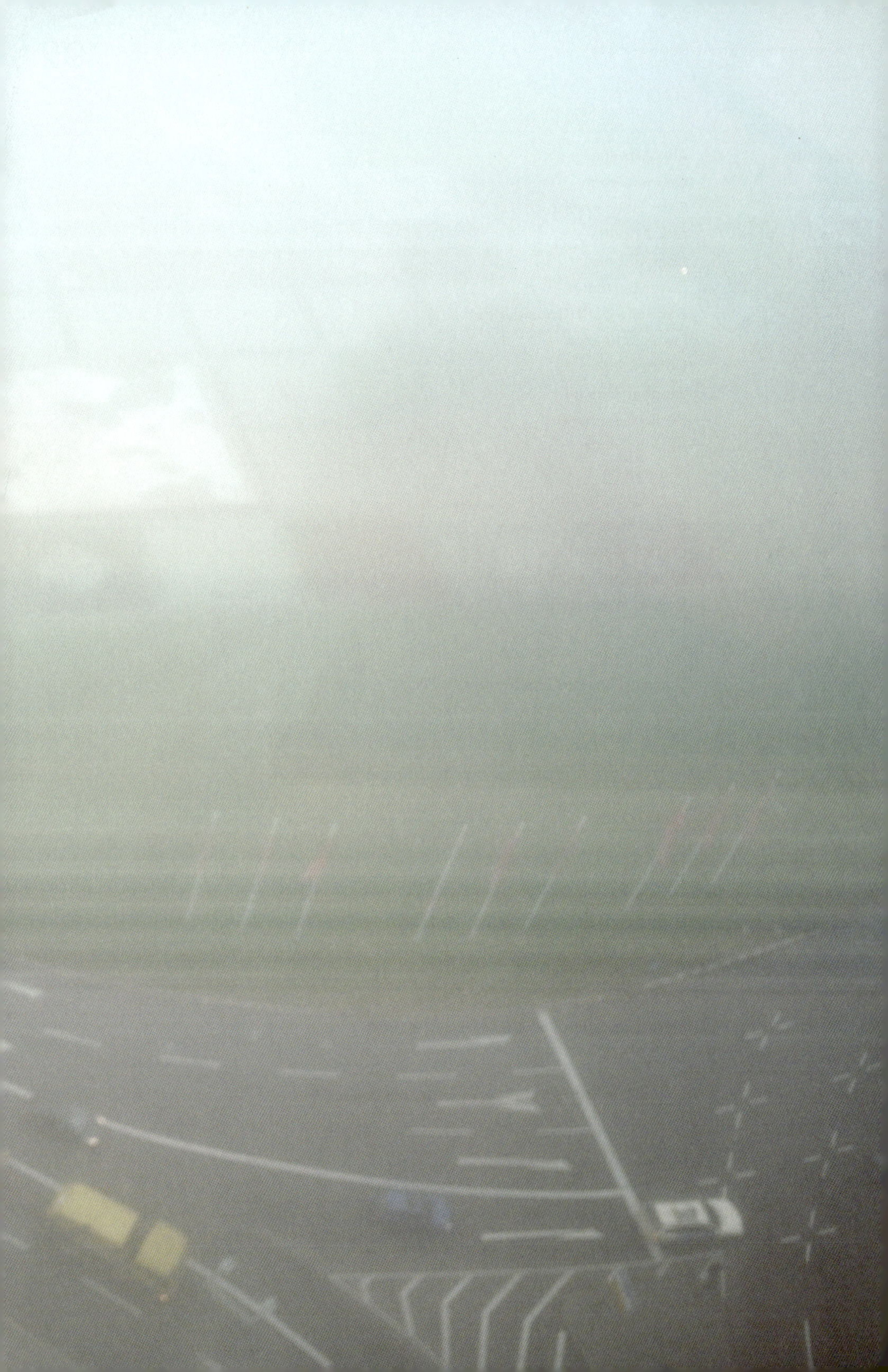

Editors: Alex Arteaga
                     Gunnar Green
                     Boris Hassenstein
Contributions: Alex Arteaga
                     Anna Bogner
                     Oliver Bormann
                     Gabrielle Dolff-Bonekämper
                     Frank Eckhardt
                     Gunnar Green
                     Stephan Günzel
                     Boris Hassenstein
                     Saskia Hebert
                     Maria Horn
                     Lucas Hövelmann
                     Marco Mattelig
Copy editor: Sage Anderson
Design: Studio TheGreenEyl, Berlin
Print: Ruksaldruck, Berlin
PrePress: Carsten Humme, Leipzig
Publisher: Errant Bodies Press, Berlin, 2016
                     Surface Tension Supplement No. 7
                     www.errantbodies.org
Copyright texts: Alex Arteaga
                     Gunnar Green
                     Boris Hassenstein
                     Anna Bogner
                     Maria Horn
                     Lucas Hövelmann
Copyright Images: Gunnar Green   (pages: 58–59, 60, 61, 62–63, 64–65, 126–127, 128–129, 130–131, 132–133)
                     Willy Sengewald   (pages: 70–71, 72–73, 74–75, 76–77, 78–79, 80–81, 190–191)
                     Lena Burmann   (pages: 134–135, 136–137, 138–139,140–141, 142–143)
                     Lucas Hövelmann   (pages: 144, 145, 146–147, 148 –149, 150–151)
                     Maria Horn   (pages: 154–155, 156–157, 158–159, 160–161, 178–179, 180–181, 186–187, 188–189)
                     Boris Hassenstein (pages: 182–183, 184–185)
ISBN: 978-0-9889375-7-4

This book has been realized in the framework of
Alex Arteaga's research project Architecture of Embodiment,
supported by the Einstein Foundation Berlin through
an Einstein Junior Fellowship.
                     www.architecture-embodiment.org